MOSS MANOR NEWS

MOSS MANOR NEWS

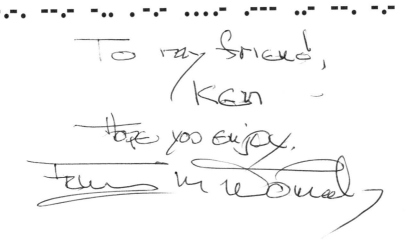

To my friend,
Ken —
Hope you enjoy.
Francis M. Womack

FRANCIS M. WOMACK, JR.

XULON PRESS

Xulon Press
2301 Lucien Way #415
Maitland, FL 32751
407.339.4217
www.xulonpress.com

Unless otherwise indicated, cripture quotations taken from the King James Version (KJV)–*public domain.*

Printed in the United States of America.

ISBN-13: 978-1-54565-039-4

TABLE OF CONTENTS

AN INTRODUCTION

Francis and Beverly Womack purchased a winter residence in the nearby Sky Lake community in early 2010. They had an Ocala residence but sought periodic escape from the mid-Florida heat to the Northeast Georgia Mountains. I met Francis by sheer accident via amateur ("ham") radio. One of his numerous friends had recently passed away, and the friend's widow asked Francis to help sell her late husband's ham radio equipment. I subsequently drove over to Francis's home in the Sky Lake (Sautee, Georgia) community and immediately fell in love with the man. While there, I also met sweet Beverly and was introduced to Lady Bean.

Francis and Beverly lived in Sky Lake for several years before moving to South Carolina for medical reasons. Francis still owns the Sky Lake home and spends time either there or in his Presbyterian retirement home in Clinton, South Carolina, where he continues to preach at the age of eighty-nine.

The grounds around the Moss Manor residence are covered in what is known as deer moss. It's like a putting green, only shaggier and a bit less green, and there's little need for maintenance, so long as a bit of rain falls now and then and the correct amount and type of fertilizer is properly applied. So the name of this novel came straight out of the moss and the newsletters. Francis and Beverly began sending more or less monthly newsletters to long-range friends and family members, and as a friend I received all of them. The newsletters slowly evolved into. . .well. . .you'll see. Early in 2018, I begged the man to let me edit the newsletters, not that any significant editing was required, and then to get someone to publish his work. Francis took me up on the offer, and as his editor I take full responsibility for all errors in this novel (I assure you that they exist).

Dr. Francis Womack is without question the finest man I've ever known in my life. Read his words and experience his vast, crystal-line-clear memory. Read and think about your own life and your own memories. Cherish your loved ones and take time to enjoy the beauty of our world.

Kimberly G. Smith
Fall 2018

DEDICATION

I dedicate this book to the many friends who walk through the pages of these stories, ramblings and remembrances. I make a special dedication to my late wife, Beverly, who not only contributed in writings but corrected my spelling and careless errors and omissions.

Lady Bean would make life miserable if I did not include her in my dedication. So, Lady Bean, I pay tribute to you for your numerous thoughtful comments and observations that many, perhaps most, readers like more than what I have written.

To my good friend and the editor of this book I offer a well-deserved dedication. It was Kim Smith who felt that Moss Manor newsletters should be published. It was at his urging and because of his offer of help that enabled the newsletters to live in print. Thank you, Kim. *FMW*

MOVING IN

Beverly and I have been in Sky Lake since the Tuesday after Easter. While we have enjoyed our time in our North Georgia mountain home and plan to spend most of the summer and part of the fall here, we do miss our friends and our family. Many of you, both family and friends, have already visited us in Moss Manor and others of you are planning, or have indicated a desire, to come. We thought it might be helpful to you for us to send a periodic report of things that are happening here in our mountain retreat. The purpose of this newsletter is to keep you informed about what we are doing, what is happening and what might be happening in the future.

THE MONTH IN REVIEW

April and May have been busy months. First we had to open the house and get things in order. The weather was cool and the trees were just breaking out in new green. We watched our cherry tree in the moss lawn bloom, saw the mountains fill with the white of the dogwood. As the dogwood faded the Mountain Laurel took its place. Some evenings were cool enough to enjoy a fire in the living room fireplace. On April 12th we had the privilege of hearing our grandson, Stephen, perform his senior Euphonium recital in Mars Hill College.

I raked and blew winter leaves every day and more seemed to come each night. On April 30 I left Beverly and Lady Bean and drove to Ocala for the Society of Antique Models flying event. On Sunday I preached at Reddick Presbyterian Church and returned to Sky Lake, pulling the Buzzard trailer full of model airplanes.

Monday, our good friends Tom and Betty came and we enjoyed the week together. The next Monday, Geert and Joy came to visit and we enjoyed talking and sharing the sights of the area with them. Activities of the church, community and home have kept us busy.

CHANGES AT THE HOUSE

Every home changes daily and Moss Manor is no exception. For those of you who have been here you will see some changes when you return. The back deck was expanded last year and the kitchen and the dining room sport a new Pergo wood floor. Just last week the cracked stone façade beside the steps was repaired and arrangements were made for some glass to be replaced. A new TV graces the living room and a headboard enhances the first guestroom. Little by little, 231 Laurelwood is changing.

VISITOR'S SCHEDULE

We like to have our friends and family visit with us, but to keep everyone from coming at the same time and having to sleep on the sofas; here is the schedule as it looks today.

- May 3 – 10 Tom and Betty
- May 10 – 15 Joy and Geert
- May 29 – 30 Mickey and Melinda
- Jun 21 - 15 Tom and Linda

Other family and friends have said they hoped to come and visit. We hope you will; just let us know and we will keep the light on for you.

FROM THE THRONE OF QUEEN LADY BEAN
(in her own words)

I had almost forgotten how nice it was to have this long hall to race up and down and all these soft beds and sofas to sleep on. It is especially nice when there is a fire in the fireplace and I can curl up at the end of the sofa.

My staff has been very nice to me. I have trained them well. They even let me go outside even though my man-staff always goes with me. It is good to have company and I am always there to protect him. Sometimes he takes me in before I want to go in but I guess you can't have everything all the time. . .although I try.

A few weeks ago a white dog with a loud voice came to visit. Being a good hostess, I gave him the run of the house and I stayed in the master bedroom. My staff brought my food and water to me on schedule. I was patient and after a week he went away and the house was mine again. LB

DISCOVERIES AND LOOKING AHEAD

While our friends were here a few weeks ago, we discovered York Falls. Everyone else knew about it but we had not found it yet. It is a beautiful little park and a quite large water fall that tumbles down the mountain and eventually fills the lake from which Sky Lake gets its name. While standing on the bridge admiring the falls, Beverly slipped and bruised and skinned her arm. It is still sore but healing well.

We are looking forward to a hike to another fall with the church next Sunday (I hike, Bev reads a book). Saturday we will go for a class at a state park on birds of the area and their songs and calls. Each Saturday evening there is music of the area in Unicoi State Park not far from here. In June there will be a hot air balloon race from Helen. We look forward to seeing the colorful balloons in the air. Lots of other events are taking place. . . we will tell you about them in future newsletters.

FROM BEVERLY'S VIEWPOINT

What can I say that they have not already mentioned? For one thing-FLOWERS! When we arrived, thc hyacinths by the little stream down by the main road had done their best, or else the deer had had a feast. All that was left was the flower stalks. BUT the cherry tree still had some bloom and after the first good rain, the ground looked like we'd had a snow storm. Thank goodness the dogwood was in bloom all through the apple-green woods.

Within the next week, the mountain laurel stared to bloom and is still going strong. Now the rhododendron is beginning to show huge heads of color. This sight will be here probably until the end of June. Some people who have planted one or two near their homes have blooms already, but the highways and byways are still full of unopened buds. I can't wait to see hillsides as full of them as the mountain laurel is now. Come and see for yourselves! B.

HURRICANE HOLES

Moss Manor News is our way of keeping our family and friends up to speed on what is happening as we spend the summer in our mountain retreat in Sky Lake. We hope you enjoy this kind of communication. Let us hear from you.

ACTIVITIES

We made a day trip to visit tour daughter, Mary Glenn, in Black Mountain. While it is always good to see MG, this particular trip was to bring back plants from her garden shop to our yard. Mary Glenn always gives us some of the things that are not selling and that she would probably have to throw away. We also bought some other plants for the yard.

A bonus for us was a visit with Lardner, a classmate of mine in Seminary and a retired missionary who served in Japan, who had invited us to meet for lunch. He and his wife, Molly, hosted us at the Black Mountain Bakery. Lardner and I had crisscrossed paths a number of times in our ministry. We enjoyed sharing experiences and family histories.

Bev and I enjoyed the beautiful mountain scenery both going and coming as we watched the new green of spring fade into the deeper colors of summer.

We had a great outing with our nieces, Ann and Melinda, and family, when we traveled north into the NC Mountains to the Brasstown Valley Resort where we enjoyed lunch. On the way home we visited Alexander's, a store that has three levels of "everything under the sun." It is amazing to find a busy department type store in the middle of nowhere.

Visits to the Annual Hot Air Balloon Race in Helen yielded some good video and pictures. Some twenty-five balloons lift off from Helen and the winner finishes by first crossing I-95 somewhere to the east.

A hike with the church hiking club to Angel Falls left me sore and winded. My aching back remembers a truckload of topsoil left on the driveway to be spread around the various planting areas. Plants from Mary Glenn's garden shop are all in the ground and hopefully growing.

Shopping and dining in nearby towns, attending clubs, crafts, and meetings, sitting on the deck in the evenings and enjoying our many trees rounds out our days.

WHAT'S NEW AT THE HOUSE

The clouded glass in the deck door and the glass in the second guest bedroom have been replaced. An A-frame and swing now stand in the yard, ready for customers. New railroad ties replace the worn ones on the back hill.

STARTING THE DAY

The alarm jumps on the bed and walks across my face. It is between seven and seven-thirty and time for me to get up, feed the cat and meet the day. It is good to get cup of coffee, sit down at the table in the breakfast room and watch the sun dispel the shadows across the front yard. It will be another hour at least before the sun makes it up the mountain and full light dances across the moss lawn. I watch an early hummingbird drink from the feeder hanging on a limb of the Japanese maple just outside the window. If I am lucky, a deer or gaggle of wild turkeys will cross the yard on their way to the creek just down the road.

I turn on the laptop and check my e-mail, look at my grandchil-dren's latest activities on Facebook and get another cup of coffee, this time with an apple sticky-bun Beverly has just made. In a little while Beverly will come in and we will get breakfast together. It is a good way to start the day.

A HURRICANE HOLE

Many years ago, when we were sailing *Karisto* and the weather forecast was that a hurricane was expected, we would immediately look for a hurricane hole in which to hunker down. This usually would be a small creek deep enough for our draft and narrow enough to tie lines to the trees on either side. Or it may just have been a spot protected on all sides by high banks and with an anchorage with good holding.

The 2010 predictions are as follow:

Across the entire Atlantic Basin for the six-month season, which begins June 1, NOAA is projecting a 70 percent probability of the following ranges:

- 14 to 23 named storms (top winds of 39 mph or higher), including:
- 8 to 14 hurricanes (top winds of 74 mph or higher), of which:
- 3 to 7 could be major Hurricanes (Category 3, 4 or 5; winds of at least 111 mph)

Now Moss Manor, tucked away in the mountains of North Georgia, qualifies, in my book, for a good hurricane hole. When the winds in Ocala or along the coastline are predicted to reach seventy-five miles per hour you will probably find us here in Sky Lake.

You might wish to join us.

THE CHURCH WE ATTEND

Nacoochee Presbyterian Church is a unique mountain church with a very diverse membership. The liturgy might well come from a high steeple church yet it is very informal in the way it is conducted. The minister is an excellent preacher, solid in reform theology and relevant application. I think he may be something of a frustrated actor and writer. The congregation is a mix of mountain people, retired or second home professionals, artists of various disciplines, valley farmers, etc. The church is too inclusive for some people, who shake their heads and wonder how we can be Christian and still include all those "sinful" people. Yet people come from miles around to be part of this vibrant congregation.

The music and choir are usually very good and might be a high church anthem or mountain gospel. Special music might be traditional piano or might include an American Indian Flute, a banjo, guitar, string bass or penny whistle. When time for the choir to sing, they get up from their place in the congregation and form around the piano, which may accompany them or they may sing a cappella. It is all done in good taste as worship and not as entertainment. You leave feeling that you have truly worshipped.

FROM QUEEN LADY BEAN *(in her own words)*

The other day I was listening to one of our visitors refer to my man-staff *as a* renaissance man. *I bristled a little and my tail fluffed up because I thought they were insulting him. As their conversation continued, I learned that being a* renaissance man *was to be a person who was skilled in many things. As someone said:* A jack of all trades and master of none. *Well, I got to thinking. . .that pretty well describes me.*

As you may know from my other writings, I am a cat that is pretty much in control of things at all times. I have taught my staff well and they provide me with what I want, even without me asking. I am able to sleep wherever I want to. . .and I do like to sleep. When my man-staff goes outside with me I am right there to protect him from any danger. My lady-staff keeps telling me how beautiful I am, which I already know but it is good to hear again. All in all, I am a very talented cat.

So I guess the term renaissance cat *describes me pretty well. My man-staff probably learned a lot of what he knows from me. But I am glad to share.* LB

VISITOR'S SCHEDULE

Beverly and I have been blessed by having a home in the mountains large enough to share with our friends. We enjoy visiting with family and friends. Our coming schedule looks like this:

- Jun 23 - 26 Tom and Linda
- July 16 - 18 (Bev and I will be away at a wedding)
- July 22 - 23 Friends from Ocala
- Aug 27 - 29 Karl and Jackie

BEAR FACTS

THE FOURTH OF JULY

Sky Lake Community celebrated the Fourth of July with an old fashion barbeque and picnic, complete with flags, patriotic decorations and almost everyone dressed in red, white and blue. Most part-time residents have come back to share the food, fun and family. While there are no fireworks, there was a time to honor those who served in armed forces, service by service. The program included singing of patriotic songs, the national anthem and taps, played to remember those who died for our country. We ate our fill, sang, shared with returning family and joined with children in games. We took part in an old fashion cake-walk, marching to the strumming of a mountain banjo. It was an event that made everyone feel good about our country and our neighbors.

OTHER ACTIVITIES

Looking back at the June calendar, it seems that we have not done a lot and yet each day has been busy. When age creeps up on you it feels like half of your time is spent with doctors or treatment. Since we will be spending half of our time here, we felt it wise for find doctors who knew about our infirmities. . .just in case. We have visited four that seem to cover us from head to toe. Beverly spends three mornings in aerobic swimming and one morning at crafts. I spend early morning and late afternoon working in the yard. Radio-control (RC) flying takes at least two evenings a week. There is always the trip to either Cleveland or Clarkesville for groceries and supplies which always seems to find us in town for lunch. We usually end up in Capt. D's, a Mexican restaurant, a Chinese restaurant or another of the many local eateries. (Bev arranges that well.) We spent three delightful days with our friends from Charlotte. We enjoyed a delightful dinner in a beautiful mountain top home with some of our flying friends. It has been a good, if somewhat warm, month even though afternoon thunder showers help cool us down.

FLYING IN THE GRAIN FIELD

A couple of times a week we gather in a field across from the Sautee Post office. It has a beautiful stand of grain, three to four feet high. The edge by the road has been mowed so we can park and launch our models. If you are good enough, and a little lucky, you can also land on the mowed strip by the fence. Usually there is very little wind, ideal for the light electrics that we fly. Often it is still hot, which is both good and bad. Bad because we get quite hot. . .good because there is lots of lift over the field. The tall grain is both good and bad. . .bad because we have to launch our planes. . .good because it is a very forgiving place when we crash. When the grasses are cut, they have promised to mow us a runway in the center of the field.

FROM YORK FALLS TO THE BARN

Early Friday morning Beverly dropped Linda, Tom and me off at York Falls. The morning coolness was a stark contrast from the usual ninety degrees of the afternoon. After moving through the small park area we crossed the bridge just below York Falls. The water spilling down from the fall high up the mountain and cascading down the smoother rock face was a good place to stop and take a few pictures before beginning the hike.

On the far side of the bridge the trail began with a sharp left climb where tree roots crisscrossed the path and helped our footing. The climb leveled off as quickly as it began and we found ourselves in a forest floored by large ferns on each side. The trail tenders had done their job well and the path was clear and clean. The stream was below us and its sound blended with the sound of birds. Blue Ridge Bog lived up to its name with green flora around and above us. We crossed a small stream and climbed gently to Rubbing Nose Rock that looks over the beginning of the upper lake. Soon we were following an old logging roadbed from the early 1900s winding through thick Rhododendron and Laurel. A few large houses looked down on the trail. Below on the left we could see the upper lake that filters the water before it flows into Sky Lake. Soon we were descending and crossing Cherokee Trail at the Upper Dam. After crossing the road, we followed the trail down to the horse barn where we saw D-day and Velvet being washed and groomed. After a short wait and visit with ladies who own the horses, Beverly met us with the van and headed home, glad that we could have shared in the beauty of the trail.

FROM BEVERLY'S POINT OF VIEW

In the last newsletter I told you about the beauty of this place. Well, I forgot to tell you of the intensive labor put in by F. We're determined to make our mountain backyard something to see and not just a mountain of rocks and weeds. F. has planted all kinds of daisies-from Shasta's, large and small; white ones with yellow centers, to yellow ones with dark centers. They're supposed to be perennials, but we'll have to wait and see next year. If they're not, we'll find some other kind of flower that will be. We discovered another plus about the moss lawn—it is producing small mountain strawberries. When I ate one the other day, I got a mouth full of teeny seeds on the outside. The inside tasted like strawberry! Surprise!

F. has moved some ferns from the front drainage ditch by the road up to several spots on the back mountain, too. We're hoping they'll spread like the others have. At least, they're living and looking great.

Finally, we have our passes to get into the swimming pool. There were quite a few neighboring folks who came to use the pool illegally. So. . .the gates were changed and the only way residents and guests can get to use the pool is with a pass which unlocks the gate and permits entry.

I go to a water aerobics class three times per week. It is amazing how much they have helped all my aches and pains and with only four sessions. I may be able to tackle some of these gorgeous trails. F. went on his own and saw more waterfalls. Come go walking with us when you can! Beverly

FROM LADY BEAN

I am not really a lap-cat. I have always felt that my staff. . .and a few chosen others. . . should make the effort to reach down or over to stroke or pet me. Now I admit I like the feel of a gentle, warm hand stroking me and I reward the stroker with a purr. As for lap-cats, I always thought of them as rather sissy.

However, this morning I almost changed my mind. It had been raining during the night and the porch was still wet. The sun was just coming up and it was still cool. I tried a few spots on the floor and then wandered over to where my man-staff was sitting. I stood in front of him, looked up, blinked my blue eyes and he said, "up." I took him up on the offer and jumped into his lap. It was warm and comfortable. I curled up and was soon napping. He seemed to enjoy it, too, and would stroke me every now and then. We both napped in the early morning sun and listened to the birds call to one another. We must have stayed there for a least an hour.

Later, I heard my lady-staff say that it was the first time my man-staff had been still in at least a year. Sometimes we cats do something good while we are trying to make ourselves comfortable. Someday I might even try it again. LB

THE BEAR FACTS

It was about 3:00 on Sunday afternoon and I was seated at the table in the kitchen with my back to the sliding glass door which opens onto our enclosed garden area. I don't know why, as there was no sound, but I glanced over my shoulder and saw something moving. Just below our bird feeder, about ten feet from where I was sitting, I saw a small black bear. He was causally licking up the seeds that had fallen from the feeder. I called for Beverly who came running. We watched as the baby or teenage bear explored the small patio. The back gate had been left open, inviting him inside.

I ran for my camera and clicked picture after picture. Our young friend finally felt he had seen enough and wandered back out of the gate and around the back deck to the steps leading up our back hill. He looked toward us as if to say a friendly goodbye and then disappeared over the hill and into the woods. We watched carefully for mama but never saw her. (I did not climb the hill to do an intense search.) Lady Bean slept in a dining room chair through the whole episode.

I eagerly punched the button to see the pictures I had taken, only to find that the memory card was still in the computer where I had been downloading pictures taken earlier. Just like in the old days we will have to rely on our memory to experience the visit of the bear. Or then, maybe he will visit us again when we least expect it.

OUR CHANGING SCHEDULE

Our schedule seems to change every day. . .here is what it looks like today. . .no guarantee that it will not change tomorrow.

- July 9 An important birthday

- July 16&17 Wedding in Raleigh
- July 18 Visit friends and my former church in Hamlet
- July 22 Visitors arrive from Ocala
- July 25 - Aug. 15 Bev and I are in Ocala to see Drs., Dentist, LB's
- Veterinarian, possibly preach, visit our friends. . .bring back what we forgot when we came to Moss Manor

TRAVELING

GEORGIA/FLORIDA/GEORGIA

The last month seems like a year compressed and crunched. It began with a trip to Raleigh, NC to attend a wedding. The grandson of a special friend had graduated and now was taking the plunge. The bride was beautiful, the wedding was special and the food was great.

After the wedding we drove through heavy rain to Hamlet where I had served as pastor for ten years. After staying with dear friends for the night and attending First Presbyterian Church the next morning, we headed back to our mountain retreat. After three days of visiting, celebrating and traveling, it was good to be home. Lady Bean was not as pleased with our trip as we were, and asked me to share her feelings with you.

HOME ALONE

I knew something unusual was going on. For the last few days my staff had been talking about going to something in a place I did not recognize. I began to worry when the red suitcase came out. Whenever I could, I curled up on it to let them know I was concerned. One night they put the red bag in the car along with some fancy clothes, and my carrier was still on the shelf in the garage. I knew I was in trouble. . .but I did not know how much.

Early the next morning they fed me a little more than usual, locked all the doors at the house, told me goodbye and drove off in the car. That night, I watched for them but they did not come back.

There were plenty of crackers in my bowl so I ate a little more than usual and went to bed.

The next morning I jumped on their bed, hoping to see them, but the bed was empty. It was a lonely house and even running up and down the hall did not help. I was watching the birds through the glass door to the deck when someone came in the front door. It was the lady they call "niece." She was nice and talked to me and put my snack in my bowl and even policed my box. Then she was gone, and it was lonely again. All night and all the next day the house was empty and lonely. I slept as much as I could but I was really worried. My staff had never deserted me this long before. Would they come back? I thought they would, but I was not sure. Right then I was "home alone."

It was almost dark when I heard our van come up the driveway. My heart pounded with hope. In a few minutes my man-staff opened the front door. I tried to let him know that I was glad to see him, but a little angry at being left alone so long. I meowed continually to express my feelings and led him right to my empty bowl. (I was not really hungry but wanted him to think I was starving.) Soon my lady-staff came in and made a fuss over me. I continued to meow and did a few welcome-home rolls on carpet. . .the kind I do when I am very happy. Right up to bed time I continued to meow and roll and race up and down the hall with excitement. It was really good to have my staff back home. They must have been glad to see me too because they let me sleep on the foot of their bed all night long.

Next time they go off, I hope they will take me with them. LB

Sorry for the interruption from the cat but she insisted on being heard.

On July 22nd we were delighted that Fran and Jerry came by to visit for the night as they made their way to a square dance convention in Commerce, GA. The next day we packed the car and on Saturday left for our home in Ocala. For seven hours, I drove, Bev was co-pilot and LB slept on the tray between us. We invested in our doctors and our dentist and Lady Bean's vet. Time went quickly and before we were ready, it was time to reverse the process and head back up the road to the Georgia Mountains. We were glad to see the trees, find a little cooler weather and settle into Moss Manor for the next three months.

On August 19 we were glad to have Cindy and Arlene visit with us for a few days. We look forward to having some of you visit us during the fall.

RETURNING TO THE PAST

It has been said, "You can't come home again," but my short visit to the church I served in Hamlet, NC proved that wrong. During our visit with Scott and Doris we talked of many good times we shared together in years past. On Sunday, the experience of worship, the love and renewed friendship, and the flood of memories reminded me that whenever you leave a pastorate, you leave a part of yourself there and you carry a part of that congregation with you, always. It was just a short visit but it proved again that "you **can** come home again."

CHRISTMAS IN JULY

I know the neighbors think we are crazy when they see a Christmas tree with lights in our living room. I know they think, *"Is it being taken down or put up?"* The truth is that when we go home at the end of November we will have little time to get ready for our Christmas activities. It will be a big help to have most of the Christmas decorating already done. Besides, I have always wanted to celebrate "Christmas in July."

REFLECTIONS ON TURNING EIGHTY-ONE

Yesterday was my eighty-first birthday. It came and went like most other days. . .there was no great feeling of being older, no sudden twinges of pain that said my arthritis is getting worse. . .no influx of wisdom that propelled me to a "Solomon status." It was a little different because my family and friends sent cards and made phone calls. Beverly made a delicious pineapple upside-down cake. My birthday present had come two months earlier in the form of a wonderfully detailed model of the ship, *Constitution*. All in all, it was a good day.

Today I am wondering what it means to be an octogenarian plus one. First of all, it was a surprise. Not the kind of surprise that jumps out at you, but one that sneaks up on you. When I was growing up, getting old was not on the menu. There were too many other things to do. . .like exploring the exciting world in which I was growing up. . .like the inevitability of school. . .and the anticipation of recess and of playing ball after school. In the years of youth was the wonder of planning for the next day, the month and the next year and, of course, there would be no end to the years to come. In adulthood there was the excitement of work and the wonder of a family. . .children growing up and the privilege of providing for them. There was the privilege of being a role model for children and a leader and an example for the people I served, a path that saw some success and some failures. There was the empty nest when children were gone, though not forgotten . . .a time of both loneliness and rejoicing. Then came retirement and I began to think seriously about my mortality and the realization that well over half my life was probably over. There were times of great sadness and great joy and even anticipation of doing things impossible before. . .time for hobbies, travel and even relaxation. But now, at the over-ripe age of eighty-one, there is the realization that life will not last forever. At the same time there is the feeling that I do not want to rush things along and there is still much that I want to do. My plate is still full and my desk is still crowded with plans and projects. That is the way I want it and the way I plan to keep it for a long, long time.

So how does it feel to be eighty-one? If you discount a few aches and pains, a large number of pills at breakfast . . .if you remember that you cannot run or play tennis and if you take your nap in the afternoon. . .if you rejoice in the great memories that are yours and the large number of friends that you have accumulated along the way. . .if you remember to give thanks to God for the eighty-one great years and for what is still ahead. . .then being eighty-one years of age IS A GREAT PLACE TO BE!

THE GUARD CAT

It was an ordinary morning. After my morning treat and a breakfast of cat crackers, I let my staff know that I would like to go outside for a little while. They complied and, as usual, told me to stay on the porch. I smiled inside because I knew I would take my usual walk around the house and come back to sunbathe on the porch. But today something was different. I thought it would be nice to move up a few steps on the back hill. On the third step I froze. . .there at the top of the hill was a deer looking down at me. With my tail straight back I crouched motionless. We stared at each other for a full five minutes. I thought it might be nice to go on up and make friends with him, but as soon as I took a step up, he turned and ran into the woods. Now, I knew better than to go on to the top because my man-staff would come up, fuming, and carry me back down.

When I came back to the porch, my man-staff patted me and told me how proud he was of me for chasing the deer away from the flowers and vegetables we had planted on the hill. I hadn't thought of that, but you take credit whenever you can get it. From now on I will think of myself as a guard cat. I will watch the woods and if I see a deer all I will have to do is make a quick move toward him and he will run. It is nice to have an official job that is as easy to do as guarding the hill from deer. Next month I will ask for an increase in treats. LB

BEVERLY'S COLUMN

Good morning, afternoon, and evening! Since I don't know just when this gets read, I'll include all greetings. Hope you and yours are surviving this weather.

We're doing fine for eighty-one-year-olds and I'm sure some of you understand what that means. We've had rain and more rain. Today it seems like all the chain saws in the county are busy cutting down or trimming brushes and bushes-and all on our street. Yesterday our friends from Reddick Presbyterian Church went to church with us before they returned to Florida. Cindy and Arlene came without their mother, Marie, who stopped in Tallahassee to visit with other daughter, Carol and her family. The service was well-attended and the music and sermon were complimentary.

F. and I plan to join the choir on Wed. with the intention of assisting. BUT we've told the director to let us know if our ancient voices don't blend, we'll dismiss ourselves. The choir is great without us, but sings the most gorgeous a cappella work we've heard. Sometimes they are missing a few folks, but maybe they'll let us help out. Let you know how it goes.

Yesterday afternoon we went to an ice cream social. Those who attended brought ice cream or go-withs (toppings, cake, cookies, brownies). It was held beside the pool in a shaded area. Some folks brought real home-made ice cream! Delicious! More later on. B.

THE SCHEDULE (as we know it)

- August 19 – 22 Cindy and Arlene
- September 3 – 6+/- Karl & friend
- October 15 - 24 Brad and Mary Lou (We will all be in Gatlinburg, TN)

Lots of open time. . . Come on up or over. Give us a call.

BYE BYE BIRDIE

A TOUCH OF PINK

As I sit at the kitchen area table, drinking coffee, I see the humming birds dipping their long beaks into the red sugar water flowers on the feeder just outside the window. As they dip their long bills into the red nectar of the feeder, their rapidly beating wings hold them motionless in mid-air and the Japanese maple leaves around them move gently.

It was in the motion of the leaves that I noticed a touch of pink on the edge of the leaves, a preface to the brilliant red that will paint them in the coming months as fall approaches. It is a signal that the summer is drawing to a close and that fall and cooler weather is on the way. Even though the last few days have brought cooler weather to Moss Manor, the memory of a hot summer makes this promise of fall a welcome sight.

In October and November, the fifteen large Japanese maples surrounding Moss Manor will turn a brilliant red with just enough yellow to temper their brilliance. The tiny spot of pink on the edges of the leaves this morning, reminds me that autumn is not far away and will bring with it the wonderful "leaf season" of the mountains, a time when the Master's brush will repaint the greens with the brilliance of fall colors.

What a wonderful, ever changing world is ours to enjoy!

BYE BYE BIRDIE

I really hate to do it, but it has to be done. We have enjoyed watching the little birds fly down to the lattice fence work on the post and then quickly hop to the bird feeder, grab a sunflower seed and retreat to the security of the surrounding foliage. The metal feeder had been given to us by a guest and it was designed to withstand all invaders like squirrels, raccoons, large birds, etc. It had worked admirably except for the big raccoon that had learned to hold the feed gate open and scatter the seed to the ground for his family. It had really frustrated the squirrels even though they tried and tried. I could see and enjoy the activity from my place at the kitchen table. When washing dishes I could see them fluttering in and out just below our window. I really hate to do it, but for the good and safety of cat and people it must be done.

Another visitor, one that is black without wings and weighing about 175 pounds, has become a customer of the feeder. Buddy Bear has found the scent of birdseed and has visited us at least four times. He is rather regular in his visits, coming in mid-afternoon. We thought we were negligent in leaving the gate open to the back garden area and he could be discouraged by the four-foot wooden fence and gate. Besides, it was exciting to watch Buddy Bear lumber around and exit up the steep steps of the mountain side. He reminded us that we have moved into his territory and we are the invaders of the mountain.

That all changed rather rapidly. I was working at the computer near the back door and Lady Bean was sunning herself on the porch just outside. I happened to glance outside and LB was no longer relaxed but rather had moved behind the lattice work, crouched down with eyes riveted straight ahead through the lattice openings. It was an unusual pose so I got up, opened the glass door and followed her gaze. There, not six feet way, just under the birdfeeder was Buddy. He had not yet accomplished his mission of knocking down the feeder and gorging himself on its contents. I stepped out, picked up Lady Bean and dropped her inside the door. The movement must have bothered Buddy as he immediately started to amble away toward the gate. It was then I noticed that the gate was closed and latched. In a swift and almost graceful movement, the bear jumped up and over the gate, using his feet to facilitate his climb and jump movement. I came inside, went to the back deck door and watched as he climbed the steep crosstie steps and disappeared into the woods on the ridge.

I really hate to do it, for my sake and the sake of the birds, but the feeder must come down. We do not want Buddy Bear to continue to make regular visits, expecting food. I do not want to surprise him on his visit or have LB try to make friends with a wild creature. So the bird feeder must come down. The birds must look elsewhere for their dinner and Buddy Bear must be disappointed when he looks for a snack. Maybe he will get discouraged.

JOINING THE CHOIR

A few weeks ago Beverly and I joined the choir at Nacoochee Presbyterian Church. Although I came along rather hesitantly, it was good to be back with a group of singers who enjoyed the privilege of praise through song and the gift of fellowship that is usually found in a church choir. Beverly fits right in with the alto section and I follow along with the excellent tenors. There is no choir loft and when it is time for the choir to sing, they get up from their places in the congregation and gather around the choir. The pianist/director is a professional musician who makes practice fun. While we miss our CPC choir, JoAnn and all our friends in Ocala, it is good to still be singing and making new friends in the church up here.

RAIN

Last month the rain came at night. We heard the thunder in the distance and if our eyes were open we saw the echo of lightning momentarily fill the room. When the cat jumped on the bed and burrowed between the sheet and the blanket for security, we knew the storm was not far away.

The sound of rain beating down on the trees with its rhythmic drumming on the roof and down the drain pipes becomes a tympanic symphony. There is something special in the rumbling sounds of distant thunder and the magic of the falling rain that makes you want to lie awake and listen yet quickly puts you to sleep.

I look out the window and see the early rising hummingbirds busily emptying the red nectar from the feeder outside the kitchen window. The driveway is wet and the bushes are quietly shaking the water from their leaves. I think to myself, "I wasted my time and water when I watered the newly planted flowers on the back hillside." It is good to be up early with my cup of coffee and with Lady Bean stretched out as close to the keyboard as she is allowed. The world is still and thoughts come easily.

These are good years and the few aches and pains that come with passing years are little payment for the wonderful years that have been ours. Last night we showed our guests a few old videos of our days on the water in *Karisto*. It is good to relive experiences that are part of our history and will live on in memory as well as in video. It is fun to remember but it is also good to look ahead. Later on today we will drive up the twisting mountain road, passing Lake Burton and Clayton, to enjoy the experience of dinner at the Dillard House. We will probably eat too much and gain a pound but once in a while it is worth it.

I hear stirring in the house so guess it is time turn on a new pot of coffee and leave my thoughts and the wet world outside until later. It has been a good night and I look forward to a good day ahead.

BUTTERFLIES GALORE

The sunshine has brought a multitude of butterflies to feast on the pink and purple buddleia and the flowers on the back porch. We get out the book and try to identify them but it is more fun just to photograph them and enjoy the fragile beauty they bring.

CUSSING IN SIAMESE

I am a very gentle and well-mannered cat, most of the time. Sometimes I get impatient with my staff when they do not do exactly as I desire and a rather agitated meow usually straightens things out. BUT. . .there are times. . .

I remember one such time. Now I like to go into the garage of my Florida home where there is a large screen door through which I can watch world go by. It is a good place to nap and enjoy the sunshine that comes through the screen. But I also like to have the door into the house slightly cracked so that when I get hungry or thirsty or need to use my box I can have immediate access. Well, this particular day I was enjoying myself in the garage. It was hot but it felt good. (We cats like to be warm.) But somehow the door to the house got closed and tightly latched. I got thirsty and tried to get in to my water but the door would not open. I scratched at the door and even meowed but to no avail. Finally, I gave up and went back and tried to sleep in the sun but I was still thirsty. I waited for my staff to open the door but nothing happened. I do not know what they were thinking but it certainly was not about me.

The longer I waited, the hungrier and thirstier I became and the madder I got. I thought, "How could they do this to the one who controls the household and is so good to them?"

After what seemed to be an eternity, I heard steps in the house and my man-staff opened the door. As I stalked through the door, I let him know exactly how I felt. In my deepest, loudest, Siamese voice I spoke to him. I would look at him and yowl, take a step forward, look up and yowl at him again. Now I do not usually cuss, but this was an occasion that called for it and I was letting him know just how I felt.

I knew he was getting the message when I heard him say to my lady-staff, "If you have never been cussed out by a Siamese cat, you do not know what profanity is."

It is good to be understood and I feel better after venting my feelings. LB

LABOR DAY IN HELEN

Helen is a great place to visit with its Alpine buildings, Bavarian restaurants and interesting shops. It is fun to watch the tubers float through town on the Chattahoochee River. But do not come on Labor Day. It seemed that at least half of Georgia was in the tiny town and driving on the one through street. Our van traveled like it was in a parade, letting pedestrians cross in front of us. (In Georgia they have the right of way to cross anywhere.) Come to Helen. It is great fun, especially during Oktoberfest, but don't come on Labor Day.

FUTURE VISITORS

We enjoy seeing our friends and have them visit with us in Moss Manor. October and November are beautiful months in the mountains so let us know when you might like to come and we will try to work it out.

- Sonny & Jerry September 22 – 26+/-
- Brad and Mary Lou October 15 – 24+/-
- Bob and Polly and others: November

BEVERLY'S CORNER

One of the advantages of a new situation is making new friends. It is not too easy, nor too hard, if you have a variety of interests. Eating has always been a favorite thing for me to do. (I'm sure you understand.) The Nacoochee Presbyterian Church has a lunch bunch and it seems their prime purpose is to eat at different places each month. This is great for those of us new to the area. We learn a lot. This month we went to Bernie's Bed and Breakfast. It's not very new, but the food and service were excellent. I had a Maryland Crab Cake sandwich which was delicious. So often I taste more bell pepper than crab, but this time the crab was outstanding! The dining area was in part of an old house. Renovations had closed in a large back porch which was available for dining in good weather. There were windows all around that area enabling guests to enjoy the out-of-doors while being indoors. I made some comment about how beautiful it was, and someone at the table said she had been there when Bernie's had first opened. She said that they had particularly enjoyed watching herds of buffalo roam out on the range! (Sing, if it seems appropriate.) You never know what you will learn when you listen to those who've been there before. More next month! B.

FALL'S COLORS

YELLOW OF SEPTEMBER

September drew to a close and fall began painting the landscape with the colors that made the mountains sparkle. Leaves are beginning to fall and although most are still light brown a few brighten the ground with a brilliant yellow. Light winds and cooler days remind us of the changes all around. The fields and clearings are bursting forth with the bright yellow of goldenrod and other light-colored weeds and blossoms.

As we drive the winding valley roads, we see whole fields that seem to be a golden mirror reflecting the sunlight. Beside the streams and on the hiking trails, other plants add their yellow blossoms to the mix.

Soon the world around us will be enriched with the reds and oranges that identify fall in the mountains. Soon, visitors will flock to the area to drink in the richness of leaf season in the North Georgia Mountains. But for now, as September melts away and October makes its colorful entry, we look around and remember the wonderful yellow of September.

THE NOSHERS ARE COMING!

Yes, on October 8, the Noshers are coming and we had better be ready for them. I understand that there will be about six of them and they will come from all parts of the Sautee Valley. More than that, they will be hungry. We had better be ready!

If you are not familiar with Noshers you are not alone for I had never heard of them either. I Goggled Nosher and found that a nosher was something to eat, therefore Noshers might well be those who come to eat. Turns out that is exactly what will be happening on Friday night.

Some weeks ago we had signed at the church to join a group who gathered to enjoy dinner together. It worked like this. Every couple that signed up was assigned a number. These numbers were placed at the points of a four-sided figure. The number on the top point was to be the host and provide the meat. The number to the right would bring the vegetable, the one on the bottom would bring the salad and the one to the left brought the dessert. Each month the numbers and positions on the diamond changed so that we go to different homes and meet different people.

We look forward to having the Noshers gather at Moss Manor and to meeting people we might have seen at church but did not really know. Besides, we look forward to a good meal.

WAITING FOR COMPANY

It is mid-morning but it seems like much earlier. The sun has not yet climbed over the mountains and the filtered shade gives a soft, early morning appearance. My first cup of coffee is almost gone and the biscotti is but a memory. Lady Bean is preening herself in the chair next to the table. She has been outside briefly but it is a little cool and damp for any respectable cat. We are waiting for company.

It is nice to have people come visit us in Moss Manor and I believe it is nice for them too. In our journey over the years we have met many people and made many friends. When they come to see us we have the opportunity to look back and relive in memory the many happy times we spent together in other places. Friends seem to be the glue that binds the fragmented pieces of life together. Like a patchwork quilt, they paint a lifetime with good memories. Like a winding road, they weave their way through the experiences, good and bad, that make a lifetime. Life would be dull and monotonous if it were not for the brightness and warmth that good friends bring.

This morning it is with a bit of excitement that we look forward to more company in Moss Manor. We have truly been blessed with friends from the past and look forward to new friends in the future.

OPEN THE FIREPLACE!

All summer long we have turned on the fans and when mid-day temperatures pushed toward ninety, even turned on the air conditioners. We have looked forward to and wished for the coming of fall with its fifty degree mornings and evenings. We have looked at the corner of the living room where the big stone fireplace stood idly by.

Three days ago, after the big rain, the temperature dropped to 50 degrees during the night and predictions were that it would stay for a while. It was time to break open the fireplace. Wood that had been split a few weeks ago waited anxiously to taste fire. Kindling was waiting in the garage and the time was right. Open the damper. Lay the fire. Enjoy the warmth of a crackling fire. It is fall again, the leaves are falling and the fireplace is burning brightly. It is good to be in Moss Manor in the fall.

FOOD FOR FRIENDS

In summer I thought I was planting a garden on the hill back of Moss Manor. The hill is about all you can see when looking out through the glass doors from the living room. We thought it would be good to have greenery and flowers looking back at us from the hill. We did our best to fill the area with plants that would be picturesque when we sat on the deck or glanced up from the living room. We planted mostly yellow or orange flowers as we were told the deer did not bother them. It all went well during July and August. Large-leafed gourd vines cascaded down from the upper tiers. Lantana and yellow calla lilies and purple-bearded iris grew well and showed off their blossoms. It was not perfect, but it was a good beginning. That was in the summer and early September.

Now September is gone and October is bringing cooler weather. With the coming of fall we watched the coming of the deer as well. No longer would they pass us on the ridge but now would venture down the hill and feast on the leafy green leaves and even yellow blossoms. Finding it good picking, mother doe brought her spotted young ones and they, too, enjoyed our plantings.

We have had to change our thinking about the garden on the hill. It is not really for our enjoyment, although we can enjoy it for awhile, it is really "Food for our Four-legged Friends." We are learning to enjoy brown and white spots instead of big green leaves, and it is really just as good!

A DAY IN THE HOSPITAL

I knew something was up. My staff was too nonchalant in the way they treated me. They would look at me and almost whisper to each other. So when it looked like something was about to happen, I retreated under their bed to safety. But it was not safe long. The long arm of my man-staff reached under and grabbed me by the scuff of my neck and dragged me out. He carried me down the hall and asked me to get into a cage. (They call it a carrier but it is a cage!) I protested with all the strength I had, but it was two against one and they finally won.

We traveled a long way. I did not know where or why we were going so I let them know my displeasure with loud Siamese yowls. Finally we stopped and I was carried, still in my cage, into a building. Inside there were two dogs, one barking and the other just holding his master. I decided it was best to be quiet and maybe they would not know I was there and would go away.

After while I was carried into a little room and was let out of my cage. I protested as much about getting out as I did about getting in I remembered this kind of room from visits to my vet in Florida, but the lady was different. She was nice enough and petted me and talked to my staff. She took me into the back and it was then that "all hell broke loose." They pulled and poked at me in inappropriate places and when they touched that place on my rear that was very sore, I really let them know it. I scored with my hind claws and almost got away but they finally overpowered me. After they talked to my staff, they took me back and put me in another little cage. What happened after that was awful! Two or three people in flowered uniforms took me out of the cage, held me down and stuck something sharp in my skin. I don't remember much after that. I just got sleepier and sleepier. When I began to wake up, I was back in their little cage. My rear was very sore and I had this awful, hard cone around my neck. I could hardly stand up. In fact, I fell over a few times but the sides of the cage caught me. I tried to clean and lick the place that hurt but the stiff cone around my neck would not let me. It was awful.

After a while they bundled me up in a towel and carried me to the front where my staff was waiting. My man-staff took me and held me tightly. When I tried to move I would feel so dizzy that I would settle back down. After talking to the people in white, my staff carried me to the car where my man-staff sat in the back seat and held me. I knew this was serious because he never sat in the back. I tried to get away but he would not let me. Once I made it to the other seat but was so dizzy I almost fell. I gave up and let him hold me.

It was good to get home. I looked around, rolled on the floor and staggered up and down the hall. My lady-staff took me to the bedroom and put me on the bed and stroked me. I even purred a little but my rear was hurting, I was still dizzy and that #@&% thing on my neck bothered me greatly. They thought it would keep me from cleaning my wounded rear but they were wrong. (We cats can conquer almost any obstacle.) Finally I won out because they took the awful cone from my neck.

Their guests came that evening. They shut me up in the bed room. When I heard the guests leave, I began to scratch the door and complain loudly. Soon they let me out. They were very loving to me and I was so glad to have things almost back to normal that I kept rubbing my head in their hands. I even let my lady-staff hold me in her lap. (That is something she always wants to do.) But tonight it felt good to be held.

It was an awful day. I hope it never happens again. LB

BEVERLY'S CORNER

Yellow, green, yellow, pink, yellow, red, and more yellow. With sunshine blasting through the woods, that's a gorgeous God-given sight that we see daily. It doesn't matter whether we're going to church just down the road from Sky Lake, or ten miles away to grocery-shop, or the other way to eat at Captain D's. We have no idea how long these marvelous views will continue, but enjoy them we do.

We are constantly amazed with the leaves whether they are just very still in the trees, lying on the ground, or being jostled by the wind. Of course, it does help if the rain has ceased. When Francis checked the rain gauge the other day, he was surprised to see that we had a total of about ten inches in three days! We know you're hoping no more hurricanes will be along, either.

Best wishes. We'll see you soon. B.

THE NOSHERS

NOVEMBER

November came in with beautiful weather in the mountains. October brought awesome colors to the trees and mountain sides. The later part of the month also brought rain, wind and storms. But November began with clear, crisp weather. Morning saw the temperature in the upper thirties, rising to the seventies. It also saw a torrent of leaves covering the moss in the front yard and demanding daily blowing to clear the yard. They are calling for temperatures in low thirties. The fireplace has felt good. Each month has its special beauty and November is no exception.

LEAVES AND LEAF-PEEPERS

The Smoky Mountains National Park is known world-wide for the brilliant colors of the leaves during the fall. We had planned to visit the Gatlinburg area during this week. Alas, almost everyone else who could possibly get away also planned to visit that week. We found the mountains filled with beautiful leaves and the roads filled with "leaf-peepers." They came on buses, in automobiles, in motor homes and on motorcycles. In the overlooks the parking places were all taken and when we were lucky enough to find a spot, we had to be careful when taking pictures not to take the head of a "peeper" instead of the orange, yellow and red of the foliage. At least we were with the vast majority who thought this was the best time to see the fall colors of the mountains.

HIKING IN THE MOUNTAINS

One of the many adventures that we experienced during our trip through the Smoky Mountains National Park was a hike in the Joyce Kilmer Memorial Forest. Brad and I looked forward to a short hike and a quick return for snacks at the picnic table by the car. This was not to be.

The trail was well-kept but was laced with spider-like roots that both helped and hindered our footing. We moved up through poplars and firs that well could have been the inspiration for Mr. Kilmer's famous poem, "Trees."

After huffing and puffing up the mountain for a while, we encountered a large, fallen tree blocking the trail. As we moved up, there were views that offered photo opportunities on all sides. Every few turns of the trail we would say to each other, "Don't you think we should be over halfway?" But the trail was still going up and passing hikers would tell us we were not halfway. We were getting tired but still determined to make it to the end of the trail.

About forty minutes on the trail we came to the big rock with a memorial plaque embedded in the center. After a brief rest, we asked for directions. Someone, who we thought was an experienced traveler in the park, indicated that we could take one of two trails but one would have much larger trees to view, so naturally we took that one. Again the trail wound upward and around and eventually we found ourselves back at the same rock. Again, we rested, talked to fellow hikers and, this time, were directed to take the right trail toward the bottom.

This half of the trail seemed infinitely longer than the first half plus the loop. The only good news was that we were going down the mountain. That brought a new bundle of muscles into play with new aches and pains. We were grateful to the trail-keepers for providing a few rough railings on the sharpest of turns and narrowest parts of the trail. Like children in the back seat of the car, we asked each hiker we met, "Are we almost there?" Finally we received the good news that the bottom was just around the next few turns. Sure enough, we soon could see the glimmer of sunshine reflecting from car windows.

As we staggered across the parking lot, we were met by almost hysterical wives and a "band of sisters" they had met near the car. "Where have you been? We were worried sick that you had collapsed on the trail! Don't ever do that again!" We were escorted to the car, but not before one of their new friends ran over shaking her fingers in my face and crying out, "Shame, shame on you! Why didn't you let us know where you were?"

Both hikers and those who waited were glad to see each other. It probably will take days or even weeks to live down the harrowing experiences of those who left for a half hour hike and three hours later returned to those who remained below and anxiously waited for the return of the long overdue hikers.

FIFTY YEARS CAN MAKE A DIFFERENCE

Beverly and I had both visited Gatlinburg, Tennessee about fifty years ago. It was a quaint, almost sleepy mountain town with many craft shops, a few hotels and restaurants. You can imagine our surprise to see the Pigeon River lined with condos and hotels, the streets packed with stores of all kinds and chain restaurants on every corner. Traffic was bumper to bumper and streets were filled with vacationers. It was still a nice place to visit but the charming little town we remembered had been replaced by a city full of attractions. There was a four lane main street from Pigeon Forge to Gatlinburg making one long strip city along the banks of the Pigeon River.

I know you cannot stop progress, but I sometimes wonder what progress really is.

THE SKY IS FALLING

I have a little bit more sympathy for Chicken Little after our experience in the swing the other day. Beverly and I were enjoying the beauty of an early fall evening as we sat in the swing under the trees in our front yard. Every minute or so we would hear the crack and rattle of falling objects from the lofty oaks and hickory trees as they hit limbs and bounced through leaves. It sounded like we were being peppered by pellets from the sky. Suddenly I felt the glancing impact of one of the objects on the top of my head. I knew, then, exactly how Chicken Little felt as he cried out, "the sky is falling, the sky is falling." We watched the object that hit me roll a little way down the hill in front of us. Retrieving it, I found it to be a big, brown acorn.

This year there is a plentiful supply of acorns and nuts covering the moss lawn in our yard. Looking across the yard, it looks almost like a sea of bubbles. The squirrels have been having a ball collecting them. The deer have been snacking on them. It looks like I will have to get out the broom and try to sweep them into a pile and carry them into the woods if I am to see the smooth green moss to which we are accustomed.

I had better wear a hard hat for protection when I am working in the yard, at least until the fall winds come and shake the projectiles loose from the trees and the sky is no longer falling.

THE NOSHERS HAVE COME

Last month I told you that the Noshers were coming. On Friday, October 8, they came to our house for dinner. I met them at the gate and led them through the winding maze that is Sky Lake to our home on Laurelwood. There were six church members that we had seen but never met. After appetizers in the living room and some getting acquainted talk, we came to the dining table. At each place was a picture placemat of Nacoochee Presbyterian Church which were favors to be taken home. Beverly had prepared the meat which was a delicious crown pork roast stuffed with sausage. Ted and Mike brought a wonderful mixed salad and wine for the meal. Kelly and Marilyn brought the vegetable dish with butternut squash, cranberries, rutabaga and other good tasting things. Ice cream and cake dessert was furnished by Charles and Barbara. It was a delightful meal and all joined in the conversation around the table. After coffee and dessert and more conversation we descended to the basement "hobby room" where Francis showed his RC planes, the model railroads and the ham station.

When it was time to leave and goodbyes were said, the Noshers were led back through the darken maze of curves, hill, and valleys to the main gate. We had new friends and had enjoyed a most pleasant evening together.

MY NEW COLLAR

I knew things were too good to last. The other day when my staff came in from one of the many day trips, I greeted them with my usual roll and request to go outside. They petted me and then opened the door. It is always good to enjoy the great out-of- doors after being shut in for most of the day. The birds welcomed me. They always make a lot of noise when I lie down below their feed box and watch them. After I made my way around the house and came in the back door, I made my way to the kitchen table where my man-staff was typing away on his computer. I stretched out right beside where he was working.

Then it happened. He did not think I knew what was going on but I did. I felt him slip something around my neck and then I heard a faint click. I moved my head from side to side and heard a sound of a tiny bell. The light feel of something around my neck and the sound brought back memories from long ago. I could not remember exactly when but somewhere in the low numbers of my nine lives, I remember wearing something like this. It was not really uncomfortable so I did not make a fuss. When my lady-staff came in, she oohed and aahed and told me how nice I looked in my new collar. She said the light pink design went beautifully with my light gray-brown fur. My man-staff also stroked me and told me what a good cat I was. I'm sure both statements were true and I was glad to please. Besides, it was almost supper time and I did not want to upset them.

The sound of that bell tinkling every time I shook my head took a little getting used to, but I soon forgot about it. Besides if it made me look more beautiful, I could put up with the slight inconvenience. LB

LOOKING FORWARD TO COMING HOME

Only one more month and the Womack's will be packing up and heading south. It has been a great spring, summer and fall at Moss Manor. Each season has its own beauty and we have watched as early leaves turned into the full green of summer, then burst into the many colors of fall. We have felt the spring breeze change to the warmth of summer afternoons and then turn to brisk fall mornings when a burning fireplace felt good. We have enjoyed friends and family who came from many places to spend a day or a week in Moss Manor. We look forward to our children with their families coming for Thanksgiving. New friends that we have made at church or in Sky Lake will be missed when we return to Florida in late November, and we will look forward to renewing friendships in Florida.

Yes, we do look forward to coming home to Florida but are already planning things to do when we return to Moss Manor next year, sometime around Easter.

LADY BEAN IS READY, TOO!

We know she is because she often gets into the car and finds a place to park. Sometimes on a seat, but more recently on the dashboard so we can see she is ready to go back to Ocala. We think she's getting a little too cool. COOL CAT! B.

A CRUISE

A lot has happened since the last issue of Moss Manor News hit the internet. As I remember, fall had fulfilled its mission of dropping most of the yellow and red leaves on the ground. A definite chill was in the air and we were looking forward to Thanksgiving and then returning to our Ocala home. We are now in Florida and I will try to bring you up to date on our activities.

THANKSGIVING 2010

Again, the children, grandchildren and dogs gathered in Moss Manor. There was good food, great confusion, a lot of fun together, a few calamities and the joy of a family being together. When the tail lights faded in the distance and the dust settled around the house, we busied ourselves with preparing for the trip home. Leaving Moss Manor is always hard. We had hoped to see at least one snowfall before we left but we were disappointed. The ice and snow would come later.

THE TRIP HOME

It is amazing how much more gets in the van for the trip home than we anticipated. Finally the car was packed, the water cut off, pipes drained and doors locked. Lady Bean was coaxed from under the bed and brought complaining to the car. After one false start and a return to be sure the garage was closed, we were on our way. The first part of the trip was uneventful and Lady Bean settled down to endure the trip. Just north of Macon, a car pulled beside us, a horn honked, and hands waved vigorously. They belonged to Lee and Sally from Countryside Presbyterian Church in Ocala, who were returning from a visit in South Carolina. We stopped for lunch with them and enjoyed the short visit with good friends. In Florida we hit hard rain but made it through and found our home in On Top Of the World (OTOW) waiting for us. It was good to get home.

THE CHRISTMAS DROP-INS

There was little time to rest since we had planned for three Christmas parties. The tree was up from a July visit but we still had lots of decorating and baking to do. The days came quickly. Friends from the Reddick Church and from Countryside Choir came on Sunday. Other friends and neighbors came on Tuesday and the Red Hats came on Friday. It was a good but busy week.

On Christmas Eve we attended services at the Reddick Presbyterian Church. Christmas Day was quiet. . .quite different from Thanksgiving when the family was all together. On January 9th I had the privilege of filling the pulpit at Beverly's church, Countryside Presbyterian.

THE CRUISE

Beverly's birthday was coming up and we had planned a cruise to the Panama Canal to celebrate. On January 14th we climbed aboard the Cruise Connection bus which would carry us to Ft. Lauderdale where the *Coral Princess* waited our arrival. *Coral Princess* is 963 feet long, over seven stories high and carries 1970 passengers with 900 crew members.

Our trip was nice with lots of luxury. Going into the Panama Canal on the cruise ship to Gatun Lake, then continuing on to the Pacific on a smaller vessel was the highlight of our trip. The *Coral Princess* then went on to its next port-of-call and we traveled by bus to meet them back in the Gulf of Mexico. We stayed on board and watched the other tourists visit the shops and do sight-seeing on the islands that we visited. (Cruising the Caribbean on *Karisto* had spoiled us for visiting tourist traps with a thousand other people at the same time.) Although it was nice, we saw too much ocean, ate too much food, and were ready to come home when the trip was over. (So was everyone else!)

FROM LADY BEAN'S PERSPECTIVE

Thanksgiving may have been good for my staff but I was glad when the confusion was over, I was let out of the bedroom and the noisy dogs went home. The next day I knew something was up because the red suitcases came out. I slept on them as much as I could but when they were put in the car, I headed for security under the bed. Alas, they pulled me out and put me in the car. It was a long trip and it made me very nervous which caused me to shed hair all over my staff's clothing. It was good to get to a familiar house.

For a while all went well, except when people came to the house for parties and I had to stay in the bedroom. Then it started all over again. The red suitcases came out I started hiding under beds. But this time my staff just left me home. A nice man from next door came over and fed me each day but it was not the same as having my staff wait on me all the time. It went on and on and on for at least a year. Then they came back. I was so glad to see them. I stayed right underfoot or beside them on the sofa and even was on the bed with them.

I hope they never go away again unless they take me with them! LB

FROM MY JOURNAL

I guess I am losing it, one faculty at a time. I had always thought of myself as growing old gracefully and prided myself on reasonably good health. Although it is true that I can no longer play tennis, walk with a slight shuffle and take too many Aleve for my back pain, I felt my faculties were pretty much together. That was until last night.

Do you remember Mr. McGoo, an almost blind comic character whose stumbling made us laugh? (Probably politically incorrect.) Well, last night I felt great sympathy for Mr. McGoo. Getting up to walk out a cramp, I thought I saw the cat sitting on the floor so I reached down to pet her. I petted my left shoe! But worse than that, I did it again a little further on. . . this time I petted my right shoe! I never found out where Lady Bean was sleeping but I did know that I felt like saying, "Move over, Mr. McGoo, here I come!"

MY TURN

One of the activities of the church in Sky Lake is to set up dinner parties in groups of eight to meet in various homes. Different couples are in charge of the main course and the other couples fill in the rest of the meal. It's a great way to meet folks and to see some great homes. One home that we enjoyed had been in their family for over a hundred years. Needless to say, it had been renovated and renovated, but beautiful and interesting anyway.

At the Christmas Eve service both Francis and David took part in leading the service and both wives played the piano. I hope Anna and I can play together on the piano and organ next year. It would add a little more interest to the service.

When Francis told me about going on to the Pacific to see the entire Panama Canal and then taking a bus back to catch up with the Princess at another port, I was worried. Slightly afraid one of us would miss the connection! I forgot the Isthmus of Panama was only fifty miles wide at this point. Our bus ride was so fast through the forest everything seemed just a green blur, but beautiful. We only spent ten days on the trip, but LB thought it seemed like forever.

I don't know if the 900 crew included the entertainers or not, but they had truly a wide variety of performers. Most of the evening shows were musicals with great dance acts and LOUD music. I gave F. a tissue once and we stuffed our ears help tone down the decibels!

On ocean trips there is always too much food. We ate until I finally asked our waiter to be sure he picked out the smallest lamb chops he could find. Everyone at our table must have had two one-pound chops each, but mine may have been only a half-pound. Delicious! B.

THE MUSIC OF RAIN

We are back in Moss Manor and glad to find everything working. We hope this newsletter will be helpful in keeping up with Beverly and me as we travel from place to place. It is still raining a little up here as it is in Ocala, but we see that spring is really coming to the mountains with forsythia and wisteria blooming wildly and new green leaves appearing on the trees and plants. As I look out the kitchen window I see a couple of deer visiting our yard. Today we finish unpacking and we should have everything in place by this afternoon (or at least by next month). Until we return or until you come to visit, we will miss you. Be safe and God bless you.

THE TRIP TO MOSS MANOR

Our return to Moss Manor began a day late. Somehow, we never seem to get everything done and all our things packed on schedule. Besides, rain was forecast all day Monday. It was good, and probably necessary, to have that extra time to fit everything into the van. By Monday night we were packed and ready to leave the next morning.

Five-thirty came early but we were soon up and moving. The food from the refrigerator still needed to be packed and the few extra bags and two airplanes had to be carefully fitted into an already full van. Finally we were ready to lock up and leave, but where was our Lady Bean? She had been sitting on the back of the sofa waiting to go, but now she was nowhere to be seen. It always happens. Just before we were to put her in the car, she would hide under the bed. This year we had foxed her and shut the bedroom doors but we

forgot about the sofa. After an episode with the broom, she reluctantly came out and we all got into the van.

Although we look forward to our stay in the mountains, it is hard
to leave our good neighbors and friends in Ocala. (Wish we could
take them all with us, but not all at one time.)

The drive to North Georgia takes about eight hours, counting
time for breakfast and a quick lunch. The skies were overcast with a
few sprinkles of rain. . .good weather for traveling. Lady Bean was
a wonderful traveler. It was the first time we had taken her in the
car without her letting us know her displeasure with a loud Siamese
protest. This time she climbed into her place between us, sometimes
changing to the back seat, where she slept the whole way.

We were all glad to see the winding road through Sky Lake
to Moss Manor and to find our home waiting to welcome us. (My
daughter, Mary Glenn, had come over the past week-end, turned on
water and heat, cleaned the house thoroughly and left flowers around
and in the house to welcome us.) Lady Bean spent the evening running up and down the hall and rediscovering her special places in
the house while Beverly and I unpacked the necessary items, rested
and relaxed.

We were also welcomed by three deer which tasted our plants
and seemed almost tame enough to feed by hand. Unfortunately, we
had no food for them and they left us for the neighbor who always
had corn for them. It is good to be in back in our second home.

VISIT SCHEDULE

Some of you have already visited with us and we hope that you
will return. Last year we had about thirty visitors, including family.
We enjoy having company and hope that many of you can spend a
few days with us.

- March 28 (now) until April 21 in Sky Lake
- April 14 – 18 Margaret, Bob and Ardis
- May 15 Return to Sky Lake for the summer
- June 24 – 27 house may be used for a reunion.

The last week in August we will return to Ocala to get ready for our trip to the Yellowstone National Park. Other times are open for your visits. Just let us know so we can co-ordinate the October-November schedules. We will probably be in Sky Lake during part of this time (during leaf season). We will keep you posted by Moss Manor News.

SOMETHING'S UP

I had known that something was up for the last week. My staff was doing unusual things, like filling boxes with stuff and putting them in the garage. When they pulled out the red suitcases, I knew they or we were going somewhere. I hoped I was included.

Now I do not mind traveling, but the thought of staying in the moving box they call a van for a whole day makes me very nervous. I begin to lose hair and look for places to hide. There are only two places the big van takes me, to the doctor and on a long trip. I really do not like either. I guess I just do not like change, so at the last minute I find a good place to hide. This time, there was only one place and it was under the big sofa. I was secure until a broom started pushing me out. I knew the jig was up so I reluctantly came out.

The trip was not too bad. My staff put my pillow between them and my food, water and box in the back. They would pet me and talk to me so I decided not to fuss at them. It was a long trip. They left me in the car alone a couple of times, but it was warm and I napped and waited patiently.

Finally, after hours of travel, I saw things I was familiar with and when they stopped, I recognized the house with the long hall. It was good to get inside and see all the good places I like. Before I went in I saw my friend, Doe Eyes, and two other deer. It is good to be here and I guess the long trip was worth it. LB

RAIN IN THE NIGHT

About 2:00 this morning I woke with my usual leg cramps. The predicted rain had come and the sound of drops peppering the tree emphasized by an occasional roll of thunder was a symphony of sound. I opened the window a little more to turn up the volume. The rush of water coming down the drains at the corners of the house added a brass section to the music of the rain. I lay back down and listened. Seeing me awake, Lady Bean jumped out of her basket bed and joined me in our bed. We listened to the music of the rain until we both fell asleep.

BEVERLY'S VIEW

Sunshine is nice, but driving all day in it can be hard on the eyes. We were lucky this time. The sky was overcast all the way. The dismal, cloudy sky was a blessing in disguise.

Thank you, God, for the beginnings of spring. The new green leaves coming, and the spring flowers blooming in the woods certainly brightened the day. First, we saw white through the dark woods and then we realized we were seeing dogwood. In small spots and then in larger and larger ones were the white, purple, and fragrant hanging vines of wisteria. (Francis probably thought I was losing my mind by the way I hollered when I saw a new clump.) We did not see any forsythia until we were closer to Sky Lake. Ours had bloomed beside the driveway and had lost most of their blooms there. Glorious yellow color! Our daffy-down dillies had produced their flowers earlier and must have been as beautiful as others we saw on the way up the mountain.

The blueberry bushes have flowers on them, but no evidence of even green berries yet. The deer in the yard seem to have their eyes on the bushes. They are waiting, probably impatiently! Haven't seen the "b'ar."

As usual the blooming cherry tree has left its blooms all over the ground like a late winter snow. One day we'll get up here in time to see them on the tree. B.

THE WELCOME MAT

THE TRIP FROM FLORIDA

Our journey to North Georgia was to begin by 7:30 a.m. At 8 a.m. Beverly's bandage from the wounded toe slipped off. By 8:45 I had poked, coerced, and finally pulled Lady Bean from under the sofa. By 9:15 we were at the Doctor's office to get the bandage back on Bev's foot and toe. By 10:00 we were finally underway. The trip was uneventful except that we left I-75, with its overload of 18-wheelers, south of Macon to pull the Buzzard Wagon (my model airplane cargo trailer) on less-traveled roads and bypass Atlanta. It was a nice secondary road with great scenery but slow. It was around 8 p.m. when we pulled into the Moss Manor driveway. Everyone was glad to get to our second home and get a good night's sleep. It is always a relief to get home safely and offer a short prayer of thanks.

THE GREEN, GREEN MOSS OF HOME

It is 7:30 in the morning and I am looking out the breakfast window over the moss lawn and into the woods that climb the gentle hill away from our yard. It must be early for the deer but the squirrels are busy scavenging for forgotten nuts. The sun is still hidden behind the mountains but the morning light is bringing out the many different shades of green on the soft deer moss that gives Moss Manor its name.

The first hummingbird I have seen this spring just settled on the feeder hanging from the Japanese maple by the window and drank his fill. He then flitted among the gold-green leaves and twig-like branches before speeding away.

The leaves of tall trees that canopy the yard begin to rustle with the first breath of morning, mimic the moss and intensify the many shades of green. The view is a perfect setting for a hymn of praise and a prayer of thanksgiving. It is good to see again the green, green moss of our mountain home!

A TELEPHONE THAT WORKS

It was frustrating to say the least, trying to decide which phone to use when we wanted to make a call. In Florida we used the regular phone for long distance and kept the cell phone for mobile use. In Georgia, we used the cell phone for all our outgoing calls but we could only receive incoming calls on our regular phone. It was enough to make me tear out my hair (and I do not have any to spare.)

Now it is different. With a paper from Habersham County, proving that I am really a senior, delivered to Windstream, we were able to get the discounted bundle which gives us TV, internet and unlimited phone calls. It will be a great relief to answer any phone and make a call whenever we wish. . .in other words to have a "telephone that works."

A RIDE THROUGH THE MOUNTAINS

The day after we arrived in Sky Lake, we drove to Cleveland for supplies. Coming home we decided to take the long way home through Helen and Unicoi State Park. Even with the price of gas, it was well worth it just to enjoy again the Alpine Village, the Chattahoochee River, the winding mountain road lined with Mt. Laurel and the valley pastures with sheep, goats, horses and cattle. Sometimes the longest road is the shortest (or most pleasant) way home.

THE END OF THE WORLD, AGAIN

Saturday May 21. . .The morning broke cool and clear. The sun danced across the new green leaves of early spring and played on the moss lawn. It was a good day to be alive, or so it seemed. The problem is that, according to Harold Camping, the world was to end at 6 PM sharp. The eighty-nine-year-old, self-taught Bible scholar had worked it all out starting from the time of Noah and the flood to the present time using apocalyptic literature and numerology. Mighty earthquakes are to come during the day and will begin a continuing judgment. It is now 9:00 AM and breakfast is ready so I will finish this later (if I am still here).

Sunday May 22. . .

The afternoon and evening of May 21 came and went. Six o'clock saw no sign of the "rapture" and even the Iceland earthquake was a minor one. A friend of mine sat in his meadow and watched. He said, "If it does not happen, I can enjoy the beautiful scenery, and if does, it should be a spectacular sight."

Mr. Camping has missed again, as have hundreds of other false prophets since the time of Christ. The sad thing about the whole "end of the world" scenario is that it tarnishes the witness of Christians everywhere. When scripture is interpreted narrowly, exclusively, entirely literally and even blatantly misinterpreted, it calls into question the truth of the word of God. Fiction, like the *Left Behind* series, leaves a false message, impugns the facts of scripture and the truth of God's word. Those of us who believe that scripture is the Word of God, that Christ will return and God will triumph over evil, also believe that NO ONE, especially not Mr. Camping, knows the day or hour of His coming.

Thank God another day is dawning that there is a Savior to proclaim and work to be done in his name. Guess I had better get off of my soapbox and enjoy each day in Sky Lake.

SUITCASES

It all started as usual. . .suitcases on the bed, boxes in the garage. . .unusual activities from my staff. They thought I did not know, but it was obvious. I tried to prepare myself by sleeping in the red suitcase but as time passed I became more nervous I knew I was about to be shut up in the van with my staff and be bounced around for a long time. I tried to prepare myself but when the morning came and the last box of food was put in the car, I could not help myself and I hid under the sofa. My man-staff tried to coax me out and even poked me with a broom. Finally he lifted something, reached under and unceremoniously pulled me out, carried me to the car and pushed me in.

We traveled all day long and I could not get out once. I tried to sleep in back, between my staff, and in both laps, but nothing was really comfortable. Finally, the air outside smelled different and I looked up to see trees almost covering the road. When we turned into our steep driveway, I knew we were almost home. As soon as the car stopped, I wanted out. My man-staff got out and I followed him. Soon I was inside my house with the long green hall and the big glass window.

I guess the trip was worth it, (all ten hours), but I hope they will stay here a long time before they pull out the red suitcases and begin to pack again. LB

THE CHAIN SAW

I like to use a chainsaw. My infatuation with it came late in life soon before my retirement when we moved to the place where hurricanes gave me lots of downed trees on which to practice. When we began spending time in Moss Manor where there was a big, open fireplace in the living room, it gave me the perfect opportunity to drag out the saw and begin cutting firewood from the fallen trees on the property.

Last week, when my doctor told me in no uncertain words to stay off of ladders and be careful with my footing, I began to wonder if it was a good idea to continue with the chainsaw. . .probably not. But desire and pride overcame common sense and today I was up in the woods attacking a recently fallen tree. I do know my limits. . .no trees over eight inches, no cutting overhead and be careful of my footing. Maybe it is because I like to see the chips fly and maybe it is because cutting fire wood is cheaper than buying it, but I still enjoy using the noisy beast. From my vantage point in life a little cutting goes a long way and I quit before I was really through. Still, I am not quite ready to give up my chainsaw.

WATERFALLS OF NORTH GEORGIA

The North Georgia Mountains hold some of the most spectacular waterfalls in the east. Just in our area there are twenty-one or more. Many of the falls are within an hour or so of Sky Lake, near a road or within a short walk. We hope to visit as many of them as possible in short day trips.

ACCORDING TO BEVERLY

As you know, we arrived at Sautee-Nacoochee (Sky Lake) last week. We were all exhausted to say the least, including Lady Bean. During the time we've been here we've seen marvelous things: A herd of black and white cattle RUNNING across a pasture (don't know why); an enormous tree or two loaded with mountain laurel; also several clumps of wild azalea; the waterfall at Sky Lake pouring forth from its highest level as the water falls from the lake; the lamb's ears blooming with their light purple cones standing up straight; AND our blueberry bushes with small green berries on them. We only hope the bear and other four-legged creatures leave more than a handful for us! The deck out back has been stained a rich brown color and looks great with the yellow/white knock-out roses, three troughs of violas, large pots of forsythia, and some troughs of red and green lettuces. On the little back porch outside the breakfast room door there are pots of more green lettuce, zinnias, two kinds of parsley, thyme and another pot of basil.

Please come and help us enjoy God's bounty in beauty and produce.

THE WELCOME MAT IS OUT

Many of you have already visited us in Moss Manor and we enjoyed having you. We plan to be right here in Sky Lake until sometime in August. We would be glad to have new visitors and revisits from our friends. We know that some are coming from the Reddick Church and others are still making plans. Right now the confirmed schedule looks like this:

- June 1&2 Herb and Melita
- June 24 – 27 Clyburn reunion (we will be at Ocean Isle, NC)

Except for side trips that we may take, you can see that the schedule is wide open so give us a call and come on up or over. The welcome mat is out.

THE LIVING PAST

Summer has not yet officially begun but it feels like it has been here for some time. Global warming is here! The months of May and June have made believers of even die-hard skeptics. Predictions of global warming have become reality, bringing record breaking heat to most of us. Tornados have wreaked havoc on many parts of the country. About thirty miles north of us at Lake Burton, we saw trees flattened as if rolled over by steam roller. We saw the remains of houses uprooted, destroyed, and tossed into the lake. We watch TV and see the devastating floods make multitudes homeless and smell the smoke of wildfires burning out of control. All this is directly related to slowly changing climate. Fortunately for us, we saw most of it on the news.

Here in Sky Lake we worried about the tinder box conditions in the woods and watched the weather channel as the boxed outlines of severe weather crawled across the screen. The last few days have brought relief for Moss Manor in the form of welcomed rain. This morning, the moss lawn is wet, the plants and flowers are still soaking up the dampness and the wild life is leaving deeper foot prints in the softened ground.

But we have seen handwriting on the wall. The higher electric bill will nudge us again. We had better make adjustments and get used to a changing climate. We have been warned.

WHAT A LITTLE HOT AIR WILL DO

The other day, skies over Helen and a little later over the Sautee-Nacoochee Valley were filled with hot air. . .hot air balloons, that is. It was the annual Hot Air Balloon Race and about thirty-two colorful balloons filled the sky. The air was light and there was little wind. Some aviators soared high but most sought the easterly wind just above the trees. No one reached the finish line, which was I-95. A few landed in strange places or fields, surprising nearby residents. However, everyone had a good time and there were no accidents.

MORE DEER FOOD!

Last week we made the beautiful drive through the Great Smokey Mountains to visit Mary Glenn in Black Mountain. As usual, she loaded the van with plants, flowers and even an apple tree. For the last few days, I have been working on the steep hill behind us, holding on to a rope to keep upright while planting shrubs and flowers. I realize that, for the most part, I am planting "deer food." But a few plants may not be on their diet and little by little the hill is looking more like a garden than an unkempt mountain side.

NOTHING TO DO

The other day, one of our visiting friends, after seeing the peaceful setting and seclusion of our mountain retreat, asked, "How to you find enough to keep you occupied during your time in Moss Manor?"

There is a lot to do, just too little time to do them all. There are the activities of the Sky Lake community, like gatherings at the club house and events like our annual 4th of July celebration. The church urges us to choir practice, book club, a hiking group, etc. The area calls us to visit waterfalls, art shows, inviting mountain towns, festivals and state parks.

Here at Moss Manor there are always projects. . .sometimes too many projects. There is always the back hill to plant, tend and weed. There is the moss lawn to feed with buttermilk and tend with

71

a weed-eater haircut. There are always pictures to take, newsletters to write, e-mails to read and answer.

I am trying my hand at painting with acrylics and oils as well as computer painting. There is always ham radio to enjoy, model airplanes to build and fly, constructing the model railroad. There must be time for reading, writing, planning trips from the bucket list. How do we find things to keep us busy? Well, just begin early in the morning and suddenly, it is time for bed and there are still lots of things that we have not finished.

ASK BEFORE IT IS TOO LATE

The older I get, the more I realize how much I have missed because I failed to ask questions and listen. The other day when I was looking through my family records in *Family Tree Make* on the computer, I realized how little I really know about the people that meant the most to me in my life. My mother and father, grandmother, aunts, uncles and cousins were taken for granted, as if they would always be there and I could always ask them questions about family. Now they are gone and with them the stories of their childhood, their early homes, their struggles and adventures.

Looking back, I can see how the crowded days of growing up, of following my own interests could easily crowd out any interest in the by-gone days of family. It was not that I did not care, I just did not have time nor did I have any real interest in what to me was ancient history. I eagerly took the present as my world and selfishly accepted the past as too far away and not something that would affect my busy boyhood schedule.

Oh, I knew a few of the facts: that my father grew up in Society Hill, SC, that my grandmother and grandfather brought my mother as a little girl from Hodgenville, KY. Now as I look back over the years, how I wish I had taken a little time from play to sit down, ask a few questions and really listen. Questions like:

- Dad, what was your day like in Society Hill, in the one room school? What games did you play? Who were your close friends? Did you enjoy growing up with four brothers?

- Mother, what do you remember about your trip to Florida or your childhood in Gainesville? Who were your friends when you moved to Fernandina?
- Nannie, tell me about Hodgenville, Kentucky. Did you know the family that raised Abraham Lincoln? What kind of dresses did you wear and what games did you play as a little girl? Introduce me to the Grandfather, whom I never knew. Tell me about my great aunts and uncles and cousins.

All I have now are names and a few dates on the pages of the genealogy. How I long to have the names filled in with flesh and blood. . .the good, the bad, the sad and the funny things that made them live. But it is too late. . .they are gone and with them stories I never had the time to hear.

Children, grandchildren, and friends: listen to me, and take advantage of the living past and history that is still available to you. There will come a time when your family history will be hidden, reduced to dry names in the family Bible. Take time to ask, listen and even write it down. Make time to know and understand your heritage and those things that shaped your genes and habits. It will be time well-spent and you will be glad you took time to ask questions and listen to voices and stories from your distant past.

The time is coming and will be here before you know it, when your history is silent and you will, like me, wished you had "asked before it was too late."

THE UPSIDE-DOWN HIKE

I missed the church hike to Duke Falls last Sunday. They all reported a great trip, so naturally I decided that I needed to make the hike and see the falls. Tuesday morning, Beverly waved goodbye to me and I drove past Helen in search of the trail. After a number of false turns, I saw the sign that led me back to the Duke Wilderness Area and Duke Falls.

The hike began on a wide, paved path with heavy wooden bridges holding it on the steep mountainside. Soon wooden steps took me down to a narrower, gravel trail which would continue for a mile to the waterfall. Tall trees and rhododendron provided shade as I slowly descended the curves and switchbacks that followed the mountain stream below me. A mile is a long way when you're almost eighty-two, and the trail moved gently downhill.

Duke Falls was heralded by the sound of rushing, falling water. A long wooden bridge took me to the observation platform, well above the two streams that joined at the base of the falls. For a long time I sat there, drank in the beauty of the scene and rested my weary legs. Then I descended to a lower platform just above the water where my rest and reverie continued.

But all good things must come to an end, and gathering my cameras and the remains of lunch, I started the climb up the steps and up the trail. That was when I realized it was "an upside-down hike." The hard climb should have come when I was fresh, not worn out. Over an hour later, 119 wooden steps up, and what seemed to be two miles not one, I emerged at the parking lot to start the drive home.

It was a great experience. I got some good pictures. In the weeks ahead, when my muscles stop aching and the never-ending trail up has become a faint memory, I might consider doing it again, but next time I will take someone with me to push, pull and encourage. Right now I need food, a hot bath and a week's rest.

SLEEPING IS MY FULL TIME JOB

The other day I heard my man-staff talking about a sermon he was preparing on "Calling." Now I had never paid much attention to being called. . .especially when I did not want to respond. But he was talking about how he spends his time as a calling or as a full-time job. Now that got me to thinking. What was my "calling" or "full-time job?"

I have lots of jobs. I protect my staff when we are outside together. I wake my man-staff by stepping lightly on his face when he sleeps too long. I play with them by pulling or jumping at the end of a silly string. I make them happy by allowing them to pet me and I purr to please them. I always remind them when it is time to eat or when I am out of my food. When they spend too much time on the computer, I get in front of the screen so they have to stop and pay attention to me.

I have very important jobs. I try to catch the little flying things like small grass hoppers that get inside and at least scare them so they want to leave. At night I race around the house making as much noise as I can, trying to sound like a horse in full gallop. When my staff is asleep, I jump on their bed and sleep at their feet to guard them against "things that go bump in the night."

But my full-time job, my vocation, as they would call it, is **sleeping**. *I can do it almost anywhere, but my favorite places include, but are not limited to: my basket, their bed, the window ledge, the sofa, the closet shelf behind hanging clothes, the shelf with towels above the dryer. When I am outside, I like to get in the van, when it is not moving, and sleep on the dashboard or on the seat. And I have a few other sleeping places that I will not disclose because I like to keep my staff guessing and looking for me.*

Yes, I am sure of my calling. . .that my full-time work, my vocation, is sleeping and I am good at it and can do it at least eighteen out of twenty-four hours a day. LB

A WORD FROM BEVERLY

As you can see from Lady Bean's last sentence, she and I have something in common. We both sleep too long, and in diverse and sometimes strange, places. I prefer my bed, but have been known to sleep in my new rocking chair in the living room, in a chaise on the deck, or even in the car whether it's moving or waiting in a parking lot for the driver to return. Even Francis has been able to sleep in these places depending upon his level of tiredness. Rarely will he sleep in the afternoon. He has to be really pooped!

He insists that he can't sleep in the daytime, but he and LB often out-snore each other!

Francis has started a fern garden on the slope in the back, and it is doing quite well. After the plant-gathering at Mary Glenn's, he has also planted a shade garden around one of the maple trees near the impatiens. M.G. gave us seven or eight hostas and he has used them beautifully.

Come, visit Moss Manor and relax. You might catch that lazy, sleepy feeling, too. B.

BEARS IN THE WRONG PLACE

A VISIT TO ALABAMA

Last Friday, August 12th, Bev and I headed out of Sky Lake bound for Jacksonville, AL where dear friends were making their home. All too often I have put off visiting with friends and have consequently lost track of them. I was determined not to let that happen again. While it is good to make new friends in new places, the deep and meaningful bonds made in former years and in different places must not be lost. As the old saying goes, "New friends are silver; old friends are gold."

We followed the winding road out of Sky Lake and soon spilled onto I-85 toward Atlanta. We were prepared by both Google maps and our friend inside the GPS, and all went well until on the busy six lane roads of the big city, where they split company. Google wanted to go on the by-pass and the GPS wanted to go through the city. Because we were in the wrong lane, the GPS won. We cruised the busy corridor at 70-80 miles per hour. (No one pays attention to the posted speed limit.) Soon we found ourselves on I-20 headed west.

We were within thirty miles of our destination when the Google map and the GPS disagreed once more. This time we followed Google and asked the GPS to recalculate. Bad decision! After going twelve miles out of the way on a beautiful, winding country road, we finally saw the city limits sign for Jacksonville. Our GPS led us to the front door of our friends' home.

Millie and Dan had been both good friends and church leaders in our Orlando church. Our children had been in the youth groups together and we had done many things together. As we visited in their lovely retirement home, we talked of mutual friends, of those in their eternal retirement home, and of the many good memories that were ours. We looked at pictures of children and grandchildren. That evening their son, who was in Junior high when we first knew him, joined us for supper. He is now a successful business man with a lovely wife and children in high school and college. After dinner we talked well into the night before retiring for a good night's sleep.

The next morning, after breakfast, our hosts took us on a tour of Jacksonville. It is a beautiful town of 10,000 until the students in Jacksonville State University return to school, when the population swells to 20,000. Large beautiful homes punctuate the rolling hills and mountain sides. We drove to the highest point and looked down upon the town nestled in the Alabama foothills and mountains. We also stopped by the Presbyterian Church which had served the community since the early 1800's.

Too soon it was time to say goodbye. After a quick snack and promises to get together again, we were on our way home. This time we followed the instructions of the little lady in the GPS and stayed on the main roads. At 6:30 we pulled into Moss Manor, glad to be home but very glad we had the privilege of reliving the past and visiting with good friends.

MY ROUTINE

I am a well-organized cat. I have my nightly, and usually my daily, routine well established. Let me lead you through a typical 24-hour period of my life in Moss Manor.

The day begins anywhere between 5:30 and 8:30. I would like it to begin when it first gets light but my staff is not as well organized as I am. Now my lady staff is pretty consistent. She sleeps late and it is around 8:30 when she makes her appearance. But my man-staff is quite different. He has no routine at all and I sometimes wonder about him. He gets up at different times during the night, mumbling something about leg cramps, whatever that is. He stomps on the floor, sometimes staggers down the hall to the kitchen. When he does, I jump down and follow him to be sure he is all right. Besides,

I can get a little snack while I am in the kitchen. On a typical night, I will sleep in my basket until he gets up the first time. Then I will get down and take my place as a sentry on the foot of their bed. From that point I can guard them against all invaders and also keep warm and comfortable.

When my man-staff finally gets up and dresses, we go to the kitchen where he heats up a cup of something and sits down at his computer to write. I take my place beside him on the edge of the table. Sometimes I ask him to let me outside to take an early morning walk around the side garden. Sometimes he comes with me and I guard him as we walk around the house. When my lady-staff gets up we eat breakfast and I go back to my basket for my morning nap which usually lasts until noon. The afternoon is much the same. It is eat, sleep, eat and sleep in a different place. (I love to sleep in special hiding places where they have to look for me.) In the late afternoon I like to go outside and I nap in the sun. (I keep an eye on my staff as I look back through the glass doors, and strangely they are usually watching me.) After supper, when it is dark outside, I sometimes lead my staff to the big sofa where I love to sleep next to them while they watch that silly television. I especially like to lie next to my man-staff and put my head in his hand. I feel very secure there and I know he is safe with me next to him.

When I get tired of the noise, I get up and go to the bedroom and climb up into my basket. Sometimes I humor my staff by jumping on the bed and letting them pet me. I purr loudly because they seem to like to hear me. Then I get back into my basket and sleep until my man-staff starts stomping on the floor again.

Well, that is my typical day. As you see, I am a very well-organized cat. LB

FLYING IN SAUTEE

As most of you know, building and flying model airplanes is one my hobbies. I was afraid that when we moved to the mountains, I would have to give that up. Much to my surprise and joy, I found a group of people who also flew RC models. A field less than two miles from Sky Lake was made available to us. Now each Saturday a group of enthusiastic flyers get together to practice their flying skills and show newly acquired models. Our group is diverse. There are old timers who have flown models for sixty years and new comers just entering the hobby. There are commercial pilots, artists, professionals and retirees plus some young people who are learning fast and flying well.

The field we use is used for grain with only a small strip when we try to land. Most of the models are launched rather than taking off. Models include electric and gas as well as gliders and helicopters. The advantage to a grain field is that it allows a soft landing instead of a hard crash.

BACK TO FLORIDA

The trip to Florida was uneventful and the miles rolled behind us. Lady Bean thought it was far too long and told us so between naps. It was good to pull into the driveway on 102nd circle.

It was good to see the folks at Reddick Presbyterian Church. We missed seeing many of our friends at Countryside Presbyterian since I was preaching and Beverly was playing each Sunday at Reddick. Tim and family came up from Vero Beach to visit and we had a good two days together. Most of our time was spent in catching up, straightening up, and preparing for the visit to Yellowstone. I did not even get a chance to go flying at the RC field. Time passed quickly.

THE TETON/YELLOWSTONE ADVENTURE

On September 11th, Beverly and I, together with our friends, Mary Lou and Brad, found ourselves packed like sardines near the back of a large United aircraft. We were on our way to our long-awaited visit to the Teton and Yellowstone National Parks. We transferred in Denver to a smaller plane which took us to Jackson Hole, WY.

When we stepped out of the plane in Jackson Hole, we were treated with the breathtaking spectacle of the Teton Mountains rising majestically beside the airport. It was a preview of the great view we would behold during our visit to the parks. The town of Jackson is a delightful, if somewhat crowded tourist town. After picking up our rental van and stopping at the visitor's center, we were glad to check into our motel for a night of rest.

For the next nine days we would be treated to powerful, majestic, awe-inspiring and picturesque scenery. We would follow the lofty Teton Mountains with their snow caps and glaciers to the mysterious world of Yellowstone with its geysers, steaming mud pots and towering waterfalls. We would see deer, elk, bison and a distant moose. Although we looked hard, black bears and grizzlies escaped us. We stopped at almost every overlook, visited almost every waterfall, and took pictures of everything we saw.

Our stay at the cabins of the Teton Lodge and in Old Faithful Inn was everything we had hoped for and then some. Old Faithful erupted on schedule and the bubbling pots continued to fill the area with a steamy mist. It was almost frightening to realize that just beneath our feet the earth was a river of fire and was venting its power in the wonders of steam and water around us.

All too soon it was over, and we found ourselves back onboard a shuttle flight to Denver and then on the giant Airbus back to Orlando and home. It was ten days we will long remember and will relive in video and pictures for years to come.

A PS BY LADY BEAN

They may have had a good time wherever they went but the place they left me was a prison from the pit. The lady in the white coat poked me and stuck me with a needle! There were dogs barking and a cat howling that kept me from sleeping. The cage where I stayed was small and the food was awful.

I was there a long time! I was glad to be liberated by my staff but I let them know exactly how I felt with my best and loudest Siamese howls all the way home. I hope they got the message! LB

LOOKING FOR BEARS IN THE WRONG PLACE

Each day in the western parks we scanned the fields, searched the fields, and watched the rivers hoping for a fleeting glance of a bear with not a single sighting. A few people reported seeing them the day before but we saw not a one. The truth is we were in the wrong place on the wrong side of the country.

Four days after we returned to Ocala, my daughter Mary Glenn called us. She and Steve had gone to our home in Sky Lake for a short getaway visit. They had cooked and eaten steaks on the back deck and had come inside to watch TV in the living room that opens onto the deck. It was twilight but the flood lights were still on outside. Suddenly, Steve pointed to the deck. There, just outside the glass doors, sniffing at the grill which still had the aroma of recent steaks, was a mother bear and three cubs. They had come up on the deck as if they had been invited for dinner. Mary Glenn, Steve and their boxer, Wallace, pressed against the glass to watch. When the bear family saw them looking from the inside, they decided it was time to leave and made a hasty retreat up the back hill steps and disappeared into the Georgia woods.

Next time we want to see bears, we will go to our home in Sky Lake and cook steaks on the deck.

Early in October we will be heading back to Sky Lake to enjoy the beauty of a brilliantly colored world. "Leaf Season" in the mountains is from early October through November. Beverly and I hope that some of you will visit us and enjoy the splendor of the season.

OF WIND, LEAVES AND WINTER

A COLORFUL GREETING

Interstate 75 from Ocala to Atlanta is the same, monotonous highway whenever you travel. Certainly there are some interesting farms and cotton fields that race by along with a multitude of billboards. An occasional rest stop breaks the trip. But after the bumper to bumper traffic of the Atlanta by-pass, you have headed Northeast on I-85, turned north around Gainesville and have begun the rolling, curving roads toward Cleveland, you are extended a colorful fall greeting. The fields take on the brown of recently harvested corn or hay. The waving fronds of straw now stand in well-packed, spiraled bundles. Although there is still much autumn green, the brown, yellow and early red of fall covers the hardwoods. If the wind buffets the woodland, there is a smattering of falling leaves.

When we turn into Sky Lake, we see early falling leaves floating on the lake and the canopy of trees that arc the road seem to become more colorful with every winding mile. While the leaves are not yet at their peak of brilliance, they welcome us home with a wonderful, colorful greeting.

IF YOU CAN'T BEAT THEM, TAKE THEIR SEAT

I knew something was going on, but I wasn't sure exactly what. The last time something like this happened I was put in prison without a trial and for twelve days I suffered the slings and arrows of outrageous fortune. Since my staff came home and bailed me out, things have been going very well. I have walked my man-servant outside around the house each day. Everything was back to normal.

Then I saw the red suitcases on the guestroom bed. My man-staff began packing the van and I knew something was about to happen. I worried about it all that night and when both of my staff got up early the next morning I knew the time had come. I waited until the last minute, hoping I was wrong, but then I fled under the big bed and hid. It wasn't long until a long arm reached under and grabbed me. I made a good fight but he was too strong. He dragged me out and took me to the van where my lady-staff was waiting. But there was something different. My lady-staff was in on the back seat with her leg propped up on the seat. I had the front seat all to myself. I was the co-pilot and it felt good.

It was a long trip but I did not use my Siamese voice at all. It was good to have the best seat in the car. Of course I wished I could have been behind the wheel but my man-staff wanted to have all the fun and would not let me drive at all. Finally, the air smelled like mountains and the road began to twist and turn. I looked out of the window and saw the trees all around us and at last, I knew we were going to my other house. . .the one with the long green hall. When we pulled up the driveway and stopped, I could hardly contain my excitement. My man-staff opened the door and carried me inside.

It was good to be in my mountain home again. My staff complimented me on how good I had been during the trip. I purred and thought to myself, "If you can't beat them, take their seat." LB

THE LORD GIVETH, THE DEER TAKETH AWAY

The hill behind the house was green and beautiful before we left for Florida in August. We had planted decorative plants, flowers, and some gourds. We had carefully weeded the invasive creeping "snake grass" that was everywhere. We watered when things were dry. We were proud of the progress and the way the hill had been transformed into a flower garden. We were reminded of the verse in Genesis, *"and God planted a garden. . ."* But alas, we had forgotten the verse that said, *"Let the earth bring forth every kind of animal. . ."*

So it was when we came back in late September, the deer, the bear, the chipmunk, birds and squirrels had laid waste to the garden. Green stubs remained where plants had flourished. Our small apple tree had only two small leaves bravely clinging to one small branch. A few gourds remained that were too hard-shelled to eat. The hill looked like a wasteland.

However, there is a silver lining to the story of the hill. We had provided for the animals whose land we had taken. We had experienced the challenge and the reward of having it for a brief time. The exercise had kept us fit. And best of all, the hill will be ready for us to plant again next spring and perhaps, next year, with the Lord's blessing, we can replenish the hill, enjoy new flowers and fruit and even provide for animals one more time.

A NEW FRONT

Sunday morning found Beverly still recuperating from her bout with gout. The medicine she was taking for pain was making her dizzy so I went to church alone. When I arrived at Nacoochee Presbyterian Church I hardly recognized the church. The entire front of the church building was covered with white and blue construction insulation, and bare 4 by 4s were holding up the front entrance. The blue door was still the same but was roped off. On the entrance steps were beautiful potted plants and flowers stretching from one side to the other.

I followed some church goers around the building to the side entrance leading to the fellowship hall. There I was greeted by an usher who was giving out bulletins and directing us back into the sanctuary. It seems as if greedy little termites have no more respect for a church than they do for a home and had eaten away the beams and trusses across the entrance.

During welcome and announcements, the pastor told of the condition and the fact that a big wedding had been scheduled in the church. The bride could not even come into the church and down the aisle from the front door. To make the best of a bad situation and brighten up the construction area for the wedding, members had decorated the front steps with flowers and had left them for church on Sunday. He said it was a beautiful wedding despite the emergency construction.

A WEST VIRGINIA VISIT

At 6:30 Friday morning the alarm informed us that it was time to get up and prepare to leave for West Virginia. Lady Bean was under-foot the whole time we were putting things in the car and eating a quick breakfast, but when we were ready to tell her goodbye at 8 a.m., she was nowhere to be found. She was following her usual pattern of letting us know she did not want to make a long ride in the car. We looked in all the old familiar hiding places to no avail. As we locked the front, we had to call out, "Good night Lady Bean, wherever you may be." We hoped she would come out when the cat sitter come in the afternoon.

The trip was mostly on interstates as we traveled from Georgia, through North Carolina, Virginia and on to the West Virginia Turnpike. We were welcomed by a dazzling display of fall colors. It was if the dark green of the mountains had been randomly spray-painted with reds, browns and flashing yellows. It was about five in the afternoon when we crossed the river, drove through downtown Charleston and wound our way up the mountain side to the home of our friends, Tom and Betty.

They had been with us on many sailing adventures in the Bahamas and other trips. It was good to relax in their lovely home and talk about the good times we enjoyed together. An evening game of "Chicken Foot" reminded us of the many evenings we had spent playing the game onboard *Karisto*.

On Sunday morning we attended First Presbyterian Church of Charleston. It is a large, historic church with many activities and opportunities for service. Both Betty and Tom have served the church faithfully for many years. Recently Betty, as archivist, has taken on the work of restoring and reviving the history of the church and larger church community. The morning service was a well done mix of contemporary and traditional worship. The pastors and people are successfully bringing together the history and traditions and new cutting edge ways of worship.

Monday came too soon and we said goodbye to our hosts and headed toward our Georgia home. The trip home was like the trip up, a journey through the wondrously painted fall mountains. We arrived home to a welcoming Lady Bean who let us know she was glad to see us and yet did not approve of being left at home.

BACK TO RADIO

It was in 1952 that the FCC issued my first Amateur Radio license. I was in seminary and was excited to be able to communicate with other hams around the country and the world. During the last sixty years I have enjoyed being an active ham and have made many friends around the world. The homes in which we've lived sprouted strange looking towers and arrays of wire that held my antennas. As we sailed the Caribbean, the radio kept us in touch with the mainland and other boaters. When we moved to On Top of the World, restriction did not allow antennas and my radio activity almost ceased. Now in Moss Manor, where antennas are hidden from sight by the trees and forest, I am again becoming active on the air and my call sign, K4JUG, again floats across the airwaves. It is good to again be active in a hobby that has given me pleasure and has been a community service for the better part of my life.

OF WIND, LEAVES AND WINTER

The last few days have felt like winter is rapidly approaching. Indian summer has been with us up until now with warm days and gently breezes. But, as the poet says, "the old order changeth, yielding place to new"; in our case, cold weather. The wind has blown hard for the last few days and the yellows, browns and reds of fall have fluttered to the ground. The rain has been light but steady for the last three days. A fire in the fire place felt good last night and this morning we woke to temperatures in the high 30s. While I am sure that some beautiful fall weather is still before us, we have had a taste of things to come. The trees are not bare, but they have lost much of their foliage and I have found their leaves covering our yard waiting for me to blow them back into the woods.

FOREVER HOPEFUL

Having spent most of her life in sunny Florida, Beverly is always hoping that the next bit of cold weather will bring snow. This morning it was overcast and forty degrees. Beverly looked out and asked, "Is it going to snow?" No snow yet, but we plan to be here until the first week in December and there is still plenty of opportunity. "Maybe tomorrow, Beverly."

BEVERLY'S BIT

He said that it was time for me to write my bit, but after these other two have had their say, what's left? Only one thing, about which I am glad to report. The gout is out! Dr. D'Angelo said when I saw him for the second time that he was glad he had made the correct diagnosis. It seems when he himself had gout, he had not done so. His bout had lasted much longer, while mine was much better in two days after I took the medication he had prescribed.

I do believe that LB was delighted to sit in the front seat when we traveled up to Sky Lake. Hope she doesn't think that's to be HER seat from now on. Beverly

SPECIAL TIMES

LEAVES, LEAVES, LEAVES

Please forgive a few fractured quotes:

. . .I think that I shall never see a poem as lovely as a "leaf."
. . .It isn't raining rain, you know, it's raining "lots of leaves."
. . .Look, up in the sky! It's a bird! It's a plane! "It's a leaf!"

The summer had been unusually warm and we were glad to have the canopy of green leaves above and around us to shield us from, at least part of the day. We had watched them change from the light new green of spring to the rich green of summer. They would sometimes wave and rustle in the summer breezes. The birds hid under them and made the nests among them. We took the leafy green wonder of the woods for granted.

But now there is a chill in the air. The leaves, once a brilliant green, have exploded in a burst of color. The red, brown, yellow and orange of the leaves have brought "leaf peepers" from all parts of the country to the mountains for this colorful pageant. Then came the wind and rain. Leaves come fluttering down, as if they were playing tag, chasing each other to the ground. It was like a snowstorm in Technicolor. They fill the gutters, hide the driveway and cover the yard. There they lie, still and colorful, like a giant patchwork quilt. The leaves cover the yard until the green moss almost disappears. Still, the trees are far from bare of foliage. Each day, each night they continue in a steady floating rhythm as if someone is shaking the trees or as if some unseen giant is throwing baskets of painted confetti from the sky. The problem is that they all have to be removed from the roof, driveway and yard.

In places I have lived before we have had to rake the leaves from the yard a few times. But blowing leaves is new to me and it offers real challenges. At least every other day I take down the well-used leaf blower, prime and pump and pull its cord until it comes to life with a sputter and a roar. As I sweep the yard, the leaves dance up and away exposing the rich green of fall moss. As I move ahead the leaves begin to roll up in front of me, making it harder and harder to push the pile ahead. Finally I come to the low split-rail fence where the pile of leaves must be blown over or through to the woods beyond. . .woods already saturated with leaves from previous years. Then I must walk back and start another roll beside the area path just finished.

Blowing leaves can become something of a game in which I compete against the last sweep. Which batch of leaves will go the farthest? Can I keep the ones I am now blowing from drifting back to the recently blown segment? Can I finally catch the leaves in the air and send them scurrying over the fence before they fall back into the yard? Can I blow them clear before the ever-falling leaves cover the lawn again? Even though blowing leaves is work, it is a pleasure to be out in the crisp fall air and become part of the spectacular beauty of the fall and leaves, leaves, leaves.

THE TREE BY THE KITCHEN

It is one of the ten large Japanese maples that surround Moss Manor. While each is similar, each has a distinctive shade of red or yellow that makes each special. The one in the enclosed area just outside our side door and kitchen window is special. To look over the sink and see the bright red leaves, tinged with a touch of orange, makes washing dishes a pleasure. When we go out the side door into the garden area, it acts like an umbrella to deflect the rain or to filter the sun. It acts as a colorful calendar marking each month with a change in color. As winter approaches, it grudgingly but gracefully gives its leaves to carpet the ground and cover the plants.

We soon will go back to Florida, but we will look forward to a display of the new green from the kitchen window when we return.

BRUNSWICK STEW

I am told that it is an annual affair, but it was a first for us and it was a great evening. The family of Richard and Jimmie has been in the area. . .in the same beautiful home for generations. Each year about this time they open their home to friends in the church and community. It is a festive time with children exercising the many rope swings and trampoline while older children (adults) visit, renew acquaintances and find new friends. Some have brought the musical instruments and the sounds of mountain music fill the hillside. There is lemonade and apple cider. The main course is Brunswick stew, served from a big, iron pot. The stew and the sound of children playing and friends talking bring back memories of the years in Robinson Presbyterian Church where an annual Brunswick stew was the event of the year. The sound of children playing and friends talking brings back memories of those days when our children were growing up and we were part of similar community celebrations in another time and place.

The dinner was good. The music was fun. The fellowship was great. We thanked Richard and Jimmie for inviting us and for sharing their beautiful home. As we drove home, we gave thanks to God for gracious friends and for a community of faith that demonstrates God's great love.

MY SPECIAL TIMES

All my time is special, but there are some times that are more special than others. Here is a list of some of my "special times" not necessarily in the order of importance:

1. *Early in the morning, before it gets light and before my lady-staff gets up, my man-staff and I enjoy sitting at the kitchen table. He works on that silly computer thing and I sit right beside the keyboard. If he is not petting me enough, I reach over and touch my keyboard. . .then he pays attention to me.*
2. *When it is time for my staff to eat, I like to sit in the chair at the end of the table and pretend I am eating with them. Usually I do not like their food even when they give me a small bit. But if they are having chicken or pork, which I like, I get a portion. It would be better if they would let me eat on the table with them, but they make me eat on the floor. Still, it is a special time.*
3. *When it is light outside, and not too cold, I like to take my man-staff for a walk outside. We usually go out the kitchen door and slowly make our way around to the back by the big hill. Once in a while, I lead my man-staff up the hill. He fusses but always climbs up, turns me around and we make our way back down. (It is good exercise for him.) Most of*

the time, we just walk slowly around the house. I stop and taste some of the good grass on the side of the house, but I always keep a sharp eye on my man-staff. Although I have never seen them, he talks about the wild animals around us. I think he makes some of it up. The front yard is always fun. There are new smells, lots of leaves, some soft green moss on the ground and there is always something that I have not seen or smelled before. My man-staff usually gets tired of exploring before I do and I have to go in to watch after him. We usually go in the front door but sometimes we go all the way around the garage and use the door where we came out. After that, I go to my basket and rest. It is a special time for my man-staff and me.

4. *I like to go to the basement room where my man-staff plays with his radio. I sit right in front of him beside the thing he talks into. Sometimes he has to move me around to work with the lighted boxes in front of him. I move grudgingly but I soon am able to work my way right back in front of him. It is a special time and I get lots of attention.*

There are many special times. . .like sleeping in the windowsill and watching the things outside. . .like taking a nap with my lady-staff in the afternoon. . .like sitting in front of my man-staff's computer until he moves me. . .like playing with a ball of paper, the end of a rope. . .like rubbing my face on my stuffed toy that smells so good. But the most special time of all is when my man-staff sits on the sofa and I lie down close beside him and put my head in his hand. When I sleep there, I feel very good and secure. I purr and sleep and dream special dreams. That is my favorite of all my special times. LB

HANGING BY A THREAD

SUNRISE IN THE MOUNTAINS

I have watched the sunlight climb down the mountainside many times and it always renews a sense of awe and reverence in me. This morning is no different. Last night was cold, down below freezing, and it probably finished off any of the tender plants that still struggled to exist. The impatiens in the side yard bend down to touch the ground and shiver with their last effort to cling to life. Outside the window, a chickadee tries unsuccessfully to get something from the empty hummingbird feeder. The little fellow's feathers are fluffed up in an effort to keep warm. On the ground below him, the red and yellow leaves sparkle with the morning frost.

As I look through the trees, now stripped of foliage by wind and rain, I see the mountain. Its gently rising and descending summit still has a touch of orange almost hidden by the rich brown and evergreen of fall. The bright sunshine at first had been only a skullcap on the highest point. Now the light crawls slowly down the mountainside as if it is hesitant to disturb a sleeping world and yet is eager to light the valley completely.

Soon the sun will climb over the back ridge that holds it down. The tops of tall trees in the yard are touched with morning fire that slowly makes it way down the trunks. In minutes our moss lawn will change from frost capped moss and leaves to a brightly sunlit yard. I watch the drama each morning and each time it is different, almost magical.

HANGING BY A THREAD

It was just outside the window by the breakfast table hanging by a thread. A rich red maple leaf had been caught by a single spider web. Both were leftovers of the season. . .the leaf, one of the last to be blown from the tree. . .the tiny thread a reminder of a full blown web designed to capture insects. Now the leaf turned and twisted in space on an almost invisible fiber. In the early morning light both leaf and web would momentarily reflect their former beauty. I wonder how long they would dance together in the morning breeze before falling and disappearing in the mysteries of yesterday's past.

They reminded me that we too are hanging by a thread. Life is transient. Like the single thread of a once beautiful and functional web, much of our work, our usefulness, our strength is in the past. Much of the web on which we depended, and on which we moved from place to place, and from friend to friend is now a memory. The leaf, caught on that single strand, reminds us how fast life passes and how precarious our journey. Aging brings its own adventures. We are no longer attached to a mighty tree. . .a network of work and family and friends . . .but are often detached and fluttering.

But as I watch nature's drama, I am also reminded of the strength of the thread that holds us. . .the thread of memories, the thread that still connects us to the wonderful web of life. . .the thread of faith that is stronger than steel. The thread that holds us is flexible enough to swing in light breezes which let both leaf and thread reflect the colors of life.

I give thanks that, even as we hang in uncertain space and time, we are caught and held by the threads of God's love. . .a gracious providence that will hold us until we fall into a better time and place.

How often, in our busy, hectic world, we miss the wonder of the common place. . .a bright red leaf, a thread from a spider's web, the sunlight coming down the mountain until it lights our day and our life.

FEEDING THE BIRDS

The Sky Lake community is dedicated to keeping things close to the natural surroundings. Houses blend into the mountains. There are no gaudily painted homes or visibly obtrusive sheds or trailers. Towers and antennas fall under these restrictions.

In order to comply with the objective to keep things natural and further the nature of the animal and bird preserve, we are getting ready to put up a series of bird feeders and small bird houses high enough to keep the bears and other predators away. Near the top of the tall trees that surround our home, we are putting a five hundred-foot loop of wire that can be lowered and lifted at any point at will. From this wire we can hang light feeders and should provide a resting place for transient birds. It should delight the aviary population. Since the wire surrounds our home, it also acts as a lightning deterrent. It is a good and effective way to further the goals of the community.

As an afterthought, I might, at times, also use the wire as a loop antenna.

ON GIVING THANKS

It was the Sunday before Thanksgiving and the children's sermon was a delightful reminder of what next Thursday should be about. Granted, there are many traditions that have come to surround the day and many of them are worthy in their own right. . .traditions like a family reunion, turkey with all the trimmings, the big football game. But the children's sermon brought the real meaning of the day into sharp focus.

The pastor began by suggesting that they write a letter to God. The letter would begin, "Dear God, today we want to thank you for. . ." He asked the children to tell him what to write down. After a few hesitant suggestions like, the sunshine, the rain, my family, other things began to pour out. They were honest and eagerly wanted to thank God for food, candy, money, for God Himself, even for the preacher and the internet. It could have gone on and on but the minister said he would put the list on a table where everyone could add to it after church. Pages were filled by both children and adults.

This Thanksgiving, it would be great if we all gave our honest thanks for the things we have, the things we do, the things we really enjoy, things we appreciate and not just for the things we think should say in a prayer of Thanksgiving. It would bring real life to the words of that old hymn, "Count your many blessings, name them one by one, and it will surprise you what the Lord has done."

Beverly and I hope that each of you have had a good, and meaningful Thanksgiving.

AN APOLOGY

I apologize for running two Lady Bean columns in the same issue. . .here is why:

It seems that LB has acquired a fan club. She tells me that her fans would rather read her column than anything else in the newsletter. She feels that she writes better than her man-staff. I am not sure if this is fact or if it is the fantasy of a vain cat. However, to keep peace in the family, this month we will run two stories that she has written and wants published.

PLEASE, DO SOMETHING ABOUT THE WEATHER

The last week has been a bad one for me. We have had company come and go. Everyone has wanted to pet me or ruff up my fur. My staff had neither chicken nor pork, my favorite foods, so I have had to eat my regular crunchy stuff from my bowl. But the worst thing has been the weather. . .dark, damp and raining.

Now you know I like to take my man-staff for a walk around the house each day and sometimes twice a day. All week, I have tried to go outside. I burst through the door and find myself sliding on wet leaves or wading through standing water. It is not a place for any self-respecting cat, so I quickly dash back into the house. It is very disappointing. I have tried every door in the house and it is raining at all of them. It seems to me at least one of them should open on a dry and sunny world. The rain does not seem to bother my little feathered friends. They still flit down to the railing where my staff puts seeds. I can sit at the kitchen door and watch them swoop down, grab a seed and fly away. I want to get out and wave to them with my paw, knowing they will be just out of my reach, but I will not sit in a puddle of water to do it.

I pleaded with my man-staff to please, do something about the weather. Please make the rain stop. Let the sun come out. Let it be dry outside, at least at one door. But he would mumble something about the fact that he, as a preacher, was in sales and not manage-ment. That did not make sense to me and the rain continued to fall.

If my staff will not do anything about the weather, I will have to solve this problem like I do most of my problems. I will get back into my warm basket, curl up and go to sleep until the rain stops and the sun comes out again. LB

I'M NOT GETTING OLD, I AM JUST MATURING

I heard my staff talking about me the other day. When I hear "Lady Bean" or "Kitty," I perk up and tune in. Of course I do not move or even open my eyes so they will not know I am listening. This way I can stay at least one jump ahead of them.

They said, "How old do you think LB really is? She is sleeping more and does not play with her toys as much." Then, they started counting. . .six. . .seven. . .eight. . .nine years and my man-staff said, "She is getting to be an old cat."

That bothered me, so I stalked out of the room and jumped up in my basket where I could think without being bothered. I don't really know how old I am but I still think of myself as a young cat. I try to remember. . .but it was all very fuzzy. There must have been a time when I was little because sometimes, just as I settle down for the night in my warm basket and doze off, I feel like there other little cats just like me in another basket. If I try real hard, I can remember another place with another staff where I lived with another cat like me. It is all very hazy and I am not sure if it is real or if it is a dream. It is hard work trying to remember and it is much easier just to enjoy the great life that I have now. I know I have had lot of adventures, done many things, gone many places and it must have taken a lot of time for them all to happen. Even with all that, I knew I was not an old cat so I stopped remembering and went to sleep.

When my staff woke me, it was almost supper time. Their remarks about me being an old cat still bothered me. I do sleep a lot but I can still jump up to the high shelf over the washer. I can still race up and down the hall and sound like a horse. I can still guard my man-staff when he takes a walk around the house. I can still watch the house when my staff goes to the store for our food, and I can still get on the bed and keep their feet warm on a cold night. An old cat cannot do all this. My staff must be mistaken.

No, I am not am old cat. I am a cat in the prime of life and maturing gracefully. LB

WALLACE COMES TO VISIT

Wallace is Mary Glenn's boxer. He was rescued recently on his way to the pound. He came for Thanksgiving and made himself right at home. He must have learned from Lady Bean that the bed is the best place in the house to sleep. Lady Bean tolerated him and he soon learned that a little "hiss" and a wave of the paw meant that she did not want to play. Wallace also enjoyed the great out-of-doors, the strange animals, the new smells and the space to run and exercise. He has been here before and I am sure will come again. Wallace, the boxer, is a welcome guest at Moss Manor.

FOOTBALL OVERLOAD

Now I like football and I look forward to the fall when the gridiron gladiators are kicking and tackling and passing all over the field. But as December rolls in, I have watched too much football. Saturday and Sunday and even Monday nights are OK, but now it is Tuesday, Wednesday and Thursday as well. After watching three or four games, I find that a half or even a quarter is enough for me. Too many games, too much of the time, is like having too much turkey at every meal. . .it makes me ill. The illness is "football overload." The good news is that I will get over it by next year and will eagerly wait for the football season to begin.

GETTING READY TO GO HOME

Thanksgiving is over. We enjoyed having Mary Glenn, Steve and Timmy with us for a few days and John, Debbie, Lindsay and Ashley over to visit us. We joined friends for Thanksgiving dinner. It was a large spread of great food. Wallace, Mary Glenn's Boxer, was with us all week-end. Even LB felt it was all right for the dog to be here (as a visitor who would soon go home). Mary Glenn and Steve spent Friday blowing and raking leaves, clearing fallen branches and helping in many ways. Moss Manor looks a lot better.

Now it is time to start getting things ready to return to Florida. We have been in Sky Lake since last Easter except for a few weeks home in August. Now we must gather up everything we will want during the winter and see if they will fit into the van. Most of the model airplanes and equipment will travel in the Buzzard Wagon. Clothes, food stuff and a multitude of miscellaneous things will fit in the van. Lady Bean is arguing with Beverly about who will ride in the front seat. There are social obligations that we have put off and must be honored and the clock is ticking faster and faster.

We have a little over a week until we leave. It will be good to finally get back to Ocala and our friends, but getting ready to go is not fun.

BEVERLY'S UPS AND DOWNS

Today it was mostly down. The rain had come down all night and it was still raining when Francis and I drove to Clarkesville to get some ceiling tile for the house and some groceries. Long John Silver's was a logical place to stop for lunch. After we finished eating it was still raining. As I was almost at the van door, I suddenly felt myself going down. Don't know why or how but I do know the pavement came up fast and my right shoulder hit hard. Two nice men helped Francis get me up and into the van. I could hardly move my right arm and it hurt, so we felt the best course of action was to go to the emergency room and get X-rays.

The Habersham Medical Center is quite new and we were treated well. I was X-rayed and told no bones were broken. Hallelujah! But the doctor continued, "Your ligaments and muscles may be bruised or even torn." Bad News! They put a sling on my arm, gave me a prescription for pain and told me to call them in the morning.

I am home now, getting ready to sleep it off, if possible. You see why most of my ups and downs are downs. Beverly

CHRISTMAS TIME

2012 is almost here. A new year begins with all its challenges and opportunities. Beverly and I wish for you and yours the best possible 2012. We hope you had a great and meaningful Christmas. This issue of Moss Manor News (or should we call it *Spanish* Moss News?) will take a quick look over our shoulder as Thanksgiving memories fade and we shift our dwelling from Georgia to Florida.

THE FIRST CHRISTMAS CARD OF THE YEAR

Thanksgiving is over and the turkey is almost gone. The family gathering is over and the laughter of children and grandchildren is just a distant echo. Outside the window the trees are bare of leaves and we can even see the neighbors' houses through the woods. Even the leaves that rained down upon the moss lawn have been blown into the woods and the driveway is clear. The cold snaps are more frequent and the warmth of the crackling fire in the fireplace feels good. The season of Advent has just begun and wreaths and candles are appearing in our neighbors' homes. It is almost time to pack up and head south to our winter home.

It is a beautiful season but it also brings a tinge of sadness. Christmas has started too early. The Christmas music started before Halloween was over and on TV we saw Thanksgiving pumpkins and turkeys adorned with bells and holly. Now the mad commercial rush of the Christmas season is in full swing. Black Friday has taken its toll and the post office is urging us to get things in the mail right away. Our gathering of friends and neighbors is over. I am a little depressed by it all. It is too much, too early.

Then it came and my mood changed. I drove down to the post office to pick up the usual barrage of pulp paper advertisements and a few bills. To my surprise the only thing in the box was an envelope rimmed with holly. I opened it immediately. It was the first Christmas card of the year from dear friends out of the past. That Christmas card changed everything. It brought back a flood of happy memories. It was the forerunner of others to come. It even brightened the overcast day and lifted my spirits. It stands on the table by the door and speaks to us each time we pass by.

Now, once more I was eager for the Christmas season to fill our home and lives. It reminded me of the many, many friends that have enriched my life. It brought back memories of many places where we celebrated the season. Once again I look forward to the days ahead and to the excitement of Christmas.

It is amazing what the first Christmas card of the year can do.

TOO WET TO TRAVEL

It is December 6th, a little after 6:00 a.m. on Tuesday and the rain has been a constant companion throughout the night. Outside it is black and wet. Even the cat refused to step outside onto the wet deck. A hot cup of coffee and the last biscotti in the jar keep me company.

Today was the day we were to travel from Sky Lake to Florida. The car is almost packed and the model airplanes are tied securely in their trailer. It was not just the rain that kept us from leaving. Those little things that were to be done at the last minute seemed to grow exponentially. There are a few clothes yet to be washed, outdoor faucets to be covered for the winter, shoes and medicines to be gathered and packed, food to be readied for transfer and a dozen other little things. Each small task could be done quickly, but together they would have worn us out and prolonged our departure. Besides, we did not sleep well. Lady Bean had sensed that a trip was imminent and she kept jumping on the bed to be sure we had not left her. It was a short night and I am up early, doing some of the things that did not get done yesterday.

Tomorrow we will try again to get possessions, people and felines in the car. It will still be raining but we will be rested after a relaxing day of final preparation.

THE GO GAME

I had known for over a week that something was about to happen. My staff had tried very hard to keep me in the dark but when the red suitcases appeared on the guest room bed and clothes filled the bed around them, I knew I was in for a long ride in the van. They thought I did not suspect, but it was obvious. I do not believe they give me enough credit for knowing what is going on.

Well, I played right along with them. I even slept in the open suitcases. The clothes were very comfortable and warm. When my man-staff went to clean out the car, I climbed onto the dashboard and pretended to be asleep. The only time he cleans the car is when we will be in it for a long time. I let them think that they were winning the "go game." I slept in my basket or on the bed as if nothing was happening. When the clothes were no longer on the bed and the suit-cases began to disappear, I knew it was about to happen. I thought we would all leave on Monday, but then the rain kept coming down and they relaxed a little, so I knew I was safe for one more day.

Tuesday morning came and it was still raining. But this time my staff was taking things out of the refrigerator and putting them in a big, red box. My man-staff kept going out carrying boxes and bags. He would sometimes leave the door open and I could have slipped out any time, but it was too wet out there for any self-respecting cat. I went back to my basket and when he carried out my litter box, I knew it was time to act.

I walked casually down the hall, making a little noise so my staff would see me. Then, when they were not looking, I slipped into my secret hiding place where I could see them, but they could not see me. The game really began when they started calling me over and over. My lady-staff looked in the closets and in the chairs under the table. My man-staff got his flashlight and looked under the sofas, even pulling them out. He crawled around the bedrooms looking under the beds and in the closets. They opened cabinets and even went outside to see if I had slipped out. I smiled as only a female cat can smile. I knew I was winning the game. After a while, he even pulled out the blue monster, turned it on and began poking around the sofa and television cabinet, trying to frighten me out. I almost purred aloud but I kept quiet. They had been looking for me for an hour and a half.

My man-staff said, "We will just have to wait until tomorrow to go!" My lady-staff said, "Let's just sit down and turn on the television and calm down."

I knew the game was over and that I had won. It was time for me to make my grand entrance. So, with measured gait and tail held high, I walked calmly into the living room. Immediately they picked me up and we all headed for the van. It was so full of stuff there was hardly room for me, so I sat up front with my lady-staff while my man-staff checked things in the house. Soon, we were off on that long trip I had known was coming. They kept asking themselves, "Where do you think that cat was hiding? She made us almost two hours late!" I just smiled and went to sleep on the pillow between them for the long trip to Florida.

I'll bet you, too, are wondering where I was hiding, but if I told you, you might tell them, and that would ruin my "go game" next year. LB

FROM SKY LAKE TO ON TOP OF THE WORLD

It was 10:30 and raining when Lady Bean finally came out of hiding and we climbed into the fully packed van. Since we were pulling the model airplane trailer we had decided to follow highway 441 going around Atlanta. There was less traffic but more stop lights and towns. When we passed Macon and joined I-75, it was still raining and the wind was blowing. Just before we entered Florida, the rain stopped. It was dark and we were glad for better weather.

About 8:30 p.m. we raised the gate of OTOW. The Bougainvillea, in full bloom, greeted us as we pulled into the driveway. It was good to get home.

CHRISTMAS IN JULY

"The weather outside is frightful, the fire is so delightful. . ." or so the song tells us it should be near the end of December. But here in Ocala it is more like celebrating Christmas in July. The sun is shining brightly and the temperature is heading for eighty degrees. But regardless of the weather, we are getting ready for Christmas . . . a season and a day that does not depend on what is going on outside. In the tropics or the land of ice and snow, we will celebrate the birth of the Christ Child and Santa will still come to children everywhere. . .so, let it glow, let it snow. A Merry Christmas to all.

A DIFFERENT CHRISTMAS SERVICE

It was Christmas morning and the little church in Reddick was prepared for worship. But things were a little different. The communion table still stood on the floor while the people and the four advent candles with the Christ candle in the center still waited for the symbolic lighting. Memories of the beautiful and meaningful Christmas Eve service still filled the sanctuary.

But on this Christmas morning, the lighted Christmas tree stood in the center aisle in front of the table. Brightly covered boxes surrounded the tree. As parishioners entered they were asked to sit on pews near the tree. The bulletin was only one page with a different order.

After greetings, a Christmas carol and the usual liturgy, the congregation was asked to get a package for each family from under the tree. Each box was numbered. While they tore off the paper and opened the packages, the pastor shared Christmas chocolates with the people. In each box was a large card with a few words of promise or a scripture passage. Returning to the pulpit the pastor asked the family with box #1 to read the card. It was a prophecy of Isaiah about a coming Messiah. A few comments were made and the card from box #2 was read. It was the angel's instruction to Mary about the name for the baby. So it continued: words about God's gifts and promises to the world. When the last box was opened these words were read, "For unto you is born this day in the city of David a Savior, which is Christ, the Lord. . .and He shall reign forever and ever." The people responded with "Hallelujah! Amen!"

The service lasted thirty-five minutes and ended with the challenge hymn, "Go Tell it on the Mountain that Jesus Christ is born."

WAITING FOR SANTA

Strange things have been happening around in my Florida home for the last few weeks. Staff kept talking about Christmas and if Christmas is doing all the things they are doing, I like it. First, they brought in a strange tree, one that did not have that good earthy smell to it. They hung all kinds of stuff on the tree and made it light up. They warned me not to bother anything on the tree, as if I would. I like to play in the boxes that the "stuff" came out of. I would curl up in a box and play like I was hiding from the big dog that lives across the street. They leave paper on the floor and I play with it and hide under it. They put a nice, red cloth under the tree and put big packages all around it. I think they were doing all this just for me because there are so many things to play with.

My staff has been talking a lot about someone named Santa Claus, whoever that is. The television tells how he comes down the chimney and brings toys and things. I kind of doubt that he will stop here, because we have a fire place but no chimney. They say that Santa comes at night when staff people are asleep. That suits me just fine because night is my special time. I wander around the house, taste things that are left on the counter, sometimes knock something over, just to watch my man-staff stagger out to see what is happening. Well, I am going to stay awake, at least with one eye, all Christmas Eve and see what happens. If Santa Claus really comes, I am sure he will bring me some toys and cat food.

My favorite Christmas sleeping place is under the tree and behind the boxes. The red cloth is soft and comfortable. The little lights keep me warm and I can see everything that is happening in the living room. That is exactly where I will be on Christmas Eve. I am not really sure about Santa, especially coming down the chimney. But you can bet I will be ready to welcome him. I am going to my favorite spot under the tree and I will be waiting for Santa. I really like Christmas time. LB

A BRAND NEW YEAR

What would I do if I had a brand new year in front of me. . .a year with no mistakes, no failures, and no victories? What if my journal had nothing but blank pages? What if I had is a whole year. . .twelve months, fifty-two weeks, 365 days, 8760 hours and 525,600 minutes ahead? That is a lot of time and it is what 2012 offers me.

I would try to plan a little better and keep things a little neater. I would like to spend a little more time preparing sermons and visiting in homes. There were so many people I meant to visit, so many letters I meant to write. There were so many places I wanted to see, and so many things I wanted to do. I did not see all I planned to see nor do all I wanted to do. I hope to see and do more in the year ahead. I would like to be more patient with people and say many more "thank yous." These are just a few of the things that I hope will fill my 365 days ahead.

Now I have no assurance that I will have all these days, but I am reasonably sure that I will have tomorrow and that is at least sixteen waking hours in which to begin. I am not making resolutions. I never was much good at keeping resolutions. . .they always seem to get broken by the second week in January. But I am going to try to do some of the things I have neglected. Maybe I will have more and better things to write about in my journal. There is a lot to do in the minutes, hours, day, weeks and months to come, so I had better get started.

What do you plan to do with a brand new year?

BEVERLY'S BLOG

It is good to be home, even with my bum shoulder and up-coming rotator cuff surgery after falling down again. This time it's my right shoulder. Being right-handed, you can imagine how hard it is to use the left hand. Thank goodness for a loving and talented husband who comes to help whenever I holler.

Between the two of us, we cooked a good Christmas dinner and enjoyed the quiet, calm afternoon. We even baked a five-layer cake. It had three layers of a white sour cream cake alternating with two layers of peppermint cheese cake. The frosting was melted peppermint combined with real whipped cream. Needless to say it had to be refrigerated to harden enough to cut. Delicious!

Since we participated in the Christmas Eve service and the Christmas Day service at Reddick Presbyterian Church, we have missed seeing many of our friends at Countryside Presbyterian here in Ocala, but there is time ahead. B.

THE TIME RIVER

SPANISH MOSS

As you know, Moss Manor News derived its name from the deer moss that makes up our yard in Sky Lake. It seems only appropriate that when we are in our Ocala home, we might call our newsletter "Spanish Moss Manor News," even though our immediate setting has been graded of all trees. Spanish moss is a plant that consists of a slender stem bearing alternate thin, curved and curly leaves. It hangs gracefully on the shaded branches of large oak trees from Virginia to Florida and even into South America.

As a boy, I remember going into the woods and bringing moss home to use as bedding in our dog house. I am sure we brought more redbugs than moss. With age, we learned to leave the moss in its natural setting and appreciate its flowing beauty as it decorates the mighty oaks along the roadways. If we only look, we can find beauty all around us.

RAIN!

It rained this afternoon and the thirsty earth eagerly drank each drop. It rained this evening, not just pitter-patter but by drops that pounded the roof with percussion music. The lakes that had been shrinking began to rise and tinder dry fields and woods rejoiced. Even the loud claps of thunder that came with the rain sounded like the heavens were rejoicing behind the dark clouds. Rain had been a long time in coming but it was here, and we were glad.

The rain has stopped and as I climb into bed the mockingbirds are rejoicing at inclement weather. I hope it will rain hard again tonight and I hear it pounding the roof and rattling the gutters. That makes real good sleeping weather.

TO FLY OR NOT TO FLY

If you can roll out of bed about 7:00 a.m., grab a large cup of coffee, load up an electric airplane and head for the flying field, chances are you will be greeted by a blanket of low- hanging fog. Never mind that it is too dense to fly, there are other early rising flyers ready to spin yarns, drink coffee and wait for the sun to burn the fog away. Some have come just to enjoy the fellowship and watch while others will be putting their small electric aircraft together eagerly watching the sky for an opening.

Early morning offers the beauty of a colorful sunrise, the magic of a field almost hidden in a soft, white cloud, the warmth of a coffee cup in hand and the anticipation of flying that new bird. It is great to share information and stories about a hobby we enjoy and even better to know the feeling of good friends being together at the beginning of a new day.

"To fly or not to fly. . ." does not matter as much as just being together with friends.

A HAPPY BIRTHDAY

Tarpon Springs has always held great memories. As a child, I remember riding on the sponge boat and watching the Greek diver put on his diving suit with big rubber gloves and a windowed helmet that bolted on at the collar. It was a thrill to watch him climb down the side of the boat, disappear into the Gulf waters and reappear with a basket full of sponges from the briny deep. We both remember eating seafood at legendary Pappa's restaurant. Just up from Tarpon Springs, in the Ancolte River, I had purchased my first large sailboat and set sail around Florida for North Carolina.

So it was a logical choice to travel the hundred miles from Ocala to Tarpon Springs to celebrate Beverly's birthday. It was overcast when we left home. It was raining when we drove along the sponge docks. Pappa's was no longer in business but we did find Mama Maria's where we had delicious lamb chops cooked in Greek style. I did not get a single picture because of the rain that was coming down in buckets when we left the restaurant. The drive home in pouring rain was difficult.

It was a great trip, a memorable meal and a wonderful birthday!

THE FILE CLERK

Since I am a cat of unusual abilities, I have wanted to do different things in my lifetime. I have dreamed of being a mighty hunter and have practiced the art of stalking my prey with birds and chameleons. I have tried my hand at writing and have been quite successful. But now, there is something else I really want to do.

Every day I watch my man-staff reach next to his desk and open a large drawer from what he calls a file cabinet. Now I have climbed behind the open drawer when he was not looking and almost was squashed when he pushed it closed. I have seen him search for things in the drawer that he has lost. (He seems very disorganized.) That is why I have decided to become a "file clerk." I think it would be fun to push the folders back and forth and even hide behind them. I am sure I could do a better job of filing than he is doing. I am not really sure what a file clerk does, but it would be fun to learn. I might even find a good place to hide or to sleep. It will take a while to be perfect at the job so for right now I will be content to move the folders back and forth and see what is underneath them.

You can address me by my new title: Lady Bean, the File Clerk

THE TIME RIVER

Today my youngest son celebrated his 50th birthday. It came to me as a surprise. I had forgotten how quickly time passes. When he was born, I was thirty-two with a lifetime ahead of me. When I turned fifty, he had just finished high school. None of my four children had finished college or graduate school. Not one of them was married. Now all are married, have moved to distant cities and have families of their own. I am proud of all of them.

It makes me stop and wonder at how quickly time passes. It rolls on like a river, sometimes rushing over the rocks of everyday events, bouncing and bruising, laughing and babbling. Sometimes it moves quickly through turbulent rapids, hardly giving time to enjoy the beauty of the surrounding scenery through which it flows. At times, that river of passing time lies motionless in deep pools demanding thought and reflection. It may even catch our tears of grief and disappointment and absorb them in waters of comfort. While it may allow for memories, it never retraces itself, but winds on through the years of our lives, offering new opportunities and adventures.

Birthdays offer a chance to look back and give thanks for the many memories that line the bank of that river of time through which we have passed, and allow us to look forward to where the river will take us in the days to come.

HAPPY VALENTINE'S DAY

Before the next MMN comes, February will be a memory. Many things will be history; things like: Ground Hog Day, Doctor visits, club activities, a trip to the vet, a visit to the dentist, Presidents' Day and of course, Valentine's Day. All this will fade into the limbo of the past.

Beverly and I hope this day and its message will stay with you. Valentine's Day represents warm greetings and a message of love. Please remember that we treasure your friendship and we would share the love that day represents, not only for February 14th, but through all the years to come.

FELINE COMMUNICATIONS

AN EARLY MORNING TREAT

Pushing back the hands of time, clock hands, that is, and with the coming of daylight saving time, brought a whole new perspective to 7:30 a.m. I drove to our flying field while it was still dark and was rewarded with a wonderful panorama of daybreak. The winds were still sleeping in the distance and a light fog framed the field. A thin, white opaqueness drifted, almost imperceptibly across the expanse of grass, giving the distant trees an air of mystery. Blue sky could be seen through the light fog, and there in areas where the fog had burned away, the sky was clear. In the distance there was a border of denser fog, looking like flimsy, rolled up lace. Behind the trees the sun was rising in a burst of color, spelling the end of the thin, white shroud of moisture that surrounded me.

Soon with the coming of a light breeze and the warmth of sunlight, the mist that painted the morning in white, would begin to lift and, like Shakespeare describes it, "fades, leaving not a wisp behind."

Getting up a little earlier has brought a wonderful, scenic surprise.

WHERE HAVE ALL THE "HOURS" GONE?

Maybe I was a little mistaken in my expectation of retirement. Maybe I just got the facts wrong. Maybe things have suddenly changed. I had always thought that when I reached a ripe old age and qualified for retirement, I would have time to do everything I had never had time to do while working. I looked forward to assigning my watch to the dresser drawer and turning the calendar's face to the wall. That is not the way it has worked out.

It seems that I am busier now that I was before. Others in my community seem to have the same problem. We are racing around like frustrated ants whose hill has been stepped on. The names of activities have changed, but the crowded calendar of events seems just as full. There are so many things to do, places to visit, clubs to join, activities to participate in, places to go, books to read, articles to write, photos to take, planes to fly, friends to visit, etc. Now, I not only wear a watch but double check it with my I-phone. I am always pushing my wife to "hurry up" or we will be late, when the truth is, it probably would not matter if we were on time or a little late.

The stack of papers on my desk gets higher and higher as I do not find time to keep up with things or to file them properly. The Internet reminds me to read this, send that, or look at a You-tube video I really should see. I find myself singing that old song (with a word or two changed): *"Where have all the "hours" gone, long time passing?"*

The truth is I should stop complaining about the many things I do or that do not get done. I realize that I am the one who chose to do these things or try to get them done. The older I get, the less time I have to empty my "bucket list" so I try harder to multi-task them all. The pile of things on my desk gets higher and my calendar fills up, but, I guess that is the way I want it. When my final time comes, I'm sure can l look back on my way up (I hope) and see a full calendar, unfinished projects and a desk piled high with things I want to write.

Maybe in heaven I can sit around, relax and have nothing to do. But for me, that sounds more like "the other place." I am sure, the Lord will have plenty to keep me busy and I might even say at the end of a millennium or two, *"Where have all the **ages** gone?"*

ON LOSING AN OLD FRIEND

On February 28, 2012, I lost an old, close friend. I do not know exactly how long we had been together. It is sufficient to say that we have been together as long as I can remember. Over the years we have traveled together, helped each other with tough situations and worked together in perfect harmony. When one of us was hurting, the other felt the pain.

Last year my friend was diagnosed with an incurable malady. I felt the pain my friend was feeling as if it were my own. Together we consoled each other and I did my best to relieve my friend's pain. In the past few weeks, I received news that my friend's malady was getting worse and together we felt the pain of what was the inevitable. Yesterday our longtime relationship ended. There was pain at our separation and I did not even get to say goodbye as the doctor told me it was best that way. Yes, it is difficult to lose an old and faithful friend, but I am sure it is for the best.

My friend's passing brought even more grief before I left the dentist's office and had to pay the bill for pulling that molar that had been my friend for over seventy years. *Rest in Peace*

SOMETIMES I JUST WALK AWAY

I like to be part of a group that has little to do but sit around and talk. It may be after church while drinking coffee. It may be at a neighborhood gathering or at the flying field when the wind is too high to fly. It could be almost anywhere, at any time, when there are more than three people chatting about nothing and spinning yarns. Often I will stay too long when I should be doing something more constructive. It is a good way to spend some time.

But there are three occasions when I get up and leave the group, making some lame excuse about having another pressing engagement. Those occasions are as follow:

When the group starts kicking religion around or arguing about what they believe. Now I do not mind discussing religion. . .there is a big difference between an honest discussion of faith and just talking about religion. I have spent most of my life talking about theology and sharing my faith, but I have learned that arguing about religion does not change anyone's thinking and usually ends up making enemies out of friends. I have heard most of it before, so I just get up and leave.

The second occasion where I make a rapid exit is when politics becomes the topic of the day. That conversation usually deteriorates into dogmatic arguments that have a great deal of sound and fury and very little truth or substance. Again, I have political leanings and convictions and will share them briefly if asked. (To this day I have never been asked.) I strongly doubt if arguing about politics ever changed a mind or did much good for the country.

The third occasion that initiates a hasty retreat is "people bashing." Whether it is the president, a governing body, or a regular member of the group that happens to be absent, I feel it is a topic of conversation that does not need my presence. I must admit, I have done my share of criticizing and even gossiping and have always felt ashamed of myself afterward. That being said, I do not have to repeat the act, either by contributing or consenting by passive listening. Again, I make an exit as soon as possible.

Oh, there are other times when I walk away. I may really have something else that I need to do. Sometimes my ears just get tired of listening to the same things over and over. Sometimes I can't get a word in edgewise in the conversation and get discouraged from trying. But most of the time, I like to be with a group that, like me, has nothing better to do and just enjoys being together.

CAT COMMUNICATION

My staff has finally learned cat communication. Sometimes they are a little slow but I am training them well and they are getting the message. I have learned that using my voice does not always work. As you probably know, we of Siamese ancestry have a loud and distinctive voice that we save for special occasions. The communication I usually use is non-verbal. Let me illustrate:

My man-staff has been working at his computer for some time and has not paid me enough attention. Using my voice has no effect on him. . .he calls it "selective deafness." But I know what to do. I jump up on the table and take my place in front of the screen with those silly symbols and pictures. I stare at the screen and anchor myself in position. He cannot see through me so he stops and pets and urges me to lie down so he can see.

Another way that I communicate is by taking aggressive action. I like the soft chair that my man-staff sits in as he works. It is usually very soft and warm. Again, I jump on the table in front of him but this time I face him, step carefully down toward him, just missing the keys on his keyboard (stepping on them upsets him). Then I put my front paws on the edge of the place where he is sitting and push a little with my head and shoulder. He moves a little and I move completely in. There is not room for both of us so he gets up and I curl up on the nice, warm cushion. He pushes my chair over, gets another one, and we are both happy. He got the message.

There are lots of ways that I communicate. Sometimes I have to speak by acting things out, like when my water bowl is empty. When my staff is fixing dinner and it smells good, I simply stand on my hind legs by the counter and look at them like I am starving. If my box has not been cleaned as well as I like, I sit in front of it and they have to step over me to get by. That usually works. When they come home from wherever they go, I roll over in the middle of the floor and wave all four legs in the air to let them know that I am glad to see them. They usually bend down and pet me.

At night, when it is sofa time. . .time for my man-staff to sit by me and hold my head until I go to sleep, I can let him know by either getting in front of whatever he is doing or by walking in front of him wherever he goes. He usually gives in and we have quality time together on the sofa. It has taken some time, but my staff has finally learned "cat communication." LB

JUST A LITTLE LONGER

We are looking forward to returning to Sky Lake and to our friends and activities in the mountains, but we have to wait a little longer. If it were not for the delay, caused by Bev's doctor who decided to take a vacation, we would be on the road. Lady Bean has checked out the car and is ready to see her Possum, Deer and Bear friends. We had looked forward to seeing the daffodils in bloom and the cherry tree budding out in pink. However, health takes priority, and although both of us are doing well, we have to wait for the doctor to return. If all is well, we will leave here around March 28th.

Once again, we extend an invitation to those of you who have come before and to those of you who would be visiting for the first time. There are many places to visit and many things to see in the area.

The welcome mat is always out at Moss Manor. Just let us know when you would like to come and we will let you know if your rooms are vacant and our schedules do not collide. Bev and I look forward to seeing you.

A NOTE FROM THE LADY-STAFF

One day I will get a head start on this newsletter and really have something to say before they do. It seems that all of our "news" is already done by LB or F. and I'm left with nothing to add. Maybe that's just as well.

Speaking of well, I'm grateful that F. is so thoughtful and caring. He's becoming a great cook, bottle-washer, and nurse. I must add, though, he's not for hire!

BLUEGRASS

SPRING CAME EARLY AND SO DID WE

It was mid-March when we started gathering things we wanted to take Moss Manor. That was a month or two earlier than our usual time of departure but we wanted to see the early spring in the mountains. We were delayed by a postponed doctor's appointment but by the end of March the car was packed and we were ready.

Early on a Thursday morning we were ready to roll. Bev was in the car; all last minute things were done. We thought we had outfoxed Lady Bean by shutting the bedroom doors and access to her under-the-bed hiding places, and she seemed to be nervously sitting on the sofa when Bev went to the car. I came back to get her and she was gone. After a brief search I located her under the sofa. . .not just under the sofa but entwined with the springs. A half-hour of lying on the floor, reaching awkwardly up and pulling and poking, I finally retrieved a vocal and unhappy cat. It was a typical departure.

The trip north was uneventful except for unusually heavy traffic around Atlanta. When we entered Sky Lake we were welcomed by early dogwoods, a yard of early green deer moss, and a wonderful hosta garden in the side yard. We were tired but we were glad to see the "green, green moss and green carpets of home."

RAIN, RAIN

It rained all night. . .not the gentle rain that is falling now, but a pounding rain that seemed determined to clear the air of all dust and pollen. Occasionally there was a rumble of thunder that brought Lady Bean from her basket to the bed. It was a good, much-needed rain, without the wind that brought destruction to the mid-west. The sound of rain tapping on the roof and then rushing loudly down the downspouts provided the setting for good sleeping.

Rain like this always brings back memories. My thoughts jump back to childhood when I was forced to take a nap and would lie awake in a bed level with a window and look down at my backyard world being pounded by an afternoon downpour. Even in the afternoon the drumming and splattering sound would hurry me to sleep.

When I was older, I remember a camping trip when we tried to sleep in the pup-tent while rain came down and drips developed from the canvas above us.

I remember traveling in the mountains of West Virginia when I would drive through and climb above the rain. At times I would pull off the road and look down at the heavy cloud and downpour below me and look up at the shining sun above me. For me, that was a parable of life reminding me that all must go through times of troubling, dangerous rain but with perseverance, and sometimes help, we will climb above the storm and find a bright, better time.

Rain seems to jog my memory. It is still raining and I remember it is time to start breakfast and get ready for the activities of the day.

MAYBE I SHOULD SEE A SHRINK

The other morning I had a conversation with Lady Bean. It had rained all night. As usual, I got up early and, as usual, Lady Bean got up with me. She led me to her feeding bowl and waited for me to fill it with crackers. When she was finished she went to the side door and asked me to take her outside. I opened the door and she looked at the water pouring down. She turned around and asked to go out the doors onto the deck. Again, she felt the rain splatter as it hit the deck and turned back inside. She went immediately to the front door and wanted me to open it. I did, and the rain was coming down just as hard there as at the other doors. Lady Bean turned, came back inside, sat down, looked up at me and began to meow. It was then that things got a little scary. I have always heard that it is all right to talk to your pets, but when they talk back and you understand them, it is time to see a "shrink." Well, I knew exactly what she was saying.

She said: *You are a powerful man-staff. When I am hungry, you just reach up on a high shelf and create food for me to eat. When my water dish is low, you tap the wall in the kitchen and water comes gushing out. When you think I have gone too far away from home, you are there to pick me up and carry me back. When I am cold, you touch a button on the wall and the wall burns with fire. When I am hot, you push another button and things get cooler. You make writing appear on a screen in front of you. You wave your hand and the pictures disappear and the sound is gone.*

Man-staff, if you can do all these things, is it too much to ask that you make the water stop coming down outside at least one of the doors? Can't you push a button and make the warm sunshine come back on just one side of the house? Please, man-staff!

I want to tell Lady Bean, "Yes, I do have some powerful connections through my profession, but I am in sales and not management." Somehow, I do not believe that she will either understand or believe me.

OVER THE HEDGE

It is early morning and the mountain to the east still blocks the rising sun. I look out of the side door and there, just over the hedge, I see the clematis. The back yard is still in deep shade but the purple of the large, perfectly designed flowers seem to have their own light. They appear to shine in all directions, both drawing attention and pointing to the hosta garden below. As I return to my writing, I feel better after seeing the flowers just over the back hedge.

MEMORIES

It is Sunday night and I am listening to Georgia Public Radio as they play some good, old fashioned blue-grass music. As I listen, it brings back a flood of memories from my childhood in the early thirties.

My father loved many kinds of music and one of his favorites was mountain blue-grass. After our traditional Saturday night supper of hot rolls and baked beans, just before 6:30, I would sit with him in his big, stuffed chair beside the upright radio and watch him carefully tune in a radio station in a nearby town. Over the airways would come the sound of a hillbilly band signing on with its theme song, "*I like mountain music, good ole, mountain music, played by a real hillbilly band.*" For the next half hour we were captivated by the sounds of guitars, a banjo, a string bass and nasal twang of the singer as it soared above the static and scratchy sounds of early AM radio.

An event that ranked almost as high as Christmas with me was the time we were invited to the studios of that small station in Gainesville, Florida. After a two-hour drive, we arrived and were escorted into the large, back room that was their studio. I watched, wide-eyed, as the band unpacked their instruments, arranged the chairs, and placed a microphone the size of a small plate in front of them. The leader, who was the singer, guitar player and announcer, came over and spoke to us as we sat on folding chairs against the wall. He welcomed us and admonished us to be quiet during the show. The band tuned up, a big red light came on and I watched wide-eyed and open-eared as the theme began, "*I like mountain music, good ole mountain music. . .*"

I do not remember much more about that night, but after almost eighty years the sound of a real hillbilly band brings that memory back and I feel something of the excitement I felt that night so long ago.

SHUBERT ALLEY IN THE VALLEY

We almost missed it. Saturday evening was sold out and there were just a few tickets left for Sunday afternoon. When the choir met to practice before church, the ones who saw the production "Shubert Alley in the Valley" were enthusiastically proclaiming its quality and their enjoyment. Over half of our choir had performed in the musical and Barbara, our choir director, was directing the music and playing. After church we rushed across the street to the Sautee Nacoochee Center to get tickets.

The Center is a complex of buildings whose purpose is "to nurture creativity and to preserve and protect the beloved resources of the Sautee and Nacoochee valleys and surrounding area." Housed in an old school building, the Center includes a history museum, art exhibits, a pottery museum and hosts plays, musicals, concerts, picnics, and provides for recreational activities. The school auditorium, converted to a theater, was the setting for this production.

For two hours we were treated to Broadway music by musicians, singers, dancers and performers who volunteered their time and talents. We came away awed by the talent that is in the valley and looking forward to many of the other activities to come. We enjoyed the show!

A NEW ADDITION TO THE LIVING ROOM

There was an old piano in Moss Manor when we moved in. It was moved to the downstairs room and was retuned. Sadly, the tuning did not help. It twanged and groaned and created discords by itself. We threatened to roll it to our drive way, give it a push and wish it well as it careened down the mountain. But then we thought of our neighbors down the hill who would not like it crashing through their house. Therefore, it still waits, unplayable, for disposition in the downstairs room.

We have been looking for a better piano for Beverly to play, but nothing we found seemed to fit the space we have. Even the used spinets that we looked at would extend beyond the appointed space. It looked hopeless.

But yesterday we drove to Gainesville, GA and visited a music store. Beverly tried all the pianos while I measured them with a tape measure. Again, the grands were too expensive and too large; the spinets would not fit our space. Finally, we came to the electronic section. There we found a new medium-grade Yamaha that sounded like a piano, played like a piano, felt like a piano and would fit the appointed space. Also, it just fit into the back of our van and soon we were unloading it at Moss Manor. It fit perfectly in the space just to the right as you step down into our living room. There it sits in all its glory, plugged in and ready to play.

Beverly is happy. Now she can not only play the piano, but a full church organ as well. I am happy because I enjoy listening to her play. We are both happy that it seems to have found a good home in our living room. However, Lady Bean is frustrated because she can no longer race down the hall and propel herself to the top of the stuffed rocker that the piano replaced, but she will get over it. Then we will all be happy and enjoy the music.

BEVERLY'S CORNER

When we left Ocala for Moss Manor, we had not expected to see the cherry tree in bloom, just hoped! Needless to say, we did see the white petals. . .all over the ground around it. However, the traveling up from Ocala did let us see spring coming south. Mostly, there were dogwoods-white and pink and red! Then, we saw purple wisteria festooning huge trees, and white single-petal roses climbing stately pines. It was magical to see stands of the dogwoods in the dark woods along the way.

Now, in the Sautee area, the dogwoods are mostly bloomed out, but mountain laurel is making itself known. As we go to church or to the grocery stores down the mountain, almost every turn brings us face to face with a huge bush of these lovely pink and white blooms. Each time we drive down, a new bush appears.

When we first arrived, we were greeted with a single blue iris in our backyard. The next day there were five, then the next, fifteen. Two days later, twenty-five blooms, up the mountain. Our dividing the main clump proved successful. The impatiens are just beginning to come up. The two clematis vines are in bloom, too. The lavender one has blooms the size of salad plates and the dark purple ones are just about bread and butter plate-size!

As usual, there are young, "teenaged" and older deer and turkeys that strut across our yard as though they own the place. Come and see.

SCRATCHING
THE WALLS

BLAZING THE TRAIL WITH
MOUNTAIN LAUREL

For the last few weeks, our mountain has been filled with beautiful bursts of color provided by the red and pink of mountain laurel. As we drive the twisting road from Moss Manor to the gate, we see them along the roadway and back in the woods. At every turn they mark our way. It is almost as if a giant master painter had blazed a trail, splashing color at every turn and dragging his brush along the roadside as he walked the straighter places of the way.

Spring came early this year and the early leaves provide a lush, light green backdrop for the vivid display of blossoms. Mountain laurel is seldom planted but grows in wild profusion in our mountain. Along the roads or in the privacy of deep woods, they bring a burst of color. They will soon be gone until next spring but for now we appreciate their presence and give thanks to the master painter who has marked with fire the way we travel.

HIP HIP HURRAY!

I think I have it reversed. It should be Hurray Hip Hip! Yesterday I went with the hiking group from the church. There was a pot luck dinner after church, after which about twenty hearty souls set out for Hemlock Falls about thirty miles up the mountain toward Lake

Burton. We parked at the trail head and after a group picture, we set forth.

On the right a good-sized mountain stream marked the way. The trail itself was well-kept by the park service. The group set a good hiking pace, and some were soon well in front of a few of us whose legs felt the wear and tear of age. Besides, I wanted to take pictures of the beautiful scenes around us. The trail moved ever upward, sometimes presenting the challenge of tree roots and rock. There were places where springs crossing the trail left their mark of mud and clay. A few places required climbing up uneven rocks where I was glad to have my hiking stick and a helping hand ahead of me.

The trail marker said it was one mile to the falls, but I am sure it was longer. I am also sure the distance was determined by age and agility. Finally the stragglers heard the sound of falling water and the voices of our group. We had arrived at Hemlock Falls. The fall was a large cascade that poured over large rocks and into a pool below that dissipated its fury into an almost still pool. It was a beautiful place to rest and eat cookies that had been brought along. We prepared ourselves for the descent. It was there that I felt like planting the flag of success and shouting, "Hurray, I have made it to the top!"

The trip down was just a reversal of the ascent. We took more pictures, saw mountain flowers like trillium and jack-in-the-pulpit. Someone rescued three baby birds which had fledged too soon and whose mother was anxiously announcing her concern.

The trail seemed even longer going down, but we finally arrived at the trail head and our cars. It was then, as I climbed into the car for the trip home that my exuberant "hurray!" turned into the complaint of "hip hip." The ache in my hips told me that I was not as young or agile as I thought I was or used to be.

Even with the reversed victory cry, I was glad I was able to make the climb and to enjoy the hike with friends. Life is good and I am fortunate.

COMPETITION FOR THE PREACHER

It was one of those beautiful Sunday mornings in early May. Since there was no air- conditioning in the church, the windows were wide open letting in fragrance, a little pollen and many accompanying sounds. From our pew we could look out and see the lush green of the Sautee valley and the blue-green mountains beyond them. The music and unison liturgy of the early part of worship kept us concentrating on the bulletin. . .when to respond, when to stand and when to say "Amen." Then came the relative silence of the sermon. Of course there were the usual distractions that come naturally to most congregations: the rattling of bulletins, a baby crying, someone slipping out the side door. This was the time when it was easy for the mind to wander and to listen to the ambient sounds that drifted in from the open windows.

But today there were different sounds to vie for attention. The chirping of birds and the raw cry of a crow called my attention from the pulpit to the world outside the window. A light breeze stirred the leaves and the pink blossoms of a tree just outside the window. Then, without warning, a car with a loud muffler passed by followed closely by a herd of motorcycles, interrupting both my outdoor reverie and the service itself. Almost as a climax, a car parked near the window began the steady blaring of its car-horn alarm. The preacher stopped. Three people got up and headed out, punching the off buttons on their auto-keys. Finally, after what seemed to be an eternity, the noise stopped; silence was restored; the preacher cleared his throat and continued as if nothing had happened.

I know the Lord, and maybe the preacher will understand if I do not remember much of what was said from the pulpit that day. But I will long remember that Sunday and the competition to the sermon.

THE YONAH BRASS

Last night we attended a concert in the sanctuary of the Nacoochee Presbyterian church. A group was made up of brass players, professional and amateur, from the surrounding area. The concert was an endeavor to raise money for charities in which the church was involved. There were twelve instruments including trumpets, flugelhorns, euphoniums, tubas, a clarinet, a trombone and piano. Our church music director was guest conductor for the featured selection. The church overflowed into the fellowship hall.

Music included *Fanfare from "La Peri"*, *Allegro Glusto*, *Rhapsody in Blue*, *Procession of the Nobles*, *Noon River*, *Stars and Stripes Forever* and *National Emblem*. It was a performance well-worth seeing and reminded us once again of the wealth of talent hidden in the North Georgia mountains.

REMEMBERING MOON RIVER

The Yonah Brass was playing *Moon River*. Maybe it was the name of the music. More likely it was the tune reminding me of a popular song taken from the music. At any rate, as they played, I was transported back over the years to a little river in South Carolina that flowed into the Intracoastal Waterway. We had been traveling the winding waters of the waterway on *Karisto*, our thirty-seven-foot sailboat. Night was falling and we needed a place to anchor. Moon River offered a perfect spot. The charts show shallow water but it was just past high tide and we could slip in over a shallow mouth and into a slightly deeper hole. We anchored, fixed supper and as we ate on deck we watched a nearly full moon cast light upon the waters of its namesake.

Our anchorage was shallower than we had thought and our five-foot keel settled into the soft mud of the bottom. There was no rocking or twisting on the anchor line that night and we slept well. The next morning, as we fixed breakfast, we were still aground but soon the predictable rising tide lifted us from our cradle in the mud. We were free to start the diesel, and watching the depth sounder carefully, we moved over the shallow entrance to the channel of the waterway.

A loud burst of music from the tubas chased away my flight of memory and I once again listened to and enjoyed the music of *Moon River* by Henry Mancini.

SCRATCHING THE WALLS

Sometimes I feel that I am scratching the wall. I have watched Lady Bean do it many times. She stretches full length up the side of the inside wall and scratches furiously. Since she has no front claws she gets no traction and leaves no marks. She turns and looks at me with a perplexed look and either sits down or walks away.

Many times I feel like I am scratching the walls of time and nothing is happening. There are many things I want to do and it seems like there is not enough time in the day or night to do them. When I was growing up, there was too much time. . .it dragged. I was always waiting for something I wanted to do or for something to come, like Christmas. The clocks ran slowly. In school, things seemed to level out and the discipline of homework or term papers kept things synchronized like the clocks in class rooms that all clicked off the time at exactly the same moment. In professional and family life there were sermons to write and children to get to activities on time, and the clocks ran fast or slow according to the situation. But in retirement, things are different.

Now I am continually "scratching the wall" and getting nothing done. There are so many things that I want to do and did not have time for in the past, and I am trying to do them all now. Guess I have not learned the art of multi-tasking since most of my projects end up unfinished; leaning against a wall or hiding in the computer. The truth is that I spend a great deal of time looking for things I have misplaced. It is frustrating.

Yet I am thankful to have the time to try many things. No one really expects a great deal from me and it doesn't really matter if everything does not get done. Still it seems that the clocks are running faster and faster and I am getting behinder and behinder. Maybe I wound them too tightly or put too high a voltage battery inside. I find I am constantly trying to catch up. I guess that is just the way life works, and time either crawls or flies.

Still, I feel that I, like Lady Bean, am just scratching the walls and leaving very few marks. It is frustrating!

MY NEW CHAIR

It came as surprise to me and I thought I would never get over it. I am talking about the time last year when my staff got rid of my sofa and chair from the living room. It had taken some time for me to break them in so that they fit me exactly and offered maximum comfort. Suddenly they were gone and in their place were two new sofas and a stuffed chair. They had a strange new smell to them and they were stiff and a little uncomfortable when I jumped up on them. Being a good and thoughtful cat, I tried real hard not to show my disappointment because my staff was so proud of the new stuff.

I am even getting used to them. My staff is heavy enough to break them in properly and the new smell has worn off. Before bedtime I bring my man-staff back to the living room so that he can sit down and watch news while I curl up next to him on the sofa with my head in his hand and do what cats do best. . .sleep.

After many naps and much sleeping practice I have decided that I like the new furniture, particularly the stuffed chair. It even matches my coloring. In fact, I am claiming that chair as my own. I have curled up in it enough to make it fit me perfectly. Of course, I will let other people use it if they ask my permission and do not stay too long.

I wonder if I should ask my staff to put my name on my new chair. LB

MY DAY!

Everyone seems to have a day. Last Sunday my lady-staff received a vase of red roses because it was Mother's Day. Now I hear them talking about Father's Day. I was feeling really bad until I saw a picture in a magazine that assured me that I was not forgotten. Or was I? My staff has been so busy about so many things that I was sure they were going to forget. So whenever I saw the magazine lying around, I would lie down on it with my paw on the picture. Surely they would see what I was pointing to, but they never seemed to notice. I was sure they would forget. BUT THEY DIDN'T!

When I woke my man-staff up on May 12th, he picked me up and gave me a big hug. My lady-staff did the same thing. Now I usually do not like to be hugged. As I have written before, I am not a lap cat nor do I like to be held, but this was different. This was MY DAY. I even got an extra portion of food. It is great to be remembered!

Did you hug your cat on the special "Hug Your Cat Day"? If you did not, shame, shame. Go immediately and get your cat a special treat or a bag of catnip or something to show that you really care.
(From *Advice to Cat Owners* by Lady Bean)

BEVERLY'S SPOT

Beverly's Spot will have to wait until next month. She has been down with a very painful hip plus some kind of a stomach virus that has kept her away from the computer.

The Doctors say the hip is fine and the pain is coming from the back. She sends her apology and will be back in the next Moss Manor News.

PUNCTURING CLOUDS

THE HILL

It is almost 7:30 and I am on the deck drinking my morning coffee. The sun is still hiding behind the mountain so the hill behind our house is bathed in gentle early morning light. The air is still. The deep bay of our neighbor's hound breaks the silence as he and his master walk the road below us. Birds are complaining about a crow that is crowding their space.

I am looking at our backyard which is a steep hill that drops from the ridge above and spills onto the narrow walkway in front of the deck. A stairway of old railroad ties divides the hill and offers a way to the top.

The steep mountainside fascinates me. It has been wrestled out of the trees and small twisting bushes that cover the mountains. We are constantly trying to control what grows there and nature is constantly trying to reclaim its own. To keep the soil from washing down the hill during rainstorms, we have crisscrossed the slope with landscape timbers. Between the timbers we have planted flowers and groundcover. But like most things that make life easier and more beautiful, there is competition. Weeds and what I call snake grass grow much easier and faster than our plants. The deer regularly follow their trail along the top and then slip down and feast on the tender flowers, as if they were planted just for them. Just when we have finally removed all of last year's leaves, fall comes again with more leaves. When my day's work is over on the hill and I am ready to retire for the night, I will find a number of new "chigger" bites.

Our hill is a constant challenge. It is difficult to keep my balance when going up the steps. As I near the top, I call out loudly, remembering the time we watched Buddy Bear go up those same steps; looking back as if daring us to follow. When it rains, water runs over our barriers and when it is dry, the shallow soil on top of rock dries out quickly and flowers must be watered. Still, with all the problems that it brings, I am glad the hill is there.

For me, it is a parable of life. . .always making us look up toward the top. . .always making us plan ahead and dream of flowers and rose bushes. . .always challenging us to plant and replant. . .always offering the opportunity to begin again and enjoy both the planting and the beauty of a blooming flower.

Like life, the hill brings disappointment and hope. It breaks my back and warms my heart. It offers hardship and rewards. As I look at the hill this morning, I know that I shall never really conquer nor tame it, but I know that I will get great pleasure from trying. I will continue to be surprised by the wonders that unexpectedly bring joy to my hill and to my mornings.

As I say, it is a parable of life.

A TRIBUTE TO MY FATHER ON FATHER'S DAY

Francis M Womack, Sr. 1891 - 1956

Good morning, Dad.

It is still raining this morning. . .the kind of morning you said was good for sleeping. Last night I opened the window and listened to the gentle drumming of the rain drops and the rattle of the water coming through the gutter from the roof. I dreamed that I was a little boy again with the whole world ahead of me. It was a good dream but a little frightening and it was good to have you near at hand to reassure me.

Now, as I sit at the kitchen table, drinking a cup of coffee, I remember how you would get up before it was light and fix your coffee in that small, dented coffee pot. You would sit by the window at the back of the table, drink coffee and read the *Times Union* paper.

This morning I wish I were there with you, or better yet that you were here at the table with me sharing a cup and talking. I never talked much with you then; I was too filled with the exuberance and perhaps the selfishness of youth. But you would listen and give advice as I poured out my plans for the day and the week. If you were at the table with me now, I would do a lot more listening and less talking. I would ask you about your hopes and dreams. . .about times when you were a boy like me. . .about your disappointments and the ways you overcame them. I would say thank you for being my father.

I would ask you how you liked Moss Manor. I know how much you liked to visit in Clayton. You would get up early to watch the sun struggle to climb over the mountains. I think you would like our place just as much. The early morning light is now outside our window. There is a misty cloud hanging on the top limbs of the trees and the moss lawn below is changing from gray to bright green. When we have finished our coffee, I would really like to show you around the house and walk with you around the yard. There is so much I want to ask and share with you.

Now I know that having you here at the table with me is just a fantasy. . .that you are just a memory. But it is good for me to talk with a memory. . .with one I loved and one who was taken home much too soon. There is so much I do not know about the place where you are now. I have read and studied and preached about heaven but it is still a mystery. . .a wonderful mystery that lives in memories and faith. I do not understand how you can hear me when I talk to you and thank you for all that you did for me. I hope that by God's great providence you do hear. Even if you do not, it is good for me to talk with a great memory.

Dad, it is good to share this time together. . .forgive me if I wipe away a tear. I hope the coffee was hot enough and not too weak. Maybe we can talk again.

I love you, Dad. Francis, Jr.

BRISTOL FIELD GETS A RUNWAY

For a number of years we have flown in the hay field as guests of the Bristol family. It is a relatively small group flying mostly electric, park-flyer type airplanes. Because of limited grass and predominantly growing grain, all airplanes had to be launched by hand. Some of the flyers still yearned for a runway from which to take off and land. Recently the Bristol family offered to allow a part of the field to be cut and a short, grass runway put in. The runway is complete, has been smoothed out and grass seed has been planted. The new grass can be seen and even though there is still work to be done, to roll, weed and cut, planes can be seen taking off and landing. It is a great gift by the Bristol family for those who enjoy flying in their field.

On Wednesday and Saturday mornings five to fifteen flyers show up to puncture the clouds with their electric planes. Veteran flyers show their ability. A number of new pilots have soloed and others are learning with a buddy-box. Flyers enjoy being together and helping one another.

Thanks to the Bristol family for allowing us to fly at Bristol Field.

MEMORIAL DAY

Memorial Day is that long holiday that marks the beginning of summer holidays and vacations. But we all know it is far more than that. It is a special day to remember those who have served and are serving our country. . .to remember their sacrifices and that of their loved ones and families. On this day we pay tribute to them and give thanks for the freedom they assure.

Maybe it was the prayers offered at church for our troops. . .maybe it was patriotic music coming from the radio. . .maybe it was the flags at the entrance to Sky Lake. . .whatever it was, I was suddenly back at the church in which I grew up. The year was early in 1942. Our nation had just been plunged into WWII. I was eleven years old; too young understand the full tragedy of war. I remembered going to church with my parents and watching as a service banner was hung in the front of the sanctuary with a number of blue stars and one gold star. My parents explained to me what it meant.

The blue stars represented members of the congregation who were fighting for our country. The gold star represented someone who had been killed while serving in the military. They explained to me that the gold star was for my first cousin who was one of the first causalities. Sgt. Henry Archer "Harry" Womack, Jr. had joined the Royal Canadian Air Force and was in training in England to hold back the Nazi threat. He was killed on July 1, 1941, in combat training before the United States entered the war.

In the months and years that followed the banner would be filled with blue stars and more gold stars. Each Sunday the banner was ever before us and we would give thanks to God for the many who served and those who gave their lives that we might live in freedom.

Since 1940 I have seen four wars and honored many veterans. On Memorial Day, may we all remember the many blue and gold stars, past and present, and give thanks for all who have served and sacrificed for freedom.

THE GOOD GOSPEL SHIP

I had forgotten that the choir was not singing this particular Sunday so I arrived almost an hour early. We usually need that much practice and warm up time to do justice to the anthem. The first service was still in progress as I made my way around the church to the fellowship hall. Through the open windows of the sanctuary came the unusual sounds of guitars, banjos and a string bass. Words of an old country hymn jogged a sweet spot in my memory: *I'm gonna take a trip on that good gospel ship. . .*floated out of the window and across the valley. It was certainly not Presbyterian but it was good, and it made me want to stop at the window and pat my foot. Then I remembered. Today was a Sunday when both the first and second service were done entirely with scripture and mountain gospel music.

On one of the pieces, the congregation was encouraged to join in the singing, clap their hands and even raise their arms and shout "Amen." As the leader put it, "It might even bring out a little of the hidden Baptist in you Presbyterians."

The service was mix of fun and reverent worship. While communion was served, a duet sang appropriate gospel music that brought a tear to many an eye and reminded us that many of our religious roots grew out of worshiping in a small, country church. While I would not want this as a regular fare, it was wonderful way to worship and remember that there is not just one way of doing anything, even Presbyterian worship.

Oh, I'm a gonna take a trip
In the good old gospel ship
And go sailin' through the air.

ALWAYS HELPING

I am a very helpful cat. When I see my man-staff or lady-staff doing something that is difficult or frustrating I jump right in and try to help. More often than not I solve their problem because as soon as I start helping they get up and leave as if the problem was solved.

My man-staff likes to put little pieces of wood together and then cover them all up. It all seems rather foolish to me but if that is what makes him happy, I am glad to jump right in and help. Sometime he says he could do it better without me, but I know that is not true.

When my staff is making up their bed, I like to help by getting under the cover and showing them where the wrinkles are. When my lady-staff is sorting clothes on her bed, I like to push the one she has rolled up off of the bed so she will have more room to work. I often test the pillows for them and get them soft and shaped. (Of course, I have to sleep on them awhile to be sure they are just right.) I test and fluff the pillows in the living room as well. I even test the bath tub to see that it is all right for my man-staff to use. (Of course, I never test it with water in it.)

Sometimes, I check the clothes in the dryer to see if they are really dry. It is warm and cozy, but I have to be careful that they see me and do not turn the dryer on. In the mornings, I can help my staff to wake up and can lead them into the kitchen and show them where they keep my food. . .just in case they forget.

I always help them find the bathroom door at night by lying down right in front of it and rolling over and over and meowing loudly as they try to avoid me. All in all, I am a very helpful cat and I know that my staff is most appreciative of my many efforts. I don't know what they would do without me! Lady "helpful" Bean

BEVERLY'S CORNER

What a difference a day makes! Even if it lasts two weeks or more. . .up here in the Northeast Georgia Mountains!

When we first came up in the spring, the dogwoods (white, red, and pink) were all blooming. Gorgeous sights! In less than two weeks, along came the mountain laurel and then all colors of iris! Last year after they had bloomed in our yard up the mountain, Francis separated some out to make a line up to the top of the ridge. When they bloomed this year, we counted about fifty beautiful blue irises. This year F. has separated some more and planted them on the opposite side of the ridge still facing the house so next year we'll have two lines climbing the mountain.

We've not seen many birds, deer, turkeys, or even bears so far this year. We do have blueberries which are still green. F. has covered the grape arbor and the blueberry bushes with netting which we hope will discourage the huge black crows from devouring the fruit before we get a chance to have one or two. Will let you know!

STATUS QUO IS PROGRESS

BACK IN SKY LAKE

We pulled up the driveway at about 8:30 p.m. on Tuesday, July 31. Almost a month ago we left for our Florida home to stay a week to ten days. Doctors and procedures lengthened our stay. It was hot. . .real hot. Even Lady Bean wanted to stay inside. It was good to be back in OTOW and especially good to see our friends.

Now it is good to be back in the mountains and be with our friends here. Split living has its advantages but it also is quite demanding. Everything we need is in the house where we aren't. Mail is forwarded back and forth until even the post office does not know where we are. Hopefully, except for a few weekend trips, we will be in North Georgia until the first part of December, so come see us. We are glad to be settled, the post office is satisfied, and Lady Bean is the happiest of all.

HAIRCUTS, HOSTAS AND HOES

It is amazing what nature can do to a yard and garden in a month of absence. When we left it the first of July, things looked pretty good. We had planned to be away only a week, but that stretched into a month. In our absence, the area was blessed with rain. When we returned, here is what we found:

The moss lawn in front needed a haircut. When your front yard has a soft, green deer moss lawn, grass likes to come up and try to take over in places where the sun breaks through the shade trees. That means I need to crank up the weed-whacker and give the lawn haircut. The weed-eater would not start and is now in the repair shop so the lawn still needs a haircut.

When we left, the hosta garden was doing well in our enclosed side yard. We were proud of the variety and beauty of the plants that were growing under the big Japanese maple. When we returned, both gates were open, perhaps pushed open by a big doe (maybe with the help of Buddy Bear), and the hostas were eaten to the ground.

The hill (you previously read about the challenge of my hill) was a mass of green weeds. The small rose bushes, canna lilies and other plants that dotted the hill were submerged in the sea of green. I have weeded for a couple of mornings and I see little progress except that I have collected a good number of the chiggers (redbugs for city dwellers). Even the wide steps, covered with rocks, had grown their own weed gardens. I guess the hill will be a good (?) summer project that will keep me busy.

Our animal and bird friends had cleaned the blueberry bushes so we did not need to harvest any berries. I could go on, but you get the idea. Thank goodness the house offered a welcome rest to tired travelers. All was in order and everything inside was working.

Still, as I look out the dinette window through the light rain I am grateful for the beauty of the moss lawn, the towering trees and the Japanese maples. When I look through the sliding glass doors in the living room and see a green hill with a few of the things we planted struggling for survival, and I see a doe with spotted fawns looking down from the ridge, I know how fortunate we are and I give thanks.

Well, guess it is time to stop writing and started on the "HHHs" . . .haircuts, hostas and hoeing.

ON TURNING EIGHTY-THREE

At my age, status quo is progress. It is good to be alive and able to get around as well as I do. I still long for the days when I could run, climb, play tennis and jump, but to paraphrase a movie title: "Eighty-threes Can't Jump." However, there are a lot of other things that we can do and I enjoy doing most of them. Sure, there are a few aches and pains; the balance isn't as good as it used to be, and I don't remember names and other things like I did. Still, I could blow out all the candles on my birthday cake and enjoy eating it with most of my own teeth. At eighty-four I probably will look back and wish that I felt as good as I did at eighty-three. As I said, "status quo is progress" and it is good to be alive and active; it was a very happy birthday.

AN OLD FRIEND CALLED

Last night the phone rang and an old friend was on the other end of the line. As we talked and reminisced, my thoughts took wings and carried me back over the years to the day when we were in school, grades one through twelve together. Those were the golden days even though we thought they were difficult and growing up would never end. We remembered family and friends, now gone from this world to the next. We wondered how many of the old gang were still around. When the call was over, I was still back in those wonderful days of memory.

Those were the days when everything seemed new and exciting. The world was fresh as morning dew. There was nothing routine except perhaps the three R's of school. It was a wonderful time even though there was measles, whooping cough and sometimes worse. These hurdles of childhood would pass and better days would take their place.

Friends were playmates, a dime was a fortune, the park was a safe place in which to play, air conditioning was a novelty and the porch was a place in which to sit and get cool. Trees were there to be climbed and the neighbor's big backyard was a place for pick-up softball or cork-ball, hit with a broomstick. The back alley was just right for kick-the-can and a good, loud shout brought kids from all around to play. Scooters made of old skates and bicycles were the transportation of choice or perhaps, of necessity. Most of our time was spent outside except when we were hauled inside to practice the piano. Things were really a dime at the dime stores. Trains still belched black smoke and rattled over the crossing down the street. Supper time came just after the half hour episode of the *Lone*

145

Ranger on the radio. There were spelling words to learn and arithmetic problems to be solved. Saturdays were too short, and Sundays required Sunday school and church and enforced rest.

It was a different world. No TV, no cell phone, and homework was written by hand, not by computer. It was the time of the depression, but we did not know it. None of us had a great deal and what we had, we shared. Maybe I have forgotten the difficulties of growing up. . .time has a way of allowing us to remember the good and forget the not-so-good.

They call the years that I am living the golden years but, at least in my case, they have it backward. The older I get, the more I dream and remember my childhood. Maybe the neurons of the brain were fresher then and stored each activity in my retrievable memory. Whatever the reason, just like the call from my old friend, more things send me back to those wonderful days some seventy to seventy-five years ago.

AN EXPANDING UNIVERSE

I remember something that my father said, "I would like to be an inventor, but most everything has already been invented." I don't think he was serious, but I am not sure. Dad would often talk about the inventions and the discoveries that had been made in his lifetime. Born in 1892, he lived through the change from real horse power to mechanical horse power. He saw manned flight become a reality. He listened as radio grew from infancy to a modern necessity. He watched the early televisions and doubted that true color would ever be possible on TV. Dad marveled at the way automobiles could travel for sixty thousand miles before wearing out. He lived through two world wars and the destruction and progress that they brought. Dad was sure that he had lived through the age of the greatest and most rapid progress. When he died in the early 1950, I am sure he felt that there was little left to discover.

Maybe every age, every lifetime feels that way. I feel very fortunate to live during a time of tremendous change. Men have walked on the moon. Knowledge is expanding in quantum leaps. We have learned that for every new invention, every new discovery, there are four more waiting just around the corner. Stop and think about what you have seen in your lifetime. We have looked inward at the tiniest building block of matter. Through the eye of the Hubble telescope we have peered back in time to the beginning of the universe. Yet we know there is much more to be discovered.

There are those who say that our discoveries and scientific knowledge have brought us to the point that there is no need for God. But for me, every new discovery, every scientific breakthrough assures me that God is bigger and more powerful than I ever imagined. An expanding universe demands an expanding faith in an infinitely powerful God.

BEVERLY'S REPORT

After spending about two months lying in bed and losing twenty pounds, we made it to a doctor in Gainesville, GA, who told us that my heart was not getting enough oxygen. I had been breathing all of my life! I guess that's the result of growing old!

So far, age has not prevented us from coming up to these gorgeous Jawja Mountains! I've been to the monthly church ladies' luncheon and to church to renew acquaintances. Our minister, Bob Prim, had an excellent sermon last Sunday. Wish you could have been here to hear him.

The birds have missed F. and are clamoring for birdseed as often as LB does for her food. The birds appear in the trees by the kitchen door and make their presence known when it's time for their food. The hummingbirds fly to the window by the breakfast table and let us know when their food is needed.

We've seen deer with food in their mouths coming up from the direction of a neighbor's yard. We suspect that she's supplying them with snacks. A few flowers are blooming. It is good to be in Moss Manor. That's enough for now. . . .more next time! B.

THE CRASH OF DELTA 879

The Delta 879 (my name for my new delta-winged RC aircraft) had been test flown once by an experienced pilot. It had been flown again successfully by someone who had never flown that kind of a model before (me). Both times someone had launched the aircraft while we were ready with the controls. I had gained confidence and was ready to both launch and control it.

I carried it to the field. Beverly came to watch the flight. I armed the motor, checked the controls which were set correctly and carried Delta 879 to the pilot's post where I planned to gently throw it into the sky. I put the plane on the ground so that I could extend the antenna on the transmitter. Trembling with excitement, I picked up the plane, tested the controls, pushed the throttle up to full speed and tossed it skyward. It flew straight and true, but I wanted it to climb quickly. I gave it up elevator. . . .and it dove straight into the ground. When I picked up the pieces, I realized what was wrong. When I launched the plane, I was holding it upside down. Naturally, when I pulled back on the control, it performed as it was designed to do and went straight down.

I have made some dumb mistakes while flying models, but I believe this one takes the cake. Maybe I should stand on my head while flying. Maybe I should take up something like playing cards where you can hold them upside down and they still look the same. I could go back to stamp collecting but I probably would put the stamps in the album upside down. It will take me a long time to forget and live down the day my plane flew upside down out of my hand, straight into the ground.

GETTING READY TO GO

I know that I am a very fortunate cat. I have two nice homes and I am very much in control of both of them. I enjoy living in both of them. But there is one thing I do not like. It is the long ride I have to take to go between them. It happens three or four times a year. I think we could all take one big jump and go from one to the other but my staff insists on piling a bunch of stuff in the van and spending a long day riding. I try to put off going as long as I can.

Last week, I knew it was about to happen again. They began to pick things up around the house. They pulled out a suitcase and began putting clothes in it. Other things went into little bags and were hidden in the garage. They think I don't know but I do. I watch their every move carefully and when they are not looking I check out my best hiding place.

Early one morning I saw them put the red bag in the van and I knew it was time to hide. I had picked out a special place. There was a tear on the edge of the cloth that covered the bottom of the bed. I crawled in there. . . above me were pieces of wood and pieces of wire. When I crawled in, the cloth cover sagged a little and was very comfortable. Soon I heard them lock the doors and say, "It is time to get the cat!" I purred a little because I knew they were too big to get under the bed and their arms were not long enough to reach me. They looked all over the house but finally he got down on the floor and spotted the sagging cloth that held me. My man-staff tried to move the bed but it was too heavy. He took a cane and poked me and begged me to come out. I just moved from side to side where he had a hard time getting to me, even with his stick. I was winning for almost an hour, but then things got quiet and I began to worry. Then he jabbed something through the cloth near me and started to cut the cloth. I slipped and almost fell out. When I did, he grabbed me by the leg and pulled. I growled and hissed and even showed my teeth, but I knew better than to bite the hand that feeds me. He pulled me out, carried me to the van and pushed me into my cat carrier. The motor started and we bounced out of the driveway.

I hate to admit it, but they always win in the end. I guess I am really glad because if they did not, they would have to leave me behind and I would be very lonely. After I complained a while and slept a little, they let me out and I took my place between them and helped them drive all the way to my other home. LB

FOR ME?

I must admit that my staff is pretty good to me. They serve my food in the morning and in the late afternoon. Sometimes, even most of the time, I have to remind them, but they always come through. My man-staff lets me take him for a walk around the house in the afternoon. Sometimes he comes in sooner than he should and I have to come in with him to be sure he doesn't get lost. My lady-staff talks to me and sometimes she combs my fur and that feels real good. They both let me sleep where I want to and try not to wake me up. My man-staff even gives up his chair at the computer when I ask for it since it is my favorite place to sleep. Of course, I let him sit in it for a while until it gets nice and warm. I let them know that I appreciate what they do for me by sitting next to them on the sofa and purring. . .they like to hear me purr.

But it was almost too much for me when they brought me a beautiful pitcher of red roses. They sat them down on my coffee table so I could smell them and enjoy them. I started to say, "Aw! Your really shouldn't have!" But then I caught myself and remembered how much pleasure I give to them and how much help I am around the house. Now that I think about it, I guess they really should have! LB

ROGUE WAVES

A TOUCH OF FALL

Today is the first day of fall and we were ready for it to come. The summer was not bad in Moss Manor which is 1500 feet up the mountain and shaded by large trees, but the middle of the day had been hot and it had been humid. Yes, we are ready for cooler weather.

As I look out of the dinette window, I see a smattering of yellow and an occasional red among the leaves. The dogwoods are leading the way toward the parade of splendor that will soon follow. The green moss lawn needs blowing where leaves are beginning to come down from their lofty habitat. During early morning hours we are pulling up the blanket and enjoying a warm bed on a cool morning.

Fall is still very much in transition, but we are enjoying its gradual approach and the touch of fall in the trees and in the air.

JOY IN THE WEATHER STATION

It has been a rather dull and boring spring and summer in the weather station. Oh, there were some droughts and floods and even a tornado or two, but for the most part it was just reporting the temperature. The Atlantic was peaceful and calm. You could almost see the boredom on the faces of those who routinely reported the weather.

But then came late August and early September. You could almost see the weather people sit up in their chairs. If you looked, you could see the sparkle of anticipation in their eyes. You could detect enthusiasm in their voices. The embryo of Hurricane Isaac was forming off the African coast. There was something out there to track. There were rain bands to color with red markers. There was barometric pressure to measure. There were storm alerts to broadcast and wind speeds to measure each hour. They almost danced to the beat, "A hurricane is coming! A hurricane is coming!" There was joy at the weather station.

Now, I am not saying that these prophets of weather are glad when impending disaster is on the way. They do a great job in keeping us aware of the danger and how we need to prepare. Weather is their business, and they are good at what they do.

But, I am sure you noticed the new sense of purpose, the new excitement as reporters waded into boiling water or swayed in syncopation with the windblown trees or almost sang in harmony with the pounding rain. The season has been saved! Isaac is a hurricane and we have something of great importance to report.

In September, there was joy at the weather station.

THE FIRST GRANDCHILD'S WEDDING

Labor Day Week-end was a long time in coming. . .like growing up. . .like the wait for Christmas Day. . .it was a long time coming and then, suddenly, it came with a rush. We were on our way to the wedding of Allison to Anthony. We had planned for our visit to Morristown where my oldest granddaughter was getting married. Our whole family was coming aunts, uncles and cousins. Most of them were flying but I, stubbornly, wanted to drive. I-64 from Ashville to I-81 offered a beautiful drive through the rolling mountains of the Shenandoah Valley and I did not want to miss it.

We left early on Friday morning with Lady Bean, hiding deep under the bed hoping we would not gather her up and put her in the van for a long ride. This time she got her wish and would be fed and cared for by a pet sitter visiting each day. It was a gray day but the sky soon turned to large white clouds and sunshine. The hills around us and the mountains on either side were lush with grass and corn fields. Six hundred-plus miles rolled under us and finally we arrived at our stop in Chambersburg, PA. We slept well and were underway again by seven in the morning. The well-kept farms of Pennsylvania slipped by on either side. By 10:30 we arrived at the Madison Hotel where the family and wedding party were gathering.

The dinner following the rehearsal was in Morristown. The entire restaurant was reserved for the wedding party. Four courses were served by formally-dressed waiters. It was a great night for all. The next morning, pre-wedding pictures were taken which included even the pets of the bride.

On Sunday afternoon at 4:00 bells rang in the Church of the Assumption of the Blessed Virgin Mary, and guests were seated as the organ played. Soon, as the oldest grandparents, we were ushered down the aisle leading the procession. Then came the groom and groomsmen taking their place in front. The beautifully-gowned bridesmaids flowed down the aisle. The bride came down on her father's arm joining the groom. Father John performed the wedding service in a dignified but almost informal way. Anthony and Allison were married in a beautiful ceremony.

The reception that followed was an affair that rivaled the wedding itself. The informal hour before the sit-down dinner was a full meal in itself with food all around the room and drinks aplenty. Mac, the father of the bride and mayor of North Brunswick, NJ had invited not only family and friends of the bride and groom, but many of the town's leadership and politically important. The dinner that followed was interspersed with toasts, music and dancing. It was still going full speed when Bev and I slipped off to bed. The next day we had a chance to visit with Mack and family before resting up for the uneventful return trip home on Tuesday. We brought with us lots of great memories.

HOUSESITTERS

When our children, Karl and Jackie, had to move from their home in Jacksonville, it was a perfect opportunity for us to have house-sitters in OTOW to use and take care of our house there. They will store their furniture and use our home, as is, for a period of time. They will move in around October 1st. We will come down from the mountains and spend the month of December and part of January with them. We welcome them to the good life in central Florida.

FIREFLIES AT THE AIR FIELD

As if it was not enough to watch our radio-controlled planes soar into the blue and sometimes touch the low hanging fog of morning, now there is something different. In the gathering darkness of evening flyers are bringing out trained fireflies. Not really, but the tiny green, red and white lights that are adorning wings and tail of aircraft look very much like giant fireflies against the darkening sky. It is a real challenge to stay oriented when all that can be seen of the planes are the sparkling lights. To people passing by in the distance, they look, for all the world, like giant fireflies over the airfield.

MY PRIMITIVE INSTINCTS

I do not know exactly how or why it happens. Usually I am a very gentle and peaceful cat, sleeping in one or more of my special sleeping places, but then, sometimes things change. Like a rogue wave on a usually calm sea. . .like a bolt of lightning out of a clear sky. . .like a primitive instinct from my distant past. . .it hits me. When it comes, I am off and running. It happens late at night when all is quiet or early in the morning before my staff is up. I go flying from the bedroom down the long green hall, my paws pounding. (My staff says I sound like a herd of buffalo, but I think they exaggerate.) I like to race down the hall, leap to the top of the sofa and fly on to the chair beyond. I once nearly had an accident doing this maneuver. My staff had replaced my stuffed chair with a piano and a piano is much harder to land on than a soft chair. I changed direction in mid-air.

Another maneuver that I like is to reverse the direction. I start in the kitchen, build up speed as I race down the hall, and launch myself into the middle of the bed. This is especially fun, early in the morning, when my staff is still asleep. Sometimes I like to hide under chairs and jump out when my staff approaches.

Another urge that comes upon me is the urge to eat. I feel it just before daylight. Then I walk up and down on the bed where my staff is sleeping, sometimes walking on top of them. If that does not work, I begin to talk with my guttural meows and unique clicking sounds. It usually works and my man-staff gets up grumpily and I lead him to the kitchen and talk to him until he feeds me.

I often wonder if my ancestors in the jungle had as much fun with their sudden impulses as I do. LB

FROM BEVERLY

When we were going to New Jersey for Allison's wedding, there were all kinds of news about the lack of corn in the Midwest from the drought conditions. Well, no newscaster was riding along with us through the miles and miles of corn fields we saw! If you like to eat corn on the cob, your mouth would surely have been salivating.

Other than what F. has already mentioned, I was delighted to see that the six bridesmaids' and two junior bridesmaids' dresses were exactly alike with a bodice laced up the back in a beautiful pink satin or taffeta. AND, wonder of wonders, when the bride came down the aisle, we saw that her wedding dress had the same lacing in the back like the bridesmaids' dresses. Beautiful!

Change of subject. Flowers had begun blooming when we returned from the north: golden rod, lots of black-eyed Susan and the ever-present white ragweed. Temperatures were still in the 70s and 80s so air-conditioning was still being used. Now fall is on the way with 60s and even 50s promised by the morning. The mountain air is marvelous! Come see us and enjoy it with us!

CONQUERING PREJUDICE

A lot of water as flowed over the dam at Sky Lake since we last put fingers to the keys to write this newsletter. This is true both literally and figuratively. A few weeks ago I emptied ten inches of weather from my rain gauge and that was just part of what had soaked the ground in the mountains. Even as I write, I hear the sound of drops peppering the roof and the rattle of water bouncing on the edges of the downspouts. Storm warnings are posted and flood warnings are in place for the valley.

It is good to sit down at the keyboard and watch the words appear on the screen in front of me. Lady Bean is curled up on the bed beside me, waiting to dictate her column. Beverly is still asleep and the sun has yet to make an appearance on the steep sides of the mountain to the east. I think of our many friends who read this newsletter and good memories dance across my mind as I visit again the good years, good places and good friends that have been part of my life.

But enough of reminiscing! Let's move on with the task of writing the belated January issue of Moss Manor News.

A SHORT ITEM OF PERSONAL STUFF

A number of you have asked, so here is what has happened to Beverly and me since last year. In October, we invited Karl, Beverly's son, and his wife, Jackie, to house sit for us while we travel and spend one winter in the mountains. Karl has been quite sick and we are glad to have them spend a year in our home in Ocala while Karl recuperated. We returned to On Top of the World for the month of December to visit our doctors and catch up on life in Florida. During our stay, I had a squamus cell removed from my face and still show the marks of the operation. It was good to preach again at Reddick, to visit our friends in Countryside P. C. and to share Christmas with our family.

Soon after our return to Sky Lake, Beverly found that she needed a full knee replacement on her good knee. She has had to keep off of the leg for the last three weeks. Today we go to the cardiologist to get clearance for the upcoming surgery.

OF DEER, TURKEY AND SQUIRRELS

While eating breakfast the other day, we watched nineteen turkeys wander casually through the front yard. They took their time, pecking the ground for a morsel or two and then saunter down toward the small creek across the road. They are regular visitors.

The deer are regular visitors, too. Sometimes we see many as eight, a small herd, and sometimes there are only one or two. They scuff up the carpet of the moss lawn, rolling back a small patch at a time, looking for something edible underneath. They soon move over to the young butterfly bushes and nibble at the tender leaves and new growth. When I open the door to get their picture, they look up, as if to say, "Why are you in our territory?" If I make a sudden motion, or they hear the camera click loudly, they sense danger and, as one, flee down the hill or into the woods, wagging their white, flag-like tails in a parting gesture.

The squirrels also think they own the place. They wait in their tree until I put seeds out for the birds. Then, as if on cue, they appear and make short work of the seeds, while the birds protest loudly. If Lady Bean ventures outside the house, these pesky squirrels join in a chorus of protest, staying well away and high up in their tree. They do not know that all she wants is to play with them as a friend.

So far this year there have been no bear sightings at Moss Manor.

THE DREAM FIELD

We had dreamed of it for years, but it was difficult to find a level piece of land in the mountains of North Georgia. Even when the mountains meet in the lush bottom lands and valleys, these areas are occupied by cattle, corn and tourists. So I'm sure you understand how excited six old-time RC fliers were when it became possible for them to lease a tract of land near the eastern end of the Nacoochee Valley. It was bordered on the east by the Sautee Creek, on the south by the Chattahoochee River, on the north by a state road, hidden by trees, and to the west by a valley extending almost to the horizon. We were to have retrieval rights over the soy bean fields and horse pastures that stretched down the valley. Someone said, upon first seeing the site, "Wow, you have leased half the Nacoochee Valley."

But wonderful as it seemed, there were challenges. The entrance road was not gated. What was to be the parking lot had in the distant past been a buffalo pen. The iron-gated entrance was prone to become a mud hole after rains. But most challenging of all were the six-foot-high weeds, bushes and small trees that covered the parking lot's uneven ground as well as the part that would be the flying area and runway. There were only six of us.

But the desire to have an AMA field, and our vision of what could be, won. Immediately papers were submitted and we became AMA sanctioned club #5123. The cost of the lease was shared among the six members. We attacked the field. Three of our members had tractors, and they descended on the weeds and brush with a vengeance. Friends and other flyers began to appear; bringing chain saws and rakes and strong backs.

The tall grass fell, trees came down; a new gate was cut in the buffalo fence. The second meeting of the club was held at the field, and the president was given a unique lectern from which to preside.

The young club grew from six, to ten, and then to twenty. Work days became a time for fellowship. In the field just beyond the parking area, the runway began to take shape. Grass was planted and soon outlined the smooth, hundred-foot-long runway.

In November the field was opened for flying. Coffee and donuts began the day. The new tables were filled with RC airplanes. It was decided that, for the present, the aircraft would be electric only. The safety officer read the club rules and reminded everyone that we were subject to AMA rules as well. It was a great opening day with no serious crashes. Regular business and program meetings were scheduled monthly.

But our flyers faced a unique situation. The property owner retained the right to allow trail riders, in groups, to follow their path on the extreme borders of the property. In order not to frighten the horses carrying novice riders, we agreed that whenever we saw horses coming, we would endeavor to fly on the opposite side of the field. Watching for horses became a major duty of the spotters. This arrangement caused no problem and is just part of learning to live together in our different worlds.

All went well until ten inches and more of rain came down in one week. Our parking lot drained miles of the valley. We needed drain ditches to be cut and gravel for the road. Our field marshal and his tractor did most of the work and, with the help of others and warmer weather, we were again flying.

Club membership has grown to twenty-one and the future looks good. Programs of interest to flyers are held monthly. Sautee RC Flyers is an example of how dreams can become reality and challenges can dissolve into a wonderful flying field and club.

MY CHAIR!

My man-staff bought me a new chair. It is big and soft with a high back that is just right for leaning against when I curl up for a long nap. He keeps my chair right in front of his new desk with keyboard, screen, noisy printer and radio. He likes my chair too, and sometimes I let him use it when I am busy doing something else or sleeping somewhere else. When he is there and I want to use my chair, I jump onto the desk, look him in the eye then put one foot gently on his keyboard and the other down on the seat of my chair beside him. Being rather smart, he knows what I want and he gets up. I quickly curl up in my chair. My man-staff grumbles as he pushes me and my chair to the side and pulls up a folding chair to use.

I like to be kind to my staff, but they need to be reminded that it is really MY house and MY chair. LB

THE PORTRAIT

"Lady Bean" arrived today in her high tech cage. After carefully taking down the bars, she emerged in life-like beauty. She is now hanging in the hallway where everyone can see her. Her live clone still thinks that she is more beautiful than the portrait, but Beverly and I think they look just alike.

Our special thanks to the talented artist, Jo Ann, who did the painting of our beloved cat, Lady Bean. We appreciate Jo Ann for what she paints on both the canvas and on the keys of the piano. Most of all we appreciate her friendship. A word of thanks also to Brad, who built the custom cage (the frame). The picture will hang in a prominent place in our home where both humans and felines can admire it.

REMEMBERING

The other Sunday our minister remembered Martin Luther King Sunday by quoting passages from his "letters from a Birmingham jail." The words took me back in memory to those days in 1963 when our nation was in the middle of the struggle for equality. We can look back from the comfort of sixty years. As I heard the words of the letter, I remembered difficult times. As ministers, we had to make difficult decisions. Could we be more effective in the front lines with the marchers, or in our pulpits urging stubborn congregations over the hurdles of prejudice toward what was right and just? Change comes hard to churches mired in the muck of "this is the way we've always done it." I made the choice and even today I wonder if I made the right choice.

As the words from prison continued from the pulpit, my thoughts flashed to other times. I remember growing up in the segregated south where Hogan Creek was a hard, fence-like border between black and white. I remember "white only" signs, I took for granted.

I grew up taking segregation for granted. As I have grown and aged, I have tried to undo and conquer my prejudice. I remember:

- the racial turmoil of the 60s
- congregations boiling over at the thought of integration
- spending long hours talking with a deacon who threatened to bring a shotgun and sit on the steps of our church just in case blacks came
- being chastised because we invited our black grounds keeper inside for lunch
- the first black teacher in the grade school. . .the best teacher John ever had
- the day my son left the Boy Scout troop because the church I served, and which sponsored the troop, would not let his black friend join the troop
- the years of violence, of bravery, of tragedy, of marches, of injustice and justice

The elegance and passion of Martin Luther King's message from prison brought feelings of guilt and pride. I could not help but look back in memory at that long struggle and the partial victories that have been made. I pray that I will continue to control my prejudices about race and many other things. *Let judgment run down as water and righteousness as a mighty stream.* (Amos 5:24)

ON WASHING DISHES

I like washing dishes. I know that it seems unbelievable since the advent of the automatic dishwasher but I really do. When we have company and when things really stack up, I break down and let Beverly file the dishes away in the dishwasher. . .she says it gets things cleaner but I doubt it. Why, then, do I like to wash dishes? Here is the story.

First, it goes back to memories. It was a ritual that after eating supper (dinner, that is, for those north of the Mason Dixon). I washed and the children dried. It was quality time for debriefing school.

Besides, there was a beautiful view of sunset over the back pasture and in another home, a view of boats passing on the waterway.

Secondly, particularly in Sky Lake, the picture outside the back window is fascinating. It is a never ending, always changing panorama of the seasons. Winter changes to the new green of spring. The leaves of the Japanese maples turn different colors. Spring greens change to fall reds and then to bare or snow covered winter canopies. Deer pass by, birds flock around the feeder, and squirrels try desperately to get inside the bird feeder, not knowing that their very weight has shut the food gate. Somehow it makes doing dishes go faster and sometimes I almost wish there were more plates and pans to prolong my stay at the window.

I don't recommend it for everyone, but for me, I like washing dishes.

IT'S SNOWING! IT'S SNOWING! AT LAST, IT'S SNOWING!

We have been in Moss Manor for five years and we have been watching and waiting for the white stuff to fall from the heavens. It happened once, briefly, just after the family had left the Thanksgiving gathering. Since then, zip. It was partly our fault since we spent part of the winter months in Florida. Yesterday afternoon it came. . .lightly at first, then gathering in size and speed. By late evening there were almost three inches on the ground.

For Floridian Beverly, it was a wonderful sight to see. In fact, for all of us who had nowhere to go, it was welcome. Our moss lawn was now white, the branches of the junipers were decorated like a Christmas painting and the fallen leaves on the back hill had changed from brown to white. Saturday night we sat by the fire and watched through the glass doors as the deck became a soft, thick blanket of white. Lady Bean watched the moving flakes with wonder but without the slightest desire to go out and investigate.

This was the kind of welcome snow that comes, hangs around for twenty-four hours, then slowly vanishes; leaving roads wet but clear and passable. Today the snow is almost gone and the sun shines brightly on the melting remnant. The temperature is rising. Soon all we will have are memories and lots of photographs. But we have had our snow and even if there is no more this year, we are satisfied with a beautiful day and night in the North Georgia Mountains.

I DO NOT LIKE COLD WEATHER

The weather here in Moss Manor has been horrible. When I first came up here, I could go outside and sit on the deck where the sun was shining and be warm, but not anymore. My man-staff will open the door for me early in the morning and I will dash out. Then it hits me. My hair stands up on my back. The wind ruffles my coat. It feels worse than it did when I jumped into the refrigerator while they were not looking. It is really cold. Even the birds do not fuss at me. The other morning, after it had rained all night, my man-staff let me out on the deck. It was real cold, but I tried to be brave. There was strange white shiny stuff on the deck and when I tried to walk on it, my feet slipped right out from under me. Somehow, I got up and hurried back inside.

The other day something happened that should not happen, even to a dog. It was a cold evening, but I had made up my mind that I was going outside for just a minute or two. My man-staff let me out when he went for firewood. It was colder than I thought so in less than a minute, I wanted to come in. But, would you believe, the glass door was shut. I walked around the house and tried every door with no luck. I went back to the door where I came out and scratched and meowed. No one heard me. I began shivering and even crying. I was sure my staff people were asleep in their warm bed and I was going to freeze. My staff would find me frozen stiff when they got up in the morning. I had almost given up all hope when I heard my man-staff calling me. He was looking everywhere but outside. Finally, he came to the door and with a surprised look, opened it. He said, "Lady Bean, I completely forgot that you were outside. I'm so sorry." But I was not going to let him off that easy. I arched my back and marched right by him and hid under the bed near a heat register. He tried to get me to come out, but I was going to teach him a lesson. He needed to suffer like I had suffered.

I stayed under the bed for a long time, but when it was time for my late-night snack, I came out. He gave me a large snack of my crunchy cereal. Food can go a long way toward making things right again, so when I finished, I jumped on his bed and curled up next to him to show that there were no hard feelings. But if that ever happens again, he won't get off so easy. LB

THE LONG, LONG TRAIL

This edition of Moss Manor News follows the medically-related journeys of Beverly as she moves from home to hospital to rehab and home again. This issue may be a little unusual; we hope it brings you information about the authors (lady-staff, man-staff and the one who really rules the house) as well as articles that might trigger a time in your memory and even a smile or two.

THE HOSPITAL

It seemed that we had just gotten into bed when the alarm sounded at 3:30 a.m. It was time to get up and start for the hospital in Gainesville, GA. I had a cup of coffee but Bev could have NOTHING. Of course, Lady Bean demanded breakfast and went back to her basket. On the road to Cleveland we met only two cars. There were a few more during the hour's drive to Gainesville.

When we arrived at the Northeast Georgia Medical Center, I wheeled Beverly inside and went on to park the car. A few early arrivals and nurses changing shifts were the only sign of activity. This was the only time I could find a parking place on the ground level. All other visits I would have to circle around underground watching for tail lights that would signal someone was leaving their parking place.

After retrieving Beverly from the lobby, we checked in and soon were escorted to a curtained cubicle for pre-op. After seeing the surgeon and a bevy of gowned support staff, I was directed back to the waiting room and Beverly was off to receive a new knee.

THE WAITING ROOM

Hospital waiting rooms are all the same. They may be larger or smaller but they have the same character. I feel like I have spent half my life in waiting rooms. . .as a pastor staying with families while loved ones were in surgery or waiting anxiously while my own family members was being treated. Yesterday I was back in the waiting room while Beverly's knee was replaced. It took me back to a hundred different waiting rooms.

In the center of the room the chairs are pulled in a circle. They are occupied by the large family of a father who is in surgery. They are drinking coffee or a Coke and reliving old times. It is almost a family reunion. Around the room people are using different ways of relieving their tension. Some are reading newspapers or books; some are trying to sleep while others are doing crossword puzzles or talking quietly. At the edge, there is a young lady, alone and wiping tears away. Announcements and calls for family members interrupt the normal sounds. Large or small; waiting rooms are the same.

I am taken back in memory to the many times I had tried to still the anxiety of parishioners. When we were called to hear the doctor report, we would stand together to hear the news, sometimes good, sometimes bad. There would be relief or disbelief, sometimes tears and always prayers.

I remember other times. . .waiting to hear about my wife and son who had been in an accident. . .anxious for my daughter who had damaged her hands. . .concerned for a son hit by a car. Waiting rooms are all the same. They are filled with people who are anxious and fearful; hoping and praying for good news.

I especially remembered being in a waiting room after my first wife had been rushed by ambulance from the doctor's office. A young man walked rapidly through the crowded room and introduced himself as the volunteer hospital Chaplain. Deep down I knew why he had come but I wanted to deny it. He was ill-at-ease; perhaps his first such mission. We made small talk until the doctor, mask still hanging from his neck, came to us. "I'm sorry," he said, "We did all we could but the heart was just too weak." He hurried off to an easier job or perhaps more complicated surgery: opening, fixing and closing. The young chaplain fumbled for words, said a prayer of comfort and walked with me to another waiting room. Then he left and I was alone, really alone.

My thoughts of times past were broken by a hand on my shoulder. It was our pastor. I was glad to see him. Having been in situations like this before, I thought I was immune to the need for care, but I was wrong. It was great relief to feel his hand and see him. We talked together until the phone at the desk brought the news that Beverly's knee had been replaced successfully. A short prayer and he was gone. . .off to minister to others. I could not help but hope that my visits in years past had been as meaningful to my parishioners as his was to me.

I took my seat back amid the gathered people in the waiting room. The family across the squared seating asked how my wife was doing. When conversation quieted down, I looked around the groups of lonely, anxious people. I almost wished that I was doing volunteer Chaplin work again and could go to them with encouragement and comfort. The desk called me and gave me a room number for Beverly. As I left, I looked back at the full waiting room and the people, each hoping, praying and waiting for news of a loved one in surgery.

Hospital waiting rooms are different, yet they are all the same.

THE HOSPITAL ROOM

The hospital room was large. The one bed backed up to a wall of plugs and switches. A metal rod soared over the bed with a bag and a trapeze towering overhead. In front was a TV, plus an array of walkers, stretchers and plastic pans. Beside the TV was a board with names and numbers. A reclining chair and a small stuffed chair were companion to the bed. Nurses and aids came in and out regularly.

The most prominent feature of the room was the large picture wind to the side. Promotion brochures depicted views of the mountain or the town and showed patience looking out. I looked forward the view from Beverly's window but when she had settled in and I had time to gaze at the mountain scene, I was in for a surprise. Instead of overlooking the town or countryside, I saw a series of stained silver roof peaks. They stretched into the distance, broken only by pipes and exhaust domes. I

167

almost expected to see the chimney sweeps from Mary Poppins come dancing with their umbrellas over the roof tops. Even without a great view, it brought brightness into a room where the gloom of pain was ever present. I was glad for the light it brought to the room.

REHAB

After three long and trying days in the hospital, Beverly was moved to New Limestone Rehabilitation Facility. The long, winding, one-story building is located, very appropriately, at the corner of Beverly Road and Limestone Parkway. While Beverly was being fitted with appropriate clothing, fitted for her wheel chair and otherwise prepared for a rather long stay, I had a chance to look around. I felt at home for in years past I had spent many hours visiting parishioners in similar facilities. This one was clean, well-staffed and equipped and noisy. Calls and announcements kept coming from speakers in the hall and together with the voices of the staff calling each other made a noisy echo that raced up and down the hall and circled into every patient's room. It seems to me that all staff working in nursing and rehab homes must take the same orientation as to how to keep patients awake both day and night.

Beverly's first room looked out on an unimpressive wall of the next building. After a few days they moved her to room just across from the nurses' station. (I think they felt they needed to keep an eye on her since the night she wheel-chaired into the hall and got lost.) Physical Therapists came in the morning and afternoon and encouraged her to stretch the knee and to walk with the walker. They were nice and helpful but Beverly thought they made her stretch too much and walk too far. They were pleasant and did their job well.

A place for rehab is necessary but it is a place where a patient works very hard to leave. Beverly looks forward to next week when, if she has worked hard enough, it might be the time when rehab is a memory.

A VISIT FROM MY SON

I stood at the top stone step with my hand on the front door and watched them drive slowly down the driveway. As I watched the taillights disappear around the winding road from Moss Manor, a flood of memories raced through my mind. Mack was my oldest son, the one who brought pride and excitement during those early days of ministry. Mack was the one who bore the brunt of parents learning to be parents. He was the child who cleared the way and made it easier for the sister and brothers who followed him.

Mack and Carol had slipped away for a busy schedule and driven the 800 miles from North Brunswick, NJ to spend a few hours with Beverly and me. . .as he said, "Just to see that she was OK in rehab and to be sure that Opa was all right."

They were gone. I came inside and realized I had been standing in the cold without a jacket. The house was empty and very quiet. It was a good time to let memories roll through my mind like a fast-changing power-point presentation. I could see proud parents bringing our first baby into the four-room manse. I remember: the first doctor visit. . . kindergarten. . .the first day of school, the accident. . .the long days in the hospital. . .the body cast. . .the day he played football again. Memories were coming so fast: days at camp and camping together, his work at Disneyworld, graduation, college and law school, a wedding on New Year's Day, grandchildren, visits to New Jersey, help bringing *Karisto* back across the Caribbean and support in sad and happy times. Details raced and circled across the screen of my mind.

Their visit meant so much to be and to Beverly. Now I worried about their safety on the way home, but I also remember worrying about all our children every time they were traveling.

As I started to clean up the breakfast dishes, memories continued and the house was no longer lonely because of them. I am very grateful for their visit and the many memories it jostled out of the past. Their visit meant the world to me.

DOWN THE LONG, LONG TRAIL

Beverly was moved from the hospital to the rehab facility on February 25th. The rehab facility was located on Beverly Road about two miles up the road toward home. Still, it takes an hour to navigate the forty miles of winding mountain highway from Sky Lake to Gainesville. Each day as I unwind the corkscrew road out of Sky Lake and travel the winding highway through Cleveland and on to the edge of Gainesville, an old song keeps rattling around in my head. It is the kind that gets stuck and cycles and circles in the brain and will not leave. It took me to a time when we would, after youth fellowship and evening worship, meet at someone's home. We would gather around a piano. Beverly would play and we would attempt to harmonize. One of the songs that we would sing now circles in my head. As I drive through the beautiful mountain countryside, I find myself singing the words over and over. *"There's a long, long trail a-winding into the land of my dreams. . . ."*

In a way, we are all traveling that "long, long trail." The scenery changes with every turn. We are lead through green valleys with cattle and grazing sheep. We follow the mountain stream and cross over still waters. There are dangerous curves and times as we move through valleys. Sometimes we are impatient when we have to wait, and sometimes scenes pass too rapidly. But there are wonderful times when, as the song says, *"The nightingales are singing and the white moon beams."* The winding trail is something of a symbol of life and a road we all must travel.

As I turn onto Beverly Road and into the rehab facility, I look forward to my visit with Beverly and again sing the last lines of the song:

There's a long, long night a-waiting until my dreams all come true.
Till the day when I'll be going down that long, long trail with you.

A SPRINKLING OF SNOW

Last month we had a good snow for Sky Lake. We got three inches and I wrote about it in the last issue of MMN. A few days ago we received what the locals call "a sprinkling of snow." There was just enough to make the hill and yard look like a large, dark and white patchwork blanket. Small flakes float noiselessly down, painting the evergreens with a coating of white. The birds are glad to find shelter and food in the birdfeeder. It stays long enough to be appreciated and then, reluctantly, it begins to change. The snow lingers a while, then turns into droplets of water; glistening for a moment and then falling to the ground. There is just enough to make us want more but not enough to cause problems. I hope we have another sprinkling of snow before the spring comes.

NOT THE SAME

Things are not the same at Moss Manor. My lady-staff is not here. I have looked for her in every room and even down in the toy shop. I miss her terribly. She had been in bed most of the time and it was a wonderful place for me to curl up and get warm. I think she likes it too because when I move or purr she strokes me and talks to me.

I get along just fine with my man-staff but he is gone most of the day and sometimes he lets me run out of food. When he is home, I stay very close to him so he will not run away too.

I hope my lady-staff comes home soon because I really miss her. Here is something that I wrote awhile back that tells you how I feel about being part of the family:

EATING TOGETHER

My staff enjoys being together when they eat. They sit, side by side, at the kitchen table and talk. I curl up in the chair at the end of the table and enjoy being part of the family. All that is very good, but I do not understand why they do not want to stay with me while I eat from my bowl. I realize that my eating schedule is a little different than theirs, but they should understand that we should do things together as a family. Here is how it goes:

About 5:00 each morning my stomach tells me that it is time to eat breakfast. My staff is sound asleep and do not seem to feel my starvation pains. I go to the edge of the bed and meow, quietly at first but with growing crescendos. My lady-staff sleeps on, but my man-staff grunts and turn over. I am making progress. Next I jump nimbly from the floor and land directly on top of my man-staff. That seems to surprise him but he still does not get up. My final move is to stand right over his face and meow loudly. After that, I need to be ready to jump because he will toss off the cover and sit up on the edge of the bed. I patiently wait near his feet while sounding a combination of soft meows and purrs. In a few minutes, he turns on the light and staggers behind me as I lead him to the kitchen and my bowl. There are still a few pellets in my bowl but I stand in front of it and look up at him until he pours more food into the plate. When I have almost finished, he stumbles back to bed.

I knew all along there was some food left in my bowl but I am a social cat and enjoy company while I eat. My man-staff seems to have difficulty in understanding why he needs to come and wait with me. I think it is only fair for one of my staff to be with me when I eat. I have watched them and they very seldom eat alone. I am just asking for the same thing. It is getting better and they are easy to teach and learn quickly. I am sure they will be with me for every one of my meals. It is only fair. The family that eats together stays together, and that means cats, too. LB

BEVERLY'S CORNER

If all wardens or jailers were as kind and caring as those who surround my stay in New Horizons Limestone/Transitional Care Center (TCC) there would be more people banging at the door to get in. I do feel a little like I am in jail with designated torturers coming regularly to pull, bend and stretch my leg. Even the bed is wired to send an alarm if I try to get up without help. I must admit that they are very caring and good to me, but it is not like home and I will be glad to say goodbye and thank all of them. Right now, that is way off in the future.

Thanks to all who have called, sent cards and food. Your thoughts and prayers have helped me through so tough times. I know there is much yet to endure, so keep me in your prayers. I am grateful for the ministries of doctors, nurses and aids and clergy. See you soon. Beverly

MOTHER'S DAY

Winter is finally over, and except few wet days and nights when the fireplace feels good, it is time to hang up the overcoats and enjoy the warmth and beauty of spring. Things are looking up at Moss Manor. Beverly is recovering nicely from her knee surgery. I am still more active than I should be. Activities keep us busy. We have enjoyed the winter and look forward to spring. "Grow old with me. The best is yet to be." *(Rabbi Ben Ezra* by Browning)

Mother's Day is here and all advertising means are telling us to remember our mothers. My mother has been gone for some forty years and there are times I still miss her. Recently, while walking through one of the super-size stores, I thought about my mother and wished I could show her some of the things she never dreamed of.

High on the list would be Walmart. Mother did most of our shopping at a small, one room grocery a half a block from where she lived. Once in a while she would go to Main Street and shop at a slightly larger grocery and meat market. I can just imagine her amazement as I showed her the long aisles of everything, stacked almost to the ceiling. The price of things would also amaze her as we moved from 1975 to 2013.

I would like to show her our summer home in the mountains. She loved the mountains, especially Montreat, NC and Clayton, GA. She dreamed of living in mountains when dad retired. I would like to point out the rhododendron in the spring and let her drink in the vivid colors of the fall. I would ask Beverly to show her around the house, especially the kitchen. She would be amazed at our refrigerator with a large freezer and ice that comes out at the press of a button. The black, glass-top stove and a microwave, together with an automatic dishwasher, would amaze her. When she lived, these things were luxuries for the very rich.

Most of all, I would like to introduce her to her grandchildren. She died while they were still in school with all the energy and activity of teens. She loved them but sometimes wondered what would become of them. She would be so proud and surprised to know that the one she thought had too vivid an imagination is an attorney and mayor of a city. The little girl that would challenge her when she thought grandmother was wrong became a forest ranger and garden shop owner. She would shake her head in disbelief when I introduced the lad who was quiet and gentle and sweet as a retired colonel in the army. She would be very proud of all, but very surprised and pleased that the little fellow who she knew would grow up to be in jail or live in a yellow Volkswagen was now the senior pastor of a large and prestigious church in Florida with multiple staff. She would be so proud of all of them and of their wives and children.

There is so much that would surprise her. . .cell phones, computers, electronic books and on and on. But there are some things I would NOT show for I know how they would upset her: I would try to shield her from the hatred and terrorism that is rampant in the world. I would not take her for a drive on the wild highways through and around Jacksonville or Atlanta. I would keep her from the immorality that seems to permeate television and I would turn her television off before the evening news. I would not encourage her to listen to contemporary music nor would I dare take her to the movies. She would be very much out of touch and out of place in the busy, mad, and dangerous world in which we live.

It is all just a fantasy and after thinking it over, I am sure the Lord knew best when he called her to a far better world. And somehow, I think she knows about the good things that have come to pass and the bad things have somehow been filtered out.

On this Mother's Day we will pay tribute to mothers everywhere but I will especially remember my mother who helped to mold me into what I am today. There is an old song that is running around in my head this morning. You may remember it:

Friends, friends, friends, I have some friends I love. I love my
friends and they love me, I help my friends and they help me,
Friends, friends, friends, I have some friends I love.

It was in our Sunday school hymn book and we sang it often. It has been taken out of the modern hymnbooks, probably for good reason, but I miss it. It sums up how I feel about friends and I hope it speaks of how they feel about me.

There are only a few of us left who sang that song long ago in an upstairs Sunday school room, but I think about them and I miss them. It has been almost a year that we have been away from Ocala. I rejoice that we have made many new friends here in the mountains, but I miss our friends in Ocala. In fact, I miss the many friends that we have made over the years in many places, in many churches. I look forward to seeing the many people who have meant so much to us over the years when we return to Ocala or visit places that have been home. I will miss those that the Lord has called home while we have been separated.

One of the great rewards that I fully expect someday in heaven will be a great gathering of our friends and we might shake the rafters of heaven as we sing together:

Friends, friends, friends, I have some friends I love. . .

THE WET WEATHER SPRING

The rain gauge outside our kitchen window shows four inches of rain in the last two days. That is a lot of water even for the mountains. It makes us glad we are high up on the side of the mountain rather than in the valley.

I braved the rain to go outside and check the wet weather spring that flows in beside our house when the mountain is saturated by rain. I stood and watched the water draining the higher mountain, pushing out from the fallen leaves and tumbling over the obstacles that had fallen into the small ditch. As I watched it make small pools then leap over small earthen dams and bounce among rocks, my thoughts traveled back almost eighty years to the time when a four or five-year-old would accompany his mother to Montreat, NC. She would attend the Presbyterian Women's Conference while I would play in a small stream under the watchful eyes of an aunt.

My father, who remained in Florida working, would build small waterwheels for me to put in the stream. I remembered getting a large, cardboard box through the mail and excitedly tore it open to see what wonderful new water toy my father had created for me. He must have spent many hours after work making these toys. Some had a number of wheels encased in small wooden tunnels. Others would drive the arm or leg of a wooden swimmer or wave the arm of a figure. I would pile up small rocks to form a pool and put the wheels in a place where the water would make them spin.

As I stood by the garage and watched the small stream of water flow by, memories flowed like the water. It is good to remember and to appreciate, more now than then, the many small things that my parents did for me to make mine a happy childhood.

THE HILL AGAIN

It seems that I am always writing about the challenge of our mountain just behind our deck. Somehow, it seems to define the things we meet in life and with aging.

This year we watched the plants we had nurtured fade and disappear. Fall leaves covered the stubborn few that survived and twice they were covered with a canopy of snow. It was a strange winter. . .cold but not bitter, continually saturated by rain. But around Easter, which came early this year, a few survivors punched through the leaves. Again, it was time to begin my struggle to restore order and beauty to the hill.

The heavy matt of leaves must be raked. The stiff and brittle remnants that did not make it must be pulled up. Tiny leaves of green must be identified. . .the weeds pulled out and the annuals carefully protected. It is time for a trip to the nursery to select what we wanted; plants that would beautify the hill and that the deer would not eat. (Dream on!) Then came the job of preparing and planting. With the help of our daughter, the plants were in the ground, 10-10-10 had been scattered, and gentle spring rains had come. As I looked up at the steep hill from our porch, I could see a patch of green and even a smidgen of color, but I was impatient and wanted to see it as it would look if they would grow and if the deer would leave them alone.

The hill gives me an opportunity to reflect and, perhaps, theologize. To me, the hill is something like New Year's Day, a time of resolutions and new beginnings. It is like Monday morning when I would begin preparing next week's sermon. . .like pushing a giant stone up the hill . . .getting it ready to roll down again next Sunday. It is like work or retirement; if you do not keep moving ahead the weeds will overtake you and ruin what you have done. As I look at our newly planted hill, I also feel the ache of tired muscles and realize that age has a way of slowing my work and dreams to a crawl.

But I am glad it is there. It teaches me that we are never too old to dream or plan. It beckons me to get my hands dirty in the opportunities that are around me. It rewards me with the pleasure of a job attempted and sometimes well done. I give thanks for the hill and its message of newer challenges and rewards. I am glad the hill is there and is never finished.

BUMPER CARS AND GROCERY BUGGIES

I guess I have come full cycle. I can remember my younger days when an excursion to the beach meant not only swimming in the surf, but going on the board walk in the afternoon or evening. Along the boardwalk there were countless booths with hawkers motioning you to try their game or buy their wares. For a little money you could throw a baseball and, if you hit the bull's eye, a man sitting above a large tub of water would fall with a great splash. You could try to knock down milk bottles with a base ball and win a kewpie doll, attempt to make baskets with a lopsided basketball or even shoot a pellet gun at a moving target. There were many wonderful ways to lose your money.

But best of all, in the next block were wonderful amusement rides, including a merry-go-round, a Ferris wheel and a rollercoaster. I loved them all. But the best thing in the block was the Bumper Car. These wonderful machines were electrically driven and could carry two riders. A pole behind the seat reached to an electrically charged ceiling with metal wheels that completed the circuit through the motor. Neither skill nor driver's license was needed. Each cart had a steering wheel that spun 360 degrees. The object was to bump the heavy rubber bumpers that surrounded each cart and send another cart spinning around and maybe go in a different direction. Your car would also be bumped and spun. It was a ride of wonderful confusion and unexpected collisions.

It all came to mind the other day when I was driving one of those electric grocery buggies designed for those of us who have difficulty navigating the grocery aisles on foot. As I dodged shoppers and their carts, navigated quick turns through narrow aisles and narrowly missed another electric cart, it suddenly came to me. I HAD COME FULL CIRCLE. I was right back where I started with the bumper cars. Oh well, I said to myself, I might as well have as much fun in my later years as I did when I was young and foolish. I turned the handle that made the cart go as far as I could and sped away, narrowly missing a stack of canned beans and two shoppers.

I have gone from Bumper Cars to Grocery Buggies. My life has come full circle and I am enjoying it.

REMEMBERING MOTHER

My staff is talking about Mother's Day. I really didn't know there was one but it seems like a good idea. I should really observe the day and think about my mother. I guess I should remember more but it was a long time ago. Sometimes, when I make circles in my basket and settle down for a good sleep, I seem to remember being in a big box with my mother and a number of brothers or sisters. It makes me feel very secure, like when I curl up beside my man-staff and sleep with my head in his hand.

My mother must have been a very good mother for I am a smart and healthy cat. I wish I knew more about my family but I have a great imagination and I can fill in my memory blanks. You may remember I wrote about how my father got to Florida.

"Since I do not remember much about my parents I can only guess at how my father got from his home in Bean Creek, Georgia, to Florida, where I was born. I once heard my man-staff say that his grandmother and mother came to Florida from Kentucky in a horse-drawn wagon. It would only be logical to think that my father caught a ride with them as they passed through Sky Lake and came with them to Florida. He must have met my mother and fell in love with her because of her outstanding beauty and elegance as a Siamese cat. I guess she must have caught a ride from Siam, wherever that is." (From *A Cat Named Lady Bean* [2009])

In Ocala, he found my mother, a beautiful Siamese cat with a wonderful personality and big, blue eyes, and he immediate fell deeply in love. She must have come from the city of Siam, which is probably in South Georgia. The rest is history and my brothers, sisters and I became reality.

I wish I knew more about my mother. When I jump on the dresser and look at myself in the big mirror I think I see my mother's blue eyes and beautiful face looking back at me. She must have looked just like me. I think she would be proud of me.

I wonder if my staff ever look in the mirror and see something of their parents. I wonder if any of you see the image of your mother reflected in your mirror. Happy Mother's Day LB

PS: My Man-staff says I made the newsletter late by not getting my column in on time. It is just that I had to wait for the inspiration to write before I could get it just right. Besides, the spring sunshine makes me sleepy and I just put it off. LB

BEVERLY'S CORNER

Since Feb.25, 2013, my dearest friend and husband has been nurse, cook, house-keeper, and shopper, too. As some of you know, when he takes on a job, regardless of difficulty, he will do it without complaining and in most cases very well. The only complaining I've heard is something like: How long before you can cook again? My answer is: When I can stand up for the time it takes to prepare a meal.

I am improving day by day and with my "Rollator" (George). George and I can walk around with ease. However, not for long stretches of time. The advantage is that when I get tired of walking, I can simply turn G. around and sit on the seat provided in the middle of his back. It is a convenient walker and it can be folded in half to stow in the back of the car. G. also has brakes for the two front wheels which is most helpful when sitting down or rising up from George's seat. (You can imagine my surprise when G. moved while I was trying to sit down. I had forgotten to engage the brakes.)

More in the next issue. We've got to retire early in order to go to the early service tomorrow. Hope you had a good Mother's Day! B.

BLACKBERRY WINTER

Last night I learned about what the local call "Blackberry Winter." They say it is as predictable as Easter. The old timers wait until after it happens to put in their gardens. Mothers' Day was a beautiful spring day, with the promise the warm days of summer to come. Flowers were beginning to bloom and we had put away our heavy jackets and warm blankets. Then came "Blackberry Winter." They say it comes each year just as the Blackberry bushes begin to bloom. Last night Mother's Day the temperature in Sky Lake dropped into the mid-thirties. I would have built a fire but I had taken all the firewood back outside and stored it away until next year. We did bring in our tender plants and keep our fingers crossed that the ones outside were strong enough to get by.

It is warming up now and maybe spring is really here, but next year I will know to watch for "Blackberry Winter." F.

NAME TAGS AND
RUBBER BAND GUNS

This issue began before Father's Day. Now it is almost the Fourth of July and it is still unfinished. Maybe it is a sign that I'm getting weary or that Moss Manor News should be a quarterly publication.

BLAZING THE TRAIL

During May and early June, it is a treat to follow the winding road from Moss Manor to the gate. The master gardener has blazed the trail with bursts of color at every turn. It is almost as if we were destined to get lost in the wilderness of Sky Lake. On every turn and beside the few straight section, the mountain laurel burned like a red or pink beacon to guide us on the way.

The brilliant blossoms are gone now but we remember them and look forward to their return next spring.

FROM ANOTHER PULPIT

It is not often that I quote a sermon from a place other than a Presbyterian pulpit, but here is an exception. Around the end of May, Pope Francis preached a sermon that drew a lot of attention. Even the Vatican had to "clarify" and in a sense repudiate what the pope said.

Maybe you saw it. It was all over the internet. I was proud of my namesake, Pope Francis. (My previous famous namesake was a talking mule.) For the most part, I shouted "Amen" and "Right on, brother" to what he said. I believe he was reflecting what Paul was saying in his letter to the Galatians as he proclaimed the message of Grace, full and free. While I do not have all the answers how God will manage grace and works or God's gift of salvation or who will be with God for all eternity, I do trust in the mercy and goodness of God to all.

There have been times when popes and I have differed greatly, but in this sermon we are "peas in a pod." (I apologize to the Holy Father for that figure of speech.) Here the Pope uses a question and answer format:

The *Lord created us in His image and likeness, and we are the image of the Lord, and he does good and **all of us** have this commandment at heart: do good and do not do evil. **All of us.***

But, Father, this person is not Catholic! He cannot do good.

*Yes, he can. . .The Lord has redeemed **all of us, all of us**, with the Blood of Christ.*

All of us**, not just Catholics. **Everyone!

Father, the atheists?

*Even the atheists! **Everyone!** We must meet one another doing good.*

RUBBER BAND GUNS WITH LOVE

As Father's Day is rapidly approaching, I am taken back in memory to days long gone and appreciate more and more the many things my father did for me. As a youngster from six to ten I was enamored with "rubber band guns." They were made of wood with a clothespin trigger. Ammunition was comprised of bands of rubber cut from old automobile or bicycle inner tubes. We would run the neighborhood playing cowboys, Indians or soldiers. If one of us was hit by a rubber band (which was rare) it might sting a little, but it was not lethal.

Dad, being a great craftsman, would keep me supplied with wooden pistols and rifles that were the envy of my friends. These toys were a labor of love and filled my holsters with pride and hours of fun. I remember a wall on our back porch that was filled with these terrifying weapons. I am sure dad would rather have been working on a table or stool or repairing furniture, but his "gun-smithing" brought joy to a young son.

I treasure these memories and give thanks for a father who I appreciate more and more as the years roll by.

BEHIND THE NAME TAG

We have all worn those plastic name tags that identify us at church, at business meetings and social gatherings. As my memory grows weaker, I am thankful for them. But a name tag tells very little about the person behind it. When we dare to venture into friendship and learn something of the person wearing the tag, we are often amazed at the surprises hidden behind them.

I think of the small lady with hair wound on top of her head and her journal always at her side. She was rather plain but always friendly. Who would have guessed that she was one of the first WWII army nurses to enter the prisons of the holocaust and one who would be a hostess at the White House for visiting heads of State?

I think of the bent-over old man who sat near the front of our church, straining to hear the music and the Word. He always complimented the choir although he probably did not hear much. He was just another nametag in the congregation until I saw, behind the badge, a man who was one of the first WWII test pilots for many of the new and dangerous war planes.

For over a year in our mountain church, we sat just behind an elderly, unimposing but friendly man. Behind his generic nametag we discovered a man who was a pioneer of helicopters; flying very early ones, developing air ambulances, training pilots in other countries and amassing at least sixteen-thousand flying hours.

Whenever we are with a group, I wonder if, beside us or in front of us, there hides an amazing story to enrich our lives hiding just behind the name tag.

A VISIT TO THE DISTANT PAST

A few Sundays ago I visited the first church I served. I had preached there while still in Seminary and they called me to be their pastor when I graduated. As we traveled to Travelers Rest, SC, I dusted off a lot of memories. Trinity Presbyterian Church boasted a few over fifty members and was located in the Bleachery community of Renfrew. The church then was a combination of Presbyterian one Sunday and Methodist the next. (The Baptists had pulled out long ago and built their own building.)

I thought I could easily find my way but back roads had turned into highways and the town had grown. My GPS led me to a large, beautiful, multi-building church. . .far different from what I expected. I had not been back for fifty years and everything had changed.

Venturing inside, I was greeted warmly as a visitor. Understandably, I did not recognize anyone nor did they recognize me. The shining moment was when I was introduced to nice-looking lady who greeted me enthusiastically. It was Shirley, who I remembered as a beautiful seven-year-old child when I left the church. It was a great reunion.

The pastor graciously introduced me during the service and invited me to pronounce the benediction. I thanked the church for their forebears knocking the rough edges from a brand new preacher and helping to prepare him (i.e., me) for future days. The visit was both surprising and wonderful.

After church we drove back to the community of Renfrew where most of my ministry was done. The mill was gone. The little brick church was still there being used by another denomination. I recognized houses in which parishioners and friends had lived. The four-room manse that held so many memories of marriage and children and pets was still there. It was run-down, with a beat-up pickup truck and a huge dog chained in the yard. I did not even take a picture as I wanted to preserve the wonderful memories of fifty years ago. Lives change and time takes its toll.

My memories of Trinity are filled with wonderful times and friends. . .with many mistakes and much learning. . .with new babies and first pets. . .with hopes and dreams of years to come. It was a good visit and I will always treasure those memories. . .the way it was in 1954 and the way time has shaped it to 2013. It was a great visit to the distant past.

THE FLYING FIELD COMES OF AGE

In the late summer of last year a handful of dreamers leased a field in which to fly. We started carving a flying field out of the tangle of head-high weeds and grasses. Fortunately the small group had skills and equipment suited for the job. Little by little the flying field took shape. The club grew and everyone pitched in to make our dream field come true. The results far exceeded our expectation. We look at a manicured runway with five flying stations. There are work and picnic tables. A forty-by-eighteen-foot canvas shelter protects us from unexpected weather. A bulletin board stands by the entrance and above is a weathervane with anemometer. Signs define areas for flying and visitors. It is a dream come true.

On the last Saturday in June, the Sautee RC Flyer, now twenty-six members strong, held the first Family Picnic and Fun Fly at the field. Everyone pitched in and there was fun flying and special flying demonstrations, including a flight using First Person View and a mass launch of Radian sailplanes.

For the picnic lunch there was fried chicken, cooked at the field, together with a variety of dishes and desserts brought by flyers and wives. As a special surprise attraction, one of the best banjo pickers in these mountains entertained us as we watched planes in the air.

Of course, nothing is ever really finished, but the field we have to enjoy is very close to being finished and is perfect.

HOW IT ALL BEGAN

Looking through a box of old model airplane parts that had followed me around from the days of my childhood, I picked up a propeller, all that was left of a once beautiful rubber- powered model. As I held it, memories, long forgotten, surged over me.

I do not even know his name or anything about him. . .I wish I did. It was in the early days of World War II and I must have been ten or eleven years old; too young to understand how the war was affecting our family, our neighbors and the people around us.

I was playing in the edge of the front yard when a man came down the steps of the house next door and spoke to me."Are you interested in airplanes?" he asked. Of course I said yes. "Then I would like to give you something. Come with me."

I should have turned away and gone back to my house, but we were living in a more innocent age, and after all he was a neighbor. I followed him into the living room of the house next door. He pointed to the windows. My heart leaped. Hanging on the curtain rods were two of the most beautiful model airplanes I had ever seen. They were the same model but one was white and other was red.

"I won't be needing these anymore. Would you like them?"

I am sure he could see my excitement and eagerness as he gently took them down. He showed me a little about them, then handed me one. "You take that one and I will carry the other."

I accepted the gift in shocked disbelief and carried the white one through his door, across the front yards and placed it on my front porch. He followed with the red one. I thanked him, still hardly believing this was happening. He walked quickly away, almost as if he was reluctant to leave them.

The only one at home was my grandmother. Quietly, I took them to my room without telling her. When my mother and father came home that evening I told them of the grand and glorious gifts I had received. Immediately they led me back to the house next door to find out more about the man who gave away such gifts to a lad he did not know. He was not there. His room was vacant.

We later learned that he had rented a room in the house but the owners knew very little about him except that he had moved his few belongings out the week before. I never saw him again nor did I learn anything more about him. My imagination conjured up different scenarios. The most plausible thought was that he was in service and was being sent overseas and could not take his belongings.

I wish I knew who he was and what caused him to give away such beautifully-built models to "a boy next door" he didn't really know. I do know that I owe a great debt of gratitude to my unknown benefactor for he started me in a hobby that would follow me throughout my life.

Together with my friend, Ed, we flew those planes many times in the park just down the street. They truly were excellent flyers and they brought much excitement and happiness. That happened seventy-five years ago but I still treasure the memories and say "thank you" to the anonymous giver. I believe I will just keep the worn and dented propeller for old time's sake.

DO YOU REMEMBER?

I was taken back the other day when one of our friend saw us take the smaller milk bottle out of the refrigerator. . .I started to say "ice box." "What kind of a container is that?" he asked. He was twenty years short of our age, but it still surprised me.

One of my earliest memories was to look on the steps in front of the house and find two bottles of milk left by the milkman who drove a horse drawn wagon. I suddenly realized that we were the privileged few that still had those wonderful childhood memories. It is one of the few perks of aging. Now when I get the milk out for breakfast cereal, it takes me back to these memories and many others.

Do you remember the clomp of the horse and the rattle of bottles of milk being left on your front porch? If so, count it a privilege that you still have both life and memory.

MY SLEEPING PLACES

I feel sorry for my staff. They have one bed that they use every night and whenever they decide to take a nap in the afternoon. I have a basket and it is very comfortable. I use it when my staff has gone somewhere and there is nothing really to do. I even sleep there part of the night. But unlike them, I have many sleeping places. They are spread all over the house and even on the deck. Some are in plain sight and some are hidden so well that only I know where they are. Let me tell you about them.

Of course, the sofa is a nice place to sleep as are most of the stuffed chairs. They are particularly good when one of my staff has warmed them up and they have gotten up to answer the phone or get something. They have lost their chair. The deck is nice when the sun is out and I can doze and enjoy the beautiful hill behind the house. The birds don't like me being outside. . .I don't know why. In the closet, behind their clothes, is a secluded and safe place to sleep. Downstairs in the workshop, there are two sofas with the softest pillows that sink down and cradle me. My man-staff bought me a wonderful chair. It sits at his desk and spins around when I jump on it. My man-staff thinks it is his, but when he gets up I seize the opportunity and it is mine! He grumbles, then he pushes my chair and me to the side and he finds another one. Oh, it sleeps so good!

There are secret places that I use when I really want to be alone or when my staff wants to take me on a trip or to the vet. I will not tell about them.

My staff has only one sleeping place but it is a comfortable one. Sometimes I wait till they are asleep. Then I pounce on their bed and curl up right where their legs bend. I am sure I sleep better than they do when we are together in their bed. It is important that we cats have many sleeping places. After all, we spend about eighteen hours a day sleeping and we need to have variety and comfort. LB

THOUGHTS FROM BEVERLY

Memories are great! Sometimes. . .I had thought of something to write, but when I sat down to type it, I'd totally forgotten what I was going to write about. That's what I meant when I said, "sometimes." It is amazing what can trigger your memory, and how walking three steps down the hallway makes you forget it as quickly as it came to you.

F. has taken care of me for the past four months, and done all those other things he's written about in this newsletter, AND has planted our backyard mountain with all kinds of beautiful flowers. We have seen ones of almost every color in the rainbow: yellow, white, pink, red, purple, and even, lavender! No green ones, but the trees with their gorgeous foliage take care of that color. Wish you would come to see what I see! B.

THE RAIN FOREST

THE OLD HOUSE

The other day, while rummaging around in the desk drawer, I came upon an old photo negative taken in the mid 1930's. When printed, the picture of the house in which I grew up filled the screen and with it a multitude of wonderful memories. As I looked at it, I was transported back to the time when I was growing up, and doing a little homework was my only worry. Share with me a few memories and it may conger up a few great memories from your childhood as well.

This was a time before air conditioning and the front porch was the place to enjoy a summer breeze. The wooden swing was the place where my early education took place. My grandmother, Nannie, would sit and read children's stories, stories from the Bible or books like *Tom Sawyer*, *Robinson Crusoe* and others. She would read until her voice slowed down and her head began to drop. I would nudge her and tell her to wake up and read on. When air conditioning came, the sense of a neighborhood community disappeared and families became isolated from neighbors and the outside world.

The grape vine behind us (really wisteria) was a place where wonderful lizards and bugs lived. . . .a place where I could cut a small brown branch and pretend it was my cigarette. I would often sit in the swing or in the rocking chairs or even on the steps and watch for my father to come home from the office in the square-backed Chevrolet. One afternoon a rubber ball got away from me and bounced into the street where it was run over and crushed by a car. It was a great lesson about not running into the street. The small passage on the left, past the old mailbox and the place where the milk bottles appeared each morning, was a wonderful private place to play and pretend. The upstairs porch held a different set of memories. From the center post to a hook near the door there hung a large, cloth hammock. It was not for sleeping but for me and my friends to take turns swinging back and forth until we tumbled out to the floor. When the fair was in town, my father would let me stay up until dark and from the left, front corner of the porch we would see the fireworks being set off a few miles away.

I wish I could sit, once more, on the front steps and watch for my father or swing and dream of wonderful adventures that were to come. This old house is now a double-deck parking lot for a nearby hospital. The oak trees my grandmother planted are pavement for a widened street, but they will always grow in my memory, and the pictures of the house will live forever in my heart.

A SUMMER STORM

It is almost 10:00 p.m. and the electricity is out all over Sky Lake. As if we needed more rain, the storms have once more rolled down upon us, the lightning knocking out power and the rain playing a staccato musical arrangement accompanied by the kettle drum sound of water racing down the drains. I am sitting in the kitchen using the laptop battery and listening to the rain rattle down the nearby gutter from the roof. The rain has cooled the air and I look forward to being lulled to sleep by the gentle patter of raindrops.

We have been fortunate here in the North Georgia Mountains. The west is burning, the middle of our country is dealing with flash floods and the northeast is sweltering in extreme heat. A few days ago, the weather report said that we had enjoyed an average of seventy-two degrees. The spring and early summer has been wet but very pleasant. While we may complain about too many rain days, we also realize that we are very fortunate to have the kind of weather that is relatively safe and very enjoyable.

JIGSAW PUZZLES

I like jigsaw puzzles. I like them best on the computer where I can use pictures that I have taken with my camera. Since I like to finish the puzzle in one sitting, there are never more than 144 pieces in the picture and I like to have the pieces all turned the right way so they slide together easily.

Sometimes I like to piece together a beautiful landscape just to watch the picture come to life. It gives me the feeling that I have had something to do with recreating it. Somehow the broken lines and shapes bring a sense of depth to the scene.

If the picture is one that we have taken on our travels and adventures, I can relive that time in history. As it comes together, piece by piece, the moment it depicts comes to life. Our sailboat, *Karisto*, comes to life and once again I almost feel the gentle motion of the ocean. The picture that appears on the monitor brings back good memories of a place we visited. As I find each piece and the picture emerges, it is like pieces of a tired memory being rejuvenated.

Sometimes a face or figure will be fitted into place and I am reminded that the pieces of my life could never have come together had it not been for my family and my many friends who tied my years together and created a wonderful picture. Maybe that is why I like to do puzzles. . .they remind me of life itself. The many different pieces must all fit together. Some are harder to find and fit than others, some take much longer than others to fit in, some seem to be lost and I wonder if they will ever be found, but in the larger picture of life and by the grace of God, each fits together to make the picture of my life.

WHEN THE PASTOR'S AWAY, THE MUSIC WILL PLAY

We parked and joined others as we walked toward the church. The pastor was on vacation and we did not know who would be preaching. As we entered the church, the associate pastor was leaving from the early service and with a smile said, "There is no sermon today." We took our seats quite confused. A look at the bulletin gave us the answer.

The morning worship was music and short passages of scripture. The music was a mix of the traditional and Gospel, played and sung with piano, guitars, and a classical harp. From classical church music, sung by a trained tenor voice, to soft, lyrical notes of the harp, to the twang of mountain gospel on guitar. Sometimes the congregation joined in the singing of hymns known and loved since childhood but forgotten by the more sophisticated hymnbooks. It was a great service. Don't tell the vacationing preacher, but we really did not miss the sermon.

It is interesting how music triggers memories. As I quietly joined the guitar player in verses of "Love Lifted Me," I remembered the many times we gathered around a piano and sang. Way back in my life, after Youth Fellowship, we would gather at a home and, with young, often off-key voices, try to harmonize. I thought of times, around campfires, at youth or family camps when singing old hymns lifted our spirits higher than the rising smoke from the fire. The music transported me back to Seminary days, when after evening church we would gather in the well- appointed lobby of Agnes Scott College and sing choruses. Light Christian music was then frowned upon by the more traditional church. It may have been the music or it may have been the light hand of an attractive date on mine, but songs like "I'd Rather Have Jesus than Anything" or "Jesus, Jesus, Jesus, Sweetest Name I know" gave me a wonderful feeling and a spiritual lift.

We had to stand for a hymn and it shook me out of my trip into a musical past. It was a great service and it reminded me of how different kinds of music influence and enrich our worship and our faith.

THE TROPICAL RAIN FOREST

I have written often about the challenge of the steep hill behind our home. It has about three inches of soil before mountain rock defines its character. In years past we have struggled to keep it green with any plant or flower except the wild "snake grass." This year our hill has magically turned into a tropical rainforest. It probably has more to do with the over-abundance of rain than magic. We have tried to pull the rapidly growing weeds, snake grass we call it, from around the plants we had put in. The snake grass grew faster than we could pull it out. The good plants are surviving. The weeds are trying to strangle them. The hill looks, to me, like a tropical rain forest.

This year, the hill is greener than it ever has been since we have been in Moss Manor. Although lush and green, it still represents the challenge of life, a place to separate the good from the bad, the acceptable from the unacceptable, and the authentic from the imposter. Like life, I enjoy the green hill with many wonderful flowers and shrubs fighting for life, and I am glad for the opportunity to learn and participate in their struggles.

RECLAIMING THE RAIN FOREST

The summer has blessed us with an abundance of rain. There were times when I longed for a rainbow and assurance from the promise that the Lord would not allow a repeat of the days of Noah. But the sun has finally found its place in the sky and it is time to reclaim the rainforest that is my hill and my challenge.

The first order of business was to a concoction that greatly reduced the redbug or chigger bites. Then, after sulfuring my ankles and bathing my arms in repellant, I was ready to attack the snake grass and other weeds that had made a home around and over my plants. I had to be careful not to step on a hidden botanical specimen as I began ripping and pulling the seeds. The weeds came out easily from the wet soil. Then came the task of bringing mulch from the garage, bucket by bucket, and spreading it around the plants that survived the rainforest attack.

The job is not finished, and when I do finish, it probably will need to be done all over again. I step back and see where I have been, what I have done and what is still to be done. The hill, with its ever-changing challenge, is for me an illustration of life. The work will never be finished but I enjoy what I am doing and take pleasure in it. Like this adventure we call life, there is disappointment, frustration and success as we seek to make the place where we live a little more beautifully. In a way, we are all reclaiming the rainforest in our lives where wrong things grow so easily and the good is hard to grow and keep. But then, I remember that we are all re-claimed and given the privilege of working on our hill of life. It is called "grace."

Enough theology: Where are my work gloves and my walking stick? It is time to reclaim the hill.

SELECTIVE HEARING

My staff tells me that I have it. They talk about it like it is some kind of disease. I really do not know what it is except that it has something to do with me coming when they call me and everyone knows that is not what a cat does. We are far too smart to act like a dog and come running every time staff snaps a finger. Oh yes, I hear the call but I must first evaluate what it really means before deciding what to do. The process works something like this. I hear my staff calling. I then decide whether they know where I am or if they can see me, and then:

- *If they do not know where I am, it is the beginning of a great game of "me hide and they seek." After they have looked all over the house and the yard and are getting upset, I decide it is time to casually appear with the look that says, "Oh, were you calling me?"*
- *If they can see me, I must quickly decide if they just want me to come or if it means there is something for me to eat. If they just want me inside, or to give me some nasty smelling stuff on my neck, then it is time to play deaf. I turn my head away or sit down and look at something in the distance. I usually lose, but it gives me dignity and buys a little time.*
- *If I am doing something I really enjoy, like eating good, green grass or walking up the forbidden steps that lead up the back hill and into the exciting woods on top, I must decide whether to stop and complain loudly or to move quickly up the steps, as if I did not hear. This last decision usually is a bad one because my man-staff climbs the steps after me. When he gets to the top, he is puffing and mad at me and*

*usually picks me up and carries me down. It is humiliating!
I rarely use this option.*

*As you can see, selective hearing is a very effective tool for cats
and I would recommend that my man-staff use the same tactic once
in a while. They may call it selective hearing but I call it, "Oh, were
you calling me?"* LB

A LETTER FROM AN ADMIRER (Grady lives with his
servants, Kim and Janice, just across the mountain from Sky Lake.)

Dear Lady Bean;
    *I apologize that I've not shared any thoughts with you in quite
some time. One of my servants usually reads me your personal
column as published regularly by one of your own servants, but I
have no excuse for not "getting back" to you before now.*
    *I hope you are still doing as well as you seemed to be doing in
the most recent picture I saw of you. I am myself doing extremely
well, especially now that I've properly trained my servants to provide grooming, feeding and petting services which meet my high
standards. I admit that I may be just the least little bit spoiled (as I
think you are yourself), but that's as it should be, don't you agree?*
    *There was a bit of excitement here at my residence (which I
allow my servants to share with me) this morning. A big and really
nasty-looking yellow cat (an intruding stranger) has been sneaking
up on my deck and eating my friend's (Miss Priss) food. I just happened to be on the deck this morning, minding my own business
and pondering the Universe, when the intruder made yet another
appearance. Understand, Lady Bean, that on my orders one of my
servants had tethered me to a chair so that I wouldn't accidentally
wound an innocent bear or deer or UPS delivery person in a blind
rage of territorial protection.*
    *But seeing this yellow intruder was too much, Lady Bean, so
I went after him even though it meant pulling the chair across the
deck and down the steps. The tether was loosed from the chair at that
instance, and my female servant managed to catch me underneath
one of my servants' vehicles.*

I don't mean to paw myself on the back, but the last time I saw that yellow cat he was running southwest at approximately 35 mph. He should be in Gainesville by this time, and still running. Enough about me! What's going on at your beautiful Sky Lake residence? I remain your friend and admirer,
   Grady

UNDER THE WEATHER

Dear Grady and other readers:
   Thanks for your letter and your thoughts. I am very proud of you for your heroic deeds. It is good to know that we have a protector of the weak and innocent in our mountains.
   I have been a little sickly lately. I pulled some hair off of my shoulder getting at some bug and I have been sneezing a lot. My staff dragged me to the doctor twice. I let them know what I thought of that. The doctor has been sticking me with needles in unmentionable places. My staff has been rubbing some salve on my bare skin while I eat. They think I do not know what they are doing. They also have been stuffing some gooey stuff down my throat. I am feeling some better now but am using my illness to get all the extra food out of my staff that is possible.
   Also, I think I am beginning to know what arthritis feels like, and I might have a little more sympathy for my staff, who moan and groan about it all the time.
   As always, Lady Bean

BEVERLY'S CORNER

Have you heard that as we age, strange coincidences occur more often? For instance, a few weeks ago, I noticed that the two addresses where I have lived (244 and 231) are directly across the street from each other on the way up the mountain to where we live now. 244 was on West 54th Street in Jacksonville, FL. and 231 Laurelwood is our address in Sautee, GA.

There was another one that could be attributed to advanced aging, but like all things, it has flown the coop. When I think of it, I'll make a note to put it in the next newsletter.

A MYSTERY INVASION

THE FIRST DAY OF FALL

Yesterday was the first day of fall. It did not seem much different since the summer had been a cool one. It was a beautiful, clear day unlike the rain that had plagued most of the summer. However, there were a few noticeable differences that heralded the gateway to fall. Leaves were beginning to flutter to the ground. . .not yet in abundance, but enough to require blowing the driveway weekly. A jacket feels good in the early morning. It is still dark when it is time to get up in the morning. The dogwoods are beginning to turn red and the squirrels are feverously gathering the nuts that remain. The harvest moon has come and gone. Halloween decorations are appearing at door posts around the neighborhood. Grass at the flying field is slowing down and needs less cutting. The deer are getting hungrier and are visiting our hill and decapitating our flowers more often.

Fall is definitely in the air and all too soon we will be turning on the heat and getting out the sweaters and coats. I hate to see summer go, even though it has been a wet one. Still I welcome fall and look forward to the brilliant colors that soon will paint the landscape.

Yesterday was the first day of fall and I am glad it is here.

CHRISTMAS IN SEPTEMBER (I'm no poet and I know it. . .but I try)

It is only September, but I know that I hear

the dancing and prancing of Santa's reindeer.
I jump to the floor,
Throw open the door
And what to my eye should appear?
Not reindeer. . .not Santa . . .
But there on the deck were six, big mule deer.
They were eating my mums and thought them just dandy.
I gestured and yelled and threw rocks that were handy.
But run. . . not at all!
The deer thought I threw candy.
When flowers were gone, deer wandered away
And I was left to replant the next day.

A few weeks ago we received the gift of a large strawberry plant jar. Since we had no strawberry plants, we filled the ten openings with little white mums. Knowing that wild things wandered the woods, we placed the jug back on the deck, knowing that no wild creature would venture that close to the house. What we did not know was that the rabbits and the deer were no longer wild. Since we live in a game preserve, they felt safe. Since some of our neighbors delight in feeding them and know them by name, they are about as tame as our cat. In fact, Lady Bean and the deer get along fine. Even the birds pay no attention to LB as she naps under their feeder. I guess it is live and let live.

But for those of us who like to grow flowers on the hill and on our deck, it is a different story. We think it is our backyard and our deck. The deer know it is their playground and they do not intend to give it up.

I guess the best thing we can say is that the deer keep reminding us, "It is Christmas all year long. . .right here on our deck!"

"BE THOU MY VISION"

It is strange how memory works. Little reminders send us spinning back over time to places long ago and far away. The hymn we sang last Sunday did just that. As we sang "Be Thou My Vision, Lord," my thoughts raced back sixty years and I was in Camp

Deerwood, near Brevard, NC. I was again a young, single pastor, leading recreation for Pioneer Camp (Junior High ages).

I had just finished Seminary, full of dreams and naïveté, and had been given the assignment of working with some one hundred and fifty young people from the churches of our Presbytery. I was asked to work with a young Director of Christian Education named Jackie, with whom I fell deeply in love and later married.

Deerwood was a beautiful camp, nestled in a narrow valley between two picturesque mountains. Jackie led the singing and I led folk games and called square dances, while others did the more difficult work of leading Bible study and keeping order in the dining room.

But what triggered my journey into memory was the music and words of the hymn. I still see it clearly. After vespers and evening recreation, tired campers went to their cabins, made ready for bed, cabin devotions and lights out. The night was still and full of beauty. Agnes, one of our young leaders, with a clear, beautiful singing voice, would take the mike of the large PA system and would fill the moonlit valley with the music and words of the hymn. I would stand, hand in hand with Jackie, my newly found love, and would look over the scenes below and around us. The vision of exciting and wonderful years ahead would fill my heart and mind and my eyes would fill with tears of wonder and anticipation. The words of the hymn would echo back across the valley:

> *Be Thou my vision, O Lord of my heart;*
> *   Naught be all else to me, save that Thou art-*
> *Thou my best thought by day or by night,*
> *   Waking or sleeping, Thy presence my light.*

The hymn ended and I was suddenly back in Nacoochee Presbyterian Church.

THE DREDGE

When I sold our sailing vessel, *Karisto*, and left my trips up and down the Intracoastal Waterway, I thought I had seen the last of the large dredges that kept the water navigable. They blocked half of the waterway and were filled with vertical light or black balls that indicated danger. We would creep by at low speed watching for signals from the tender which moved through the web of floating pipes that carried sand from the bottom to the shore. So it was a great surprise when a small replica of those sand-sucking monsters appeared floating along the shore of our small mountain lake. Like its larger cousin, this dredge carried a boom that lowered its mouth to the lake bottom and boasted a long, floating tail of pipe to carry away the dredged material.

It seems that it was less expensive to Sky Lake to have the dredge remove the silt than to have drag-pans lift it into trucks to be carried away and dumped. In this system the unwanted sand that was carried into the lake by the streams which fed it was pumped through long tubes to part of the pasture land. Here it was fed into large filtering mesh containers to drain and dry out. When finally dry, it was to be spread out with tractor blades, raising the level of the pasture a number of feet. It would be seeded and soon would return to grass land.

The process lasted all summer and was interesting to watch. The best thing about it was that it did not interfere with the roads and we did not have to slow down and pay attention the signals, whistles and bells as we did on the waterway.

THE LOST TWENTY

Last Sunday I went to the airfield before church and while there I was given a twenty dollar bill to pay for a current project. I stuffed it in my pocket and went to church.

At the beginning of the service the pastor held up a twenty dollar bill and said that it had been found in the parking area. Immediately I emptied my pocket and found only a few coins and keys. There was some humorous banter in the congregation about the Lord providing. I was about to raise my hand to claim the bill when a young lady from the other side of the church raised her hand and said, "It is mine." Now, it may well have been hers. She may have also lost a twenty while parking. If it was not, I hope she put it in the offering plate, as we both probably could have afforded another twenty to the church. Certainly, I was glad to write it off as either lost or a gift to the church. The preacher even told us that we needed to think more about storing up spiritual treasures rather than storing up twenties.

Maybe my lost twenty blew across the road and was picked up by someone who really needed it and the young lady really claimed what was hers. I hope that was the case of my lost twenty.

WE FINALLY MADE THE PAPER

I have always felt that if you got your name in the paper, in a place other than the police blotter, you were doing well and had finally reached fame. Well, the Sautee RC Flyers not only made the front page but also had received a whole page of coverage.

Thanks to Billy Chism, editor of the *White County News*, we received a great deal of coverage. The editor came to our field and spent an hour or so taking pictures and recording history and names. We waited anxiously to see what might be published. Last week, when the paper came out, the coverage was more than we expected. On the front page was a picture of Mikey's *Old Timer* airplane. The Mountain Life page was devoted entirely to pictures of SRCF. It was great coverage and we have gotten promises of new members because of it. Our special thanks to Billy Chism and the *White County News* for great coverage of our field and our hobby.

A NEW MASCOT

The parking lot for our airfield was in the past a pen for buffaloes. The iron fence is constructed of heavy tubes that could hold the strong, heavy animals. Our kiosk and tables are fastened to the railing and it holds them well.

The other day we were surprised to see a beautiful, red-tailed hawk using the rail just past our last table as a perch. He was scanning the uncut areas for his next field mouse dinner. He allowed us to come within fifteen feet of his perch before spreading his wings and showing us how to really fly. From time to time he soars with us and sometimes returns to his iron rail perch.

We have named him our honorary mascot.

THE MYSTERY INVASION

It started out as a mystery. The biscotti jar was empty except for a few crumbs. I knew I had not eaten more than my usual one or two for breakfast. Beverly claimed that she had not raided the jar. Then the raisins disappeared from their jar. A few days later we noticed that a banana left on the counter had been partially eaten. Something was stealing our goodies. But what? There were no signs of mice or rats that usually left tell-tale droppings. We knew Lady Bean roamed the house at night, but these things were not on her items for consumption list. The mystery was deepening.

Then the bomb dropped! I was looking under the sink where we kept cleaning supplies, looking for some steel wool way in the back. . .when I found it. There, back in the corner, was the stash of stolen supplies. There were the stolen biscotti, the raisins and much more. The steel wool I was looking for was there. There was a sprung mouse trap, a big pile of seed from the bird feeder, some brightly colored pieces of cloth, an old banana peel, and other unidentifiable odds and ends. In all, there must have been a full bucket load of stash. Things were too big for one mouse and an odd collection for a rat. The same night wires were cut on four of my chargers both in the kitchen and in the downstairs toy room. I remembered seeing a cartoon where an army of mice carried off everything in the kitchen.

Beverly did not want to use the kitchen until the mystery was solved. I spent a morning soldering wires together. It was crisis time so I immediately called the exterminator. He came the next day with his traps and equipment. He cleaned a shop vac full of stuff. He scratched his head and finally said, "I think it is a chipmunk." He set big traps, some sticky pads, and a few small mouse traps just in case.

The first night, a big trap was sprung, the bait eaten from all traps, but no sign of the culprit. From then on, nothing has happened. There have been no more piles of food, no sprung traps, no wires eaten, no nibbles from fruit. . .no chipmunk, rat or mouse.

It is still a mystery. We will remain watchful, see that food is put away and we are hopeful that all the traps and activity frightened our night raider away but we will be ever vigilant and will wonder who the villain really is.

THE DAY I CLIMBED THE HILL

Usually I am a very good and obedient cat but there are times when I want to do what I want to do and go where I want to go. Today was one of those days. It started out in the side yard. I asked to go out and my man-staff opened the door and told me to stay in the yard. The yard was full of those noisy birds getting food from their green box. There was nothing exciting in the yard so I slipped through the fence and started up the mountain to some real good grass. Before I could get to the grass my man-staff was calling me and getting ready to come after me. I gave up and came back.

But the day had just begun, and I was determined to get up the hill. I sat by the living room glass doors and pleaded. It took lots of wistful looking and a few meows but finally my man-staff relented and opened the doors. I bounded out and he followed me. I dutifully sat on the porch while he pulled up some weeds. (It is a silly thing to do because they grow right back.) I saw my chance and moved, quietly up the hill. He saw me when I was half way up and told me to stop. I did and waited until he was intent on pulling snake grass. I climbed to the top and disappeared into the woods. Soon I heard him calling me but I stayed where I was, tasting the clump of weeds and exploring the twisted mountain laurel shrubs. It wasn't long before I heard my man-staff coming up the hill, huffing and puffing, fuming and fussing, calling me every other breath. I knew the jig was up but I wanted to extend my exploration as long as possible, so I did not make a sound. I watched as he pulled back branches and called me unflattering names. Finally he spotted me. It was not my nature to run; it was too undignified, and so I waited for the inevitable. He reached down and tried to pull me from the twisted branches that protected me. I refused to budge. He grabbed my tail and pulled. That was the last straw. The blood of my Bengal ancestry boiled up. I snarled, and bared my teeth. (I would not have bitten the hand that feeds me, but he did not know that.) He let go my tail and stepped back. I knew I had gone too far, so I relaxed and let him pick me up. He struggled to carry me through the thick bushes. Finally, he put me down at the top of the big steps that came down the mountain. He was still fussing and worse. When I stopped, he would lightly push with his shoe and I would respond with a Siamese yowl. I was embarrassed and he was mad. It was not a pretty scene. We reached the deck, he pushed open the glass door and I rushed in and went directly to a hiding place in the closet.

When supper time came, I did my best to ask forgiveness yet keep my dignity. I purred and rubbed against him. (He is a pushover when I act like that.) He muttered but he reached down and stroked me and went to the cupboard, got my food and put it in my bowl. It was over and I was forgiven.

I still want to explore the big hill but will have to wait until he can go with me and think it is all his idea. LB

THE ARCH OF TRIUMPH

November came in with wind and rain. Last night it started lightly about 9:00 but by midnight we could hear it battering the brightly colored foliage and rattling the downspout by our bedroom. From a partially opened window we could, at intervals, hear wind rattling the branches. It was a good night for sleeping.

As I look out of the kitchen window I see a blanket of red, orange and brown leaves covering the moss lawn. I am glad we drove through the mountains yesterday to see the leaves. They were at their peak making each bend in the road an exciting vista of the fall pageant.

Each year either wind or rain places a period on leaf season and ushers in the time for raking or blowing leaves from the yard. This year it came on the first of November. . .a reminder that the peak season of nature and of life is short but magnificent while it lasts.

AN ARCH OF TRIUMPH

One of the places on my bucket list of things to see is the Arc de Triomphe in Paris. But until I am able to make the trip across the Atlantic and see this historic monument to victory, I will settle for Arches of Triumph right here at home.

Yesterday as I was making a trip to a neighboring town, I had the privilege of driving on a country road. . .a road less taken. It is late October and here in the mountains the trees are at their peak of color. I drove past fields of soybeans, bright yellow as they neared maturity. Rolls of newly-bailed hay emphasized the season as they lay scattered on grass still green. As I accelerated down a long hill and crossed the bridge just around the bend from the old dam that turned the backed up lake into wild, white water, I entered an arch of triumph to rival any structure in the world. Trees, their leaves bursting with fall colors, joined hands above the road to form the arch. From time to time, through the vacillating leaves, I could see the still blue water of the lake beside me. For at least a mile of twisting turns I drove, transfixed by the wonder of the leafy tunnel through which I drove. I was glad the twisting road demanded a slow speed so that I could drink in the wonder of my own Arch of Triumph. I cannot close my eyes for I am driving, but I still give a prayer of Thanksgiving for the beauty and wonder of the world not far from each of us.

If I ever travel to distant lands and visit historic and wondrous structures like the Arc de Triomphe, I wonder if they will compare in majesty with the arch through which I have just driven.

TIME IS MY ENEMY . . .TIME IS MY FRIEND

Time has two faces. On one hand it is something that is a friend, filled with exciting times, wonderful memories, and great anticipations. On the other hand it is something that rushes by, stealing the hours and years, and taking from us the treasure of future plans. The challenge is in reconciling the two.

Certainly time has been my friend. From the lofty precipice of eighty-four years, I look back and marvel at the many things time has given me. There are so many good memories packed into what is but a fleeting moment in the grand scheme of history. The years have allowed me to do many things others only dream of. I think of times spent with a young family. . .taking trips, camping, fishing, playing, riding horses, canoeing, caving, climbing mountains, enjoying all manner of pets, and a hundred other things that filled the good years.

Time has been my friend when it gave me the loved ones and friends I needed. My childhood was filled with friends and mentors and wonderful parents. There was a best friend, like the brother I never had. Though I did not realize it at the time, the adults who taught and gently reprimanded me were part of the good times.

There were wonderful experiences at schools, grade one through seminary, filled with friends and good times. Time was my friend when it provided me with life partners who were the best that could happen to me. As I look back over the seventy-plus years that I remember, I know that time has been my friend.

But I also feel that time has been my enemy. Like two sides of a coin spinning in the air, one side of the coin has been my enemy. As a child, there was too much time and I could not wait for it to pass. . .for Christmas to come. . .for summer vacation to begin. As I grew older it speeded up and there never was enough of it. I found myself crowding the days with too many things. . .quality time with family, work, community, play, travel, and on and on. I only understood what a thief time really was as I watched children turn into young men and women and realized time had been stolen away, never to come again. There were things that I could have done for and with my life partners. . .opportunities that time has stolen away. Now, as I realize that my lifetime is past the average and there are only so many years left, I am beginning to cram each hour and day with things that I want to do. Some call this the "bucket list." So many places to go, so many things to do, so many friends yet to meet, so many planes to build, so many doctors to see, so many things to write about, and only so much time. In this way, time is my enemy. And ironically, that enemy is stealing my ability to finish many of the things I want to do. We call it failure of memory. We blame it on "Arthur" or "Burt" or other pick pockets of our health and ability. Even now, there is a long list of things about which to write and Lady Bean is pulling at my pants leg because she has more stories to dictate. What will I do first? What will I put off? What will I just forget? Time is my enemy and I have few weapons to ward him off.

I know that I will continue to move back and forth between *time-friend* and *time-enemy*. But I also know that time, my friend, will eventually win. All the things that time, my enemy, can bring will, like a fleeting cloud, dissolve and my friend, time, will continue on with me for all eternity.

A SURGICAL ADVENTURE

I had a strange problem with my foot. A large and sharp corn that kept recurring between my big toe and the next toe was getting more and more painful. It was painful to walk and I was developing a decided limp. The podiatrist and I had decided on a surgical procedure to fix the problem. Ever since the decision, I had been both looking forward to and dreading the procedure. I was extremely nervous because the last time I was cut upon by a doctor was over seventy-five years ago when he removed my tonsils.

We arrived at Dr. Rose's office at 2:15. Almost immediately I was ushered into a back room, seated in a comfortable patient's chair that leaned back far enough to be comfortable but remained high enough so that I could watch as the nurse scrubbed my foot, especially my ailing toe. After explaining a little more about the procedure, Dr. Rose sprayed my foot with the coldest freezing spray I had ever felt. I lay back, closed my eyes and prepared for the agony to begin. I felt no pain at all as she cut and picked at the toe. As she worked, we continued to talk about various things. I learned about her children and told her about mine. We talked of our faith and church activities. I learned of their Bible study classes. We shared some of our history and the things we enjoyed. From time to time I would look down and see a long cut on the top of my toe and would watch her dig around inside for the things that had been hurting me. Then I would relax and continue the conversation. It was more like talking with friends over dinner than having surgery. Before I knew it she had sewn up the cut and was showing me a small piece of bone she had extracted.

I was fitted with a temporary walking shoe and reminded of my post-op instructions. I was given her e-mail address so she could receive a Moss Manor News. It was the most unusual surgical adventure I had ever witnessed. Now I do not want to make this a regular event but I must say it was the most unusual and the most pleasant doctor's visit that I have ever made. Thank you, Dr. Rose, for a great surgical adventure.

FLASHES

There are all kinds of flashes. There are hot flashes and cold flashes. There are lightning flashes and camera flashes. I remember waiting on the Key West seashore to see the green flash as the sun settled into the sea. (We never saw it.) But I write about memory flashes.

I am not sure what triggers these sudden trips into the past. Probably it is when similar situations, separated by sixty years or more, are experienced. Sometimes they repeat themselves at given times or with certain activities. Then, sometimes they come with no explanation at all.

Just yesterday, as I was putting our van into the garage and the door was noisily coming down, I was suddenly driving our 1940 Chevy around our half block in Jacksonville, FL, into the dirty, dusty alley and to our old tin garage. In my flashback, I was fourteen with a learner's license and delighted to get a chance to drive the family car. I remembered tugging at the heavy tin doors, then carefully inching the car forward, careful not to allow the fenders to touch the cardboard storage boxes on either side of the garage. In memory I struggled with the dragging doors. Then I worked my way through the tight space between the car and the doors and hurried back to the house where my supper was waiting. Just as quickly my memory flash was gone.

This kind of thing is happening more and more. Maybe it is that recent memory is not as deeply imbedded in my brain as those that were stored up when I was young. I am not sure why, but flashes of memory come from nowhere.

When I take a bath, I am back in the old, iron tub upstairs in the home I knew as a child. When I use my jigsaw to cut a thin sheet of plywood, I am back in the workshop above the garage where my father had rigged a toy jigsaw by attaching a leather belt to a rotating shaft. When I am easily printing pictures from the computer, I am drawn back to a darkroom under the back steps where we spent many hours printing and enlarging pictures from my brownie camera. On and on it goes. . .flashes from the past. . . sometimes unpleasant. . .like the time I received my first spanking in the first grade, but then comes a flash of good times. . .like the time I was chosen to be the engineer of the cardboard train in that same first grade.

These memory flashes are welcome windows into my history and I am sure there will be more to come.

WHAT DOES IT TAKE?

It was a beautiful afternoon with little wind and clear skies. A member of the Sautee RC Flyers was standing beside me, flying his beautiful new Radian sailplane with all the bells and whistles of a real sailplane. At the far end of the soy bean field, adjacent to our flying field, something happened and the sailplane flipped over and went straight down. The pilot searched for two hours, walking carefully between the five-foot high bean plants with no luck. The next morning by 9:30 three members were searching again. They were barely visible from the flying area. The horses on a trail ride came by about 10:30 and the leader felt our searchers were in the wrong place. They were asked to leave the bean field. Later, by good negotiation, the misunderstanding was resolved. By that time another member of our club had taken to the air in his full-sized aircraft, had flown low over the field and spotted the missing sailplane. The sailplane was recovered, in a number of pieces, and brought back to the field. Restoration may soon begin. After the incident, I posted the following on the Yahoo Group:

What does it take to find a downed Radian in the bean field?

. . .*Pointers as to approximately where the plane went down*
. . .*Two hours of searching in the bean field*
. . .*Three searchers looking again the next morning*
. . .*Radio communication with the searchers*
. . .*Offers of help with quad-chopper video*
. . .*Negotiation with horses and trail riders*
. . .*A full scale aircraft joining the search and finally spotting the downed plane*
. . .*Retrieval of the remains and hope for repair*

MY MAN-STAFF IS THE ALPHA CAT

I do not know exactly how it happened but I do know when it happened. The past is rather hazy but I remember there were some bad days and some big cages and lots of other noisy animals. I remember first meeting my lady-staff. They came in. . .she looked at me and I looked at her. I knew something good was going to happen. I remember going to a new house and I immediately hid under the sofa. That evening, when I ventured out, my man-staff was sitting on the sofa patting for me to come up. I immediately jumped up, curled up beside him and put my head in his big hand. I knew right away things were going to be all right. It was a kind of bonding and I knew from that moment he would be my "alpha cat."

A lot of catnip has gone under the bridge since then. He has acted very strange for an Alpha Cat, but I have been patient with him and tried to teach him.

He seems to have his days and nights mixed up. Every cat, whether alpha or rank-and-file, knows that the daytime is for sleeping and the night is for prowling. I think I am making progress but he still fusses about getting up at four in the morning to feed me and again at six to watch me while I finish breakfast. I am making progress, because sometimes he takes naps with me in the afternoon.

He is also learning to go outside on warm days and lead me to the best patches of green grass. Of course, I am really doing the leading and he is following (not very typical of an alpha cat).

Like any A.C., he feels that he knows it all and I have to submit to his authority. I can voice my dislike when he is calling me down from the hill or to come inside, but since he is my leader, I must finally submit. I will admit that he feeds me, morning, noon and night, even though he is often grumpy about it. Guess that is the way with alphas.

Still, in the evening, when I ask him, he sits down on the sofa and I curl up next to him and put my head in his big hand and go sound asleep. (So does he, sometimes!) I am glad that my man-staff is also my alpha cat. LB

IT IS HARD TO BE AN "ALPHA CAT" (a man-
staff response)

I am not sure how it started. . .maybe it was during those early days when Lady Bean first came to live with us. . .but there is no doubt that she thinks of me as the "alpha cat." Now I do not look like a cat, nor do I act like a cat. I did not think like a cat until LB started teaching me. Now, even though we look quite different, Lady Bean definitely thinks of me as the leader of the pack, the one who not only provides for her, but caters to her every whim. I think it must have begun right after we adopted her and she came out from under the sofa. I was the first thing she spotted and my hand offered her security and comfort. It must have been a "bonding" experience. Whatever it was, it changed my life.

To say she is spoiled is an understatement. But for Lady Bean it is not a matter of being spoiled, but a matter of receiving what is due to her from her "alpha cat." This is what I have become and what I am expected to do:

- Wake up at 4:30 because she is hungry; I go to the kitchen to fill her bowl.
- Later on, go with her to the kitchen, not because she is out of food but because she wants company while she has her snack.
- Let her take me for a walk around the house whenever it strikes her fancy.
- Play hide and seek, particularly if I do not know if she is in or out.
- To know exactly what she is saying when she starts talking in cat language.
- At our mealtime, pull an extra chair near to the table where she can curl up and not feel left out.
- Step over or around her when I move from place to place.
- Give her a bit of food whenever she expresses a hunger pang.
- In the evenings, she reminds me that it is "sofa time" and replays that time long ago when she put her head in my hand and felt secure.

This, and much, much more is expected of me as an alpha cat. At times it is exasperating and frustrating, but I have come to realize that it is indeed an honor to be chosen as an "alpha cat."

BEVERLY'S CORNER

Since this is nearly Thanksgiving, my only thought for my column in this newsletter is: Happy Thanksgiving!

THE IN-BETWEEN

OUR NEW HOME

We are finally here. It was a hard decision, but we finally agreed that it was time to move to a place where we would be cared for in the years to come. After looking around, we decided to find a place that was comfortable, affordable and near enough to Moss Manor that we could use it as our vacation home.

Clinton Presbyterian Community seemed to fit our needs. The CPC is one of six retirement communities in South Carolina operated by the Presbyterian Church. It is less than three hours from Sky Lake. We were able to get a comfortable, independent cottage near the main buildings that offered meals, health care and other amenities. After consulting with the family, we made the move and here we are.

Clinton, SC (pronounced "Clinon" by the locals) is a delightful small town. Some buildings date back into the 30s and earlier, but new things, like McDonalds, have moved in. It is the home of Presbyterian College and Thornwell Home for Children. The railroad runs through the town and freight trains blow regularly for each crossing. It is the kind of town where your banker and insurance agent know you by your first name. There seems to be a church on every corner. The Clinton Presbyterian Community is well known and respected here.

SMALL OUTSIDE – BIG INSIDE

The home that we chose in the Clinton Presbyterian Community is one of the smallest of the houses when you look from the outside. The red brick cottage is the first in the circle of cottages located behind the main building on Edinburg Drive. In back of the house two large Magnolia trees dominate the outer boundary of the yard where the hex-beam antenna looks down from the place of honor in the middle of the yard. Behind the yard, the pine and hardwood forest goes on and on. The covered carport to the side gives a place to keep a golf cart and Bev's Rascal, as well as a place to work.

The nice thing about our new home is that it is bigger on the inside than on the outside. Amazingly, it absorbed almost all the furniture from our Florida home without looking crowded. The living room has two sofas, the electric fireplace with TV on top, the electric piano from Sky Lake, a china cabinet, two end tables, two small round tables and three chairs. The kitchen boasts our round dining table with four chairs, a TV and small end table. This is surrounded by the over-under washer/dryer, stove and microwave, counters, dishwasher and refrigerator. The biggest rooms in the house are the two bedrooms. One is the master bedroom with chest, TV, dresser, book cases, queen bed, two bed-side tables and two smaller tables. The master bedroom has a large bathroom with a shower, and an entire end of the room is devoted to two large closets. The other bedroom, while it has a large bed, features an entire wall filled with ham radio equipment including three radios, three computers and two monitors. Other items include a chest, a game computer, a dresser and a bathroom with a tub. Of course, there is a TV for use when the room is used by guests. Closets fill the other end of the room. It may be a small house outside but once inside, it gets bigger and bigger. It is just right for us!

DINING AT CPC

Our home, Clinton Presbyterian Community, is different in many ways. Most of the residents have come with the knowledge that this is their last home. Four long hallways house individual apartments and different levels of assisted living. Behind the main lobby is the dining room. Behind the main building are around thirty duplexes and individual cottages. Ages of residents range from the sixties to 107. The dining hall displays the different stages of health needs. While there are some who still enjoy health and independent living, the majority come with walkers or electric wheelchairs. There are those who have trouble walking and are served dinner by the staff. Some push walkers through the cafeteria line or dinner is ordered and brought to the table by staff. Others seem much like those you would see in any restaurant. Some enjoy conversations while others eat in the loneliness of failing memory. We have come, not because it is essential at present, but because we know that soon we will need the help offered by the facility. The home gives us the assurance that, although they are willing, our children will not have to "find a home for mom or dad."

We usually go to the noon meal as it is the largest with the biggest variety. We often sit with friends we have made and enjoy conversation across the large, round table. But there are other times we look around for a table where residents seem isolated or lonely. . .there is a lot of loneliness in a retirement facility. There is a need for listening to stories from someone's past. Meeting new people, listening, and visiting, give us a sense of purpose and even calling.

MOSS MANOR IN SKY LAKE

It was difficult to leave Moss Manor. Of all the places we had lived, our mountain retreat was the favorite. The consolation and one of the reasons that we chose the Presbyterian Retirement Community in Clinton, SC, is that it is less than a three-hour drive from Sky Lake. We have left Moss Manor fully furnished, equipped and powered up so that we can return for visits. Although we will return often, we hope that family and friends will use MM for vacations and visits. Mary Glenn and Steve have already spent a week there in September. We have friends coming for the month of February. We would encourage family and friends to schedule a time to visit Moss Manor. If you are interested, let us know and we can arrange a time for your visit. Right now the schedule looks like this:

September 12-15   Francis (Preaching)
September 26 – October 12   Francis & Beverly (Preaching)
November 16 – 25   Francis and Beverly
January 16 – 19   Francis and Beverly (Doc visits)
February   Friends

Even if we are home in Moss Manor, there are two guest rooms on the main floor and sofas in the basement. We look forward to hearing from you.

BEVERLY'S ELECTRIC TRANSPORTATION

Beverly has a new chair. This one has four wheels and one seat. She drives it with a small joystick much like the ones we use when flying RC models. She uses it only outside. Although her walking has been improving, she still has trouble walking longer distances and the electric chair (not to be confused with chairs of higher voltage) enables her to ride from our house and right into the dining room a hundred yards or so away. We still have the golf cart when we want to ride around the campus together.

THE IN-BETWEEN

I guess I am luckier than most cats. I have a staff that I have trained well and usually give me what I want. I even have two houses, one in the mountains and one in the rolling country of South Carolina. I like them both. They have carpet on the floor, beds and sofas for me to lie on, windows where I can watch either animals or people outside and, most importantly, my food and basket. Both homes are cool in the summer and warm in the winter.

BUT. . .I tell you what I do not like. It is "the in-between time!" I hate to ride in the van that is crowded and bumpy and sometimes noisy. I hate going back and forth between my homes.

It starts a few days before they put me in the car. A suitcase comes out. (I try to make the most of a bad situation so I curl up and sleep on the suitcase.) They pack little boxes and put them in the car. My staff tries to hide what they are doing, but I know. The day before the in-between begins, they hang clothes in the car and straighten up the house. The last thing I watch for is when they take things out of the refrigerator and put them in a white box. My lady-staff gets in the car. It is time to hide! I make them look for me for a long time. When they find me (they always do) they pull me out, and I am carried, protesting, to the van.

The in-between time seems to last a long, long time. I complain, move from lap to lap and even try the back seat. Nothing helps. After an eternity, I sniff the air and know we are near one of my homes. I am tired! My staff is tired! When the van stops, I am allowed to jump out and march into my home (whichever one it is).

I love my two homes but I hate the in-between! LB

We apologize that this issue of MMN is filled with personal information. Since this was a major step in our lives, we feel it was appropriate to let our family and friends know where we were. Next issue will be back to the normal mix of musing, memories, random thoughts and stories by Lady Bean. F.

A PICKET FENCE

Autumn has faded into fall. The colorful foliage above and around us told us we were well into fall. The wind and rain reminded us that winter was on its way. Last week it snowed in Clinton. Now there is a real chill in the air and coats feel good.

It has been a busy season for Beverly and me as we are meeting new friends and are getting involved with the activities of our Clinton home. We have gone back to Moss Manor a number of times but our trips to Sky Lake will be fewer and fewer as winter settles in. This year we will spend Thanksgiving in our new Clinton home. Our home here is comfortable and warm. Even Lady Bean likes her new home and has quickly taken possession of it. We hope our friends will drop in and spend a day or two with us when traveling I-16 between Columbia and Greenville, SC. When spring comes, we will be spending more time in Moss Manor. Until then, Clinton Presbyterian Community will be our home.

AGING AIN'T FOR SISSIES

I have heard it said over and over, "Aging ain't for sissies." Now we are learning the truth of that statement. Oh, things could be a lot worse and we are thankful to be as able and healthy as we are. As I sit at the kitchen table and pour ten different pills out of my pill carrier, I think to myself, "Could there be that much wrong with me?"

In the morning, after I shake off the effects of sleep and drink a cup of hot coffee with a breakfast of cereal and toast, I feel ready to take on the world. I begin to think that I have moved into this facility too soon. Then, after a day of piddling around the house, I feel the aches and pains appropriate to my age and think to myself, "I should have moved here earlier." There are more doctors to see, more medicines to order and more aches and pains to challenge both doctor and pharmacist. The walkers do not seem to be such a bad idea and it is reassuring that hot meals will be prepared for me and medical help is just across the street.

TIME, LIKE A PICKET FENCE

Today I walked beside a long, white picket fence. Each picket reminded me of a year or more gone by. I walked very slowly, remembering a time when days were long and the picket fence of time stretched ahead almost forever. With each picket there came the memory of a special time, place or event. Because of the press of time, I walked more rapidly and the memory pickets began to fuse together and fade into the past. I began to run and the passing pickets whizzed by in a blur. As aging slowed me down, the individual pickets again took shape and molded precious memories to be visited and treasured. There are still pickets ahead, but when I look back most of them are behind me. Time is like a picket fence.

LAST WORDS

Our friend, Bea, sat across the round dining table. She was small and frail but sharp and full of life. We enjoyed talking with her. Soon after that she fell and was taken to the hospital where she died a few days later. I tried to look back, remembering the last time I saw her and wondering what I had said to her. What were my last words? I hope they were kind and caring, but I do not really remember.

Words are important. First words make impressions that follow us. Conversations establish friendships which grow and become bonds. But simple greetings or goodbyes may be our last communication. Life is very fragile. Living in the retirement community makes me very aware of how fragile it really is. As residents pass by our table, some are alert and walking upright; others are bent over, slowly pushing walkers. I will never know if my greeting to them will be the last words between us.

Last words may go in either direction but they will be remembered. Age is not the only factor. A young person or parent visiting a loved one will pass within feet of a head-on collision that could snuff out life as they travel home. Whatever the circumstance or direction, our last words should be remembered. They are important to the speaker and the recipient. While last words seem more urgent in a setting where the years ahead are few, they are important throughout life. I think back to times long past when we would send the children off to school, perhaps fussing because their hair was not combed or because their room was a mess. I would have been better off with words of love and assurance. I remember times when last words may have been spoken with criticism or in anger. In most cases, we have time to rethink and soften our words but then. . .

I will remember Bea, a bright and fragile little lady, and our passing greetings, never knowing it would be a last goodbye. I do not remember my words, but I hope and pray they were words of encouragement and even a blessing. In the days ahead, I will speak to many "Beas" as they pass by. I will try to remember what I have learned. Words, which may be last words, are very, very important to all of us.

THE MYSTERY RIDE

Usually, I like to know where I am going but today was different. As I climbed on the CPC bus, I had no idea where I was going, how to get there nor what we would do when we got to wherever we were going. It was billed as a "Mystery Ride" and we had signed up out of curiosity.

There were about twelve of us, some with walkers and some just slow in walking. As we rolled toward Greenwood, we talked and tried to guess our destination. A little over halfway to Greenwood we slowed for the only light and turned left. The sign welcomed us to the community of Cross Hill. A little way in we stopped at a small building under a sign that read "Railroad Diner." The proprietress unlocked the back door and we entered our mystery destination.

The Railroad Diner is a small but interesting diner, often over-looked by travelers. Inside we found railroad memorabilia and historical artifacts. After being seated around a long table, the owner told some of the history of Cross Hill stretching from Civil War days to the present.

At the end of the room was a table of lovely desserts from which we could choose our refreshments. After enjoying our afternoon snacks, we again climbed aboard the bus and headed back toward Clinton. It had been an informative and enjoyable "Mystery Trip" and we all looked forward to more in the future.

THANKSGIVING

The First Presbyterian Church of Clinton, SC is a beautiful old church. Its ministry reaches back into history and brings the gospel to the modern world. Beverly and I have been worshipping here since we moved to Clinton Presbyterian Community.

Last Sunday, the minute for mission focused on Thornwell Home for Children. It brought back many memories from seventy-five years ago. The speaker held up a small folder in the shape of a turkey with places for quarters inside. (It was dimes back then, but inflation hits everything) Suddenly I was back in the Springfield Presbyterian Church in Jacksonville and was being given a similar paper turkey to fill and give for the support of Thornwell Orphanage. My family had a special tie to the home, as its president in the early 1930s, Dr. Ross Lynn, was the minister who had married them. As a little boy, I visited Thornwell with my parents a number of times and was fascinated with the beautiful gray stone buildings, the farm and the children of the home. First Presbyterian Church has worked with Thornwell since its beginning in 1875 and has been instrumental in its growth and success over the years.

This Thanksgiving, I look forward to filling my turkey folder and giving thanks for the many years of service Thornwell has given to children who have needed its help.

LIFE IN THE JUNGLE

Life has settled down since we moved into the new house. It is smaller and there are fewer places to hide, but it is big enough. I can still race around from room to room, jump on to the beds and chairs. There is still time when I feel like I am in a jungle and need to chase imaginary rabbits or flee from imaginary tigers. My staff looks around in bewilderment as the furniture shakes with my pouncing. They will never understand what it is like to be a cat with wild impulses.

I like the warm carpets in the bedrooms and the cool hardwood floors in the kitchen. The back of the living room sofa gives me a great view of the outside world. I still take my man-staff to walk in the early morning and late afternoon. (There is a nice clump of green grass just outside the back door where I always stop for a bite or two.) He sometimes cramps my style and limits the places I want to go, but then, I have to make allowances for an over-conscientious human. He is really my alpha cat and I try to obey him. (It is very difficult at times.) He sometimes even lets me stay outside if I stay on the steps or porch. I still hide when the cleaning ladies come. One wants to pet me but she smells like dogs, and I hide under the bed. I'm sure she means well, but she just does not understand cats.

Well, it is time for my morning nap so I must jump down and ask my scribe to stop for now. LB

CHRISTMAS IN CLINTON

PREPARING FOR CHRISTMAS IN A NEW HOME

As most of you know, Beverly and I have recently moved into the Clinton Presbyterian Community home. Most of the residents come from the Clinton area and know each other's histories and families. We have come from the distant mountains of North Georgia and the flat-lands of Florida.

Coming as strangers in a foreign land gave me a new understanding of what it must have been like for Mary and Joseph on that first Christmas. They left their home and came to Bethlehem, not sure of what they would find or what would happen. They were strangers in a town where people knew each other well. Perhaps they made a few friends on the journey, but these friends had already taken the few places there were to stay in the town. In those circumstances the glory of the first Christmas would unfold.

We have been warmly welcomed by those here in the home and in the community, but in a way we are still strangers in a foreign land. It does give us a little more understanding of the happenings on that first Christmas.

TAKING DOWN THE TREE

It was almost time to take down the Christmas tree. Christmas had been different this year. We were in our new home, probably our last. We had put up the tree and decorated it with decorations we brought with us. The house looked warm and like Christmas. We had invited a number of new friends over for our usual Christmas drop-ins. Still, Christmas was different and a little lonely this year.

It was time to take down the Christmas tree. Beverly volunteered at the desk in the main building and it was my job to take down the tree. There was no use complaining. . .no one would hear me. . .so I pulled out the step-stool and began the job. First to come down was the little stuffed girl that had adorned our tree for many years. She was given to us because of our work with children from Social Services. Decorations were next to come down. Some had been with us for a lifetime and brought back memories of my childhood and the wonderful days when the family was together at Christmas. There were special wooden decorations, painted the Christmas the children were sick and housebound.

Sand dollars reminded me of friends from the coast and little sailboats reminded me of our adventures in the Caribbean. As I wrapped each symbol of a friend or adventure, my thoughts jumped back and forth over the years: the year we moved on the day after Christmas with a tree on the roof and children, dogs, cat and fish in the van. I remember the Christmas after the wreck with Jackie and Mack still recovering and the family recovering emotionally, looking for a tree in the snow of West Virginia, the Charlie Brown tree, and the Christmases at Disney and Christmases together and alone.

I carefully wrapped the figures of the manger scene. The little donkey with a missing ear reminded me of little fingers helping. Packing the manger scene brought back many memories of Christmas Eve and Christmas Day services. Eighty Christmases blurred together in my memory.

In years past we would take the tree out to be recycled so that, from the chips, other trees might grow. This year we folded the limbs and but it back in the long box. Garlands came down, destined for the attic. The boxes of ornaments and garlands would soon follow the tree.

All the Christmas decorations are down and stored away, but memories are alive in my heart and the reality of what Christmas really means is with me. Christmas can never be packed away until next year. The hope and renewed faith it brought, the joy brought by family and friends and the hope for peace renewed by angels' songs, can be with us every hour and every day of the New Year if we let it.

THE PASTOR'S VISIT

For the first time in many decades I found myself on the other side of pastoral visitation. Beverly and I had just moved into the retirement home in Clinton, SC. Our neighbors had invited us to the large First Church in downtown Clinton. (Downtown means near the intersection of two state roads and along the railroad). On our first visit we were surprised to find a beautiful old stone structure with a full program of activities. The church had recently called a new pastor. She led the worship well and her sermon was excellent. We signed the guest register and returned home, pleased with the church we had visited.

The next week we received a call from the church saying that Dr. Perkins would be in our area and would like to stop by. The next day the pastor came to call. She came bearing the gift of a loaf of fresh bread and time enough to sit down and visit with us for a good thirty minutes. In this age when the pastor of a large and busy church is caught up in myriad duties, and usually delegates first visits to assistants or lay people, it was a pleasant surprise that she not only came but took time to get to know us. She is not only the senior minister but a pastor as well.

I wonder if, in the quest for efficient administration and polished sermons, many of today's clergy have lost sight of their call to be pastors. I know the pressures of ministry and the difficulty of balancing and prioritizing things to be done. I also know the impression that was made by a new minister who took time to visit a couple of newcomers to the area, to welcome and invite them to the sheepfold.

Thank you, Jeri Perkins. You will see us at church.

WHAT HAPPENED TO MY FRIEND "CQ"?
(for our ham radio friends)

    As I search across the amateur phone bands, trying to find a place to land, I rarely hear the cry of a lonely ham looking for a new friend or an operator trying out a new rig or antenna. Unless my memory is failing, along with my antique Heathkit equipment, I seem to remember bands filled with lonely sound of "CQ CQ" or in Morse "dah-di-dah-di dah-dah-di-dah." (CQ is ham speak for "hello anyone.")

    For over sixty years I have enjoyed the multi-faceted modes that amateur radio offers. From days as a tender-eared novice to today's almost complete station, I have been active in the hobby and service. I am not really complaining. I enjoy and take part in many of the nets that fill the bands. I talk, type and sometimes use a key. I even hear my lost CQ on the weekend contests, but nobody wants to take time to talk or visit. I thought I had found my answer on the digital bands, as I see CQ float across the screen, but to my disappointment, I find that the CQ, the report exchanges and the 73s (best wishes) are often generated automatically by Macros. I do not blame anyone because maybe I am part of the problem by default, but it seems to me we have lost something valuable. For those of us who like to talk, one on one, who like to throw a hook into the air and see who bites, who have just gotten a new license and hesitate to join well-established nets, the old-fashioned CQ is a good way to fish in the vast sea of ham radio.

Whatever happened to my friend CQ? It is still alive, perhaps a little weak and waiting to be strengthened. It may be hiding behind the nets, the DX (distance) pile-ups, and the automated responses, but I am sure CQ is waiting to be re-discovered.

Let's get out there, jump in, make a new friend and learn about that person and their station. CQ CQ CQ from K4JUG (me).

CHANGES

My staff has made lots of changes around the house in the last few weeks and I do not like them. They took my sofa. . .the one by the front window that I like to sleep on. I can lie down on the back, soak up the sunshine and see everything that is happening in the neighborhood. It was in the perfect place. Now they have moved it across the room when nothing is happening and in its place they put a fake tree with a lot of lights on it. When I walked over to it and stood up to see what it was all about, they picked me up and fussed at me. They changed the kitchen all around, too. There are lights in all the windows and it is hard to see through them. If I knock them, they fuss at me. I hope the staff will get tired of that silly tree and move my sofa back where it is supposed to be.

But one thing I do like. There are lots of empty boxes around and I like boxes. I can get in one and pretend it is my special play house. Sometimes they leave clothes in the bottom and I can keep warm in the box when the house is cold. Sometimes there is paper in the boxes and I can turn them over and scatter paper all over the floor. Why do they keep bringing me toys like little mice or balls or fluffy things when I would much rather have a nice box? The other thing I like is an open drawer. I can jump into a drawer and scratch around in it. You would not believe the fun things I can find in a drawer. One time I even got in the back of a drawer and went to sleep. My staff looked all over the house before finding me.

I will be glad when things get back to normal around here and my sofa gets back where it belongs. LB

TO FRIENDS, FAMILY AND PEOPLE EVERYWHERE

May the memories of Christmas and God's great love live in your hearts and be expressed in what you do; May the promise of peace, that seems so far away, draw nearer and be reality in the coming year; May 2015 bring you good health, new hope and great adventures. Most of all, may the love of God, the grace of Jesus Christ and the guidance of Holy Spirit be with you now and in the year to come. HAPPY NEW YEAR!

SAINTS OF THE RANK AND FILE

BRRRRR!

Winter has arrived with a vengeance! South Carolina is not supposed to have temperatures hanging around twelve degrees. While we were spared the snow and ice that our northern cousins are experiencing, it is still cold enough for us and to spare. Lady Bean tries the front door and finds it too cold. She puts her nose out the back door, but her tail remains inside. As for us, the short excursion to the main building for dinner is the extent of our outing. Inside, it is warm and cozy. We will venture outside when it warms up. Stay warm!

CRAWLING IN MY BRAIN

A while back, I received a note of appreciation for our newsletter. (It always makes me feel good to know that somebody actually reads my stuff). But this note made me sit up in my chair and start thinking. It read: *We so enjoy crawling into your brain and knowing your inner thoughts from the simplest unseen magic of everyday life to your philosophic outlook of "why."*

I was never aware that people were crawling around in my brain, nor that there was magic in my philosophic outlook. However, if my ramblings are meaningful or helpful and sometimes even enjoyable, it makes my efforts at journalism worthwhile. The note made my day and it also gave me something to write about.

I had never thought about it, but what we put down on paper does provide a pathway into the secret places of our mind and heart. It is not so much the exact words or sentences but rather things that can be read between the words. The way I say things, the themes I write about over and over, the sensitivity I show, the anger or hurt that bubbles up, the tenderness and love that hides under the print; all of these allow my readers to "*crawl around in my brain*." Like an expert analyzing my handwriting, more comes across than is really intended. I guess this is a good thing because the blogs and articles that find their way into Moss Manor News speak of things I want to share. In writing, I guess I am trying to share something of myself. . .my concerns, my hopes, my frustrations and my dreams. In a sense, what is said and what is put down on paper do provide a pathway into my thoughts and into my mind. It provides a "wormhole" into who I am and what I really believe.

When I have moved from one church to another, one home to another, I have always felt that I have taken with me a part of every person I have known and that I have left a part of me with them. My hope and prayer were that I had left something of value, some of my love, with them and I know that I carried something from each of them that made me a better person. Maybe that is what I am trying to do with my ramblings and miscellaneous writings. Maybe that is what *simplest unseen magic of everyday life* was trying to describe. If words bring back good memories, if words can bring hope and encourage harmony, if Lady Bean can bring a smile, then maybe that is magic. I do not mind readers crawling around in my brain as long as they will also crawl around in my heart and find therein love for them and hope for days to come.

Guess this is my feeble *philosophic outlook* or maybe it is just the ramblings of a scrambled brain that has been crawled into once too often. . .only time will tell.

TV OR NOT TV; THAT IS THE QUESTION!

The weather has been either too wet or too cold to do much outside, so I have been watching more TV than usual. I have been getting a little "football overload" but since I enjoy watching football that is OK. The news is interesting, if somewhat depressing. My complaint is that they seem to *beat a dead horse to death,* over and over. Commercials seem to be interrupting things more frequently. The other night we were timing commercials and as the movie progressed, more commercials got crammed into the program and equaled the time the movie was on. It is amazing to me how little the content of a commercial has to do with what is being sold. Beautiful pictures of cycling, sailing, playing with animals, hiking or even rock climbing often advertise a medicine or medical procedure for people far too sick to do any of those things. Besides, the potential side effects are far worse than the ailment they seek to cure. Automobile ads spend more time on beautiful scenery and luxurious interiors than on whether the car is dependable or affordable. The pharmaceutical ads really get to me when they urge me to tell my doctor about what I am taking and tell him what to prescribe. If my doctor does not know what I am taking, I had better find another doctor. He also knows much more about what will help me get well than my TV. Just watching TV can give me ulcers!

Do you remember the days when the cable companies advertised that if you paid their fees, you would not have to watch commercials? Do you remember the days when it was unethical for doctors, dentist, hospitals and attorneys to advertise on TV? Oh, how things have changed.

I do have a Blu-Ray player and I think I will watch Netflix or my DVDs. I may see some previews on the DVDs but fewer commercials. I can always get the news from Google but there are commercials on the side. Guess there are certain things we just have to live with in our modern world.

THE HARDWARE STORE

There are two hardware stores in Clinton. One is near the center of town. It is part of a chain, is well stocked and the place to shop if you want the latest tool or current item. It is always busy. About two blocks up from the center of Clinton there is an old, two-story building that shows both age and the need for a facelift. A proud but faded sign across the building reads: "Buddy Copeland Hardware." It is seldom busy and for me, it is the place to visit.

The display windows on either side of the entrance proudly display an old iron cook stove and used bicycles. In the other window are a plow and more bicycles in different stages of repair. Upon entering, one is confronted with a long counter on the left and about ten counters extending out from the right wall. Everything is filled with dust-covered merchandise. Tools of all descriptions, half-filled spools of wire, and bins of screws, nails and gadgets fill the counters and line the walls. The large room is dimly lighted by hanging fluorescent tubes. As you follow the left counter toward the back you will come to the office. It, too, is open with an ancient cash register and an old, black safe. As you look down each row to the right, you see things that were used to build the town of Clinton. . .pipes and clamps, drills and sandpaper. It is a challenge to find just what you might need, but with a little patience and a little help, it will be discovered.

Near the back of the store, just past the side door, is the heart of the hardware store. There we find a round, iron woodstove. Nearby there are a number of chairs, usually filled with friends and customers, getting warm and telling tall stories. The owner of the hardware store sits near the stove and faces the front, seeing all that come in and all that goes on. Mr. Buddy Copeland has owned and operated the store for many years. I found him in his usual chair where he was putting a handle on a shovel. Walking is hard for Mr. Copeland, so when you tell him what you want, he will point you to a certain aisle or tell one of his friends to help you find it. The hardware store is a classic. When you walk in, you leave the present and find yourself in the thirties again.

I like to go in, not only to buy, but to drench myself in the past and remember spending time in stores like Mr. Copeland's when I was young.

OUT OF THE DISTANT PAST

I was twelve years old, going on thirteen. It was a lazy summer afternoon. Ed, my best friend, was spending the day with me and we were sitting in the front porch swing looking at the latest issue of *Popular Mechanics*. Among the descriptions of things to fix and build, we spotted an article telling us how to build a cruising sailboat. Immediately we started planning to build the boat and began thinking of the tools and materials we would need to collect in order to do the job. Soon the practical gave way to dreaming of where we would sail in our boat. We had fished together along the St. Johns River, so our first voyage was to sail down the river exploring the many Florida towns along its way. Next we planned to sail down the inter-coastal waterway. We pulled out road maps and plotted our course. Our imagination took us under the bridge we had crossed over each time we went to the beach. We dreamed of sailing on the Indian River and of exploring the chain of small islands that border the canal in central Florida. We dreamed of dropping the sails and using our small outboard motor to take us through the narrow cuts of Miami and then sail through the expanses of Biscayne Bay and on to the Florida Keys.

It was the beginning of a dream that would follow both of us throughout our lives. It would begin when, at age sixteen, we would together purchase an old and rather decrepit nineteen-foot-long sailboat we named *Bad Girl*. Strange how memories and dreams follow us and sometimes become reality. Often these memories and dreams provide the raw materials from which we build the adventures of the future. It was true for both of the boys who sat in that swing and dreamed of spending wonderful days ahead. I have thought of that afternoon many times in my life and how it became the springboard of many adventures in my life. But that is another story for another time.

A TRIBUTE TO THE CHURCH

The church in which Beverly and I grew up was typical of many Presbyterian Churches. It was medium in size and in a middle-class suburban community. I cannot remember not going to church. . .I was taken, sometimes against my will to Sunday school each Sunday. The sermons were long and boring to a youngster who usually went to sleep or counted the exposed ceiling rafters. The people in the church did not always like the hyperactive kid who dropped chewing gum in the pews, wriggled and whispered during services, aggravated teachers and tried their patience and in many ways was definitely incorrigible. But they accepted him and even loved him, and in that setting, passed on their faith, rooted in Scripture and tested through the ages. It was my cradle of faith, and they were truly "saints of the rank and file."

Today I look back and pay tribute to that church for starting seven new churches, participating in missions and faithfully proclaiming the word of God. But even as I look back with gratitude, I realize that many things they did or did not do were very wrong. Perhaps because of these failures the church was unable to fulfill its opportunity of mission. That particular church has now faded into history. But I give thanks to God for people of that church who, by grace and patience, molded and shaped a rebellious boy. They instilled in him a faith that would eventually lead him into ministry and a far deeper faith.

The church, this church, our church, any church may not be perfect, but it is the gift of God, held in God's hand and heart. The church is the body of Jesus Christ, redeemed by the cross and resurrection. The church is the agent of Holy Spirit who gives the church power to become more than it is and to be the mother of faith for this and coming generations.

When we repeat the words in the Apostles, let us do so with humble pride and renewed commitment because I am the church, you are the church, we are the church, together.

I'LL NEVER WIN THE BIG ONE

I read, or maybe it was on the infallible internet, that an individual has one, maybe two, chances of winning something big. Well, I have used up my chances. When I was about fifteen years old, my friend and I went to a fishing show. We got there late and our tickets must have been on top in the barrel, at any rate, he won an outboard motor and I won a fishing reel. That was win #1. Last week I went to the D-Star University in Aiken, SC and won an Icom 880H, a UHF/VHF digital transceiver. (If you are not in the amateur radio community, you won't know what that is all about.) It is a very nice and fairly expensive mobile radio. That used up my last chance to win something big. Guess I will never win the "five-thousand-a-week-forever" prize, or even the chance to become a millionaire. There are two reasons why I will never win again. First is that "I have used up my chances" and second, "I never buy a ticket or register for the prize." Oh well, such is life!

I'M A LAP CAT NOW

You may remember that, some time ago, I wrote in my column: I'm NO lap cat. That was during a period of my life when I valued my independence more than my comfort. Times have changed and so has my attitude. While I am still quite independent and I still have to keep my staff in their place, I have decided it is time to pamper myself and indulge myself with the comforts every cat should have. So, I swallowed my pride and jumped into a lap. I found it warm and comfortable with the bonus of being stroked and told how beautiful I was. Mind you, I still do not come just when they call me and pat their laps. I still pick my own time to jump up, usually when they least expect it.

I guess it's all right for a cat of my stature to have a change of mind and enjoy the creature comforts that laps offer. Whatever, I am a lap cat now and am enjoying it. LB

RAILROAD TOWNS

A DUSTING OF SNOW

For the last few weeks we have been hearing dire forecasts of the "big one" that will bury Clinton in a soft white blanket of snow of up to four inches. The other night we were all set. The car was pulled as far into the car port as the Buzzard Wagon, the golf cart and Beverly's electric chair would allow. The girls in the Health Clinic called and offered to bring our dinner to us if we did not want to brave the elements and come to the dining hall. We were all set and waited.

In the wee hours of the morning it came. Not the blizzard that was predicted but a dusting of snow that disappeared as soon as it touched the ground. The temperature was cold enough to freeze the rain that came with the snow on bushes but the ground and roads were warm enough to leave only water. When daylight came, we were treated with some decorative ice and snow but nothing like the predicted deluge. We were both thankful and a little disappointed.

Next time the weather prophets predict a blizzard, we will look forward to a dusting. But if they forecast just a dusting, we will stock up on groceries and look for a blizzard.

TRAINS, TRAINS EVERYWHERE!

Clinton is not really a railroad town. There is not station, no passenger trains, no work-train headquarters and yet it is full of trains. A mainline freight track cuts the town in half and then divides again, chopping it in thirds. The tracks parallel one of the main streets and then cut across it. Last night I was awakened at about 2:00 in the morning by some extra long and loud blasts on the horn. Trains come through every night, blowing for every crossing, but I seldom hear them. Maybe the soft rain and overcast skies caused the sound to come pounding into our bedroom.

As we rode the bus that carries us from our home to First Presbyterian, we were stopped by a parade of ninety-seven tanker and freight cars. During morning worship, the pastor had almost finished a powerful sermon when we heard it coming down the track in front of the church. As it passed a little over a hundred yards from the church, its whistle sounded a loud "Amen!" over and over.

Trains have always been part of my life. As a boy, the tracks ran about a half mile from our house. On Sunday afternoons, my father would sometimes take me for a hike along the tracks, pointing out the signals, the siding turn-outs, the watering stations. He would move me to a safe distance as the steam locomotives thundered by, belching black smoke and hissing steam. Sometimes the engineer, with the big, red neckerchief, would even blow the whistle for me and wave. I remember a visit to the large train depot, where engineers would be squirting oil from large oil cans around the bearings and moving parts of their steeds.

In later years, I lived in a number of railroad towns where members of my congregation worked for the railroad. Hinton, WV, was a town where coal trains thunder through the valley, depositing their dust in every crevasse of the houses that lined the hills. Hamlet was the home of a large sorting yard, known as "The Hump." Here, cars were pushed to the top of the hump, cut loose, sorted and then braked as they coasted down the gentle hill. They were made into trains for the engines to pick up and deliver. There are many stories yet to be told of my adventures with trains in Hamlet.

Trains have marked my life with happiness and tragedy. Perhaps it is only fitting that, in these golden years, I still hear the trains interrupting my sleep, invading my dreams, blocking my travel and even disturbing my worship.

MARIE HAD A BIRTHDAY

Marie is a regular at our dining table. She usually comes in late and makes a grand entrance with her designer outfits and special hats. She hails from the coal mines of West Virginia and retains the determined and knowledgeable qualities that I knew when I worked with people in that state. She is special and keeps us on our toes and in our place.

Last week, Marie had a birthday. She was 59. (Oops, I turned those numbers around.) We surprised her with balloons and streamers. She had arranged for a birthday cake to share with the entire dining hall. Together with Marie and her family, we celebrated together. Here's to Marie! May she enjoy many more anniversaries of her birth, and may we continue to enjoy her company and her saucy hats for a long, long time. HAPPY BIRTHDAY, MARIE!

A NEW HYMNAL

The hymnal called "Glory to God" has been out for a number of years, but it is still new to me. I am just beginning to appreciate the mix of old and new hymns that are in it. I am not sure of the schedule, but is seems that about ever double decade they come out with a new hymnbook. My life can be marked and defined by the publication of hymnals.

When I was growing up I remember the smaller maroon book called The Premier Hymnal. I sang from it in Sunday school and it had what we now call the "good ole" hymns. Of course they used a larger, dark blue book called Presbyterian Hymnal at 11:00 in the big church. The Hymnbook came out in 1955 with laments about hymns that had been omitted. In 1972, about the time I learned the words and tunes in that book, they published The Worship Book. That book gave way in 1990 to The Presbyterian Hymnal with the same complaints about leaving out some of the hymns we all knew and loved. About that time, they started leaving off the Amen's. Now, with the new Glory to God hymnal, I hear something of the same complaints. But some of the oldies that I missed in the previous edition are back in. What I am excited about is the wealth of new hymns that are great. Some of the tunes leave me a little cold, but I will probably warm up for them, too. So, in the words of an old church camp song:

Let us sing together, let us sing together, one and all a joyous song. Amen!

MY BAPTISM

I may have been two or three months old when I was baptized, yet I remember it as clearly as if it were yesterday. It is not that I have that great a memory. Rather I owe that memory to my mother who told me the story of that day over and over, every detail in living color. Through her voice, it became part of my life experience and I remember it as if I were sitting on the front pew watching it unfold.

Last Sunday we sang a new hymn at church. At least it was new to me. It spoke to me of my baptismal experience and of many other times in life. The words were written by John C. Ylvisaker in 1985 and can be found on page 488 of the Glory to God hymnal. You may already know it, but let me share the imagined conversational voice of God in the words of the hymn.

I was there to hear your borning cry; I'll be there when you are old.
I rejoiced the day you were baptized to see your life unfold.
I was there when you were but a child with a faith to suit you well;
In a blaze of light you wandered off to find where demons dwell.
When you heard the wonder of the Word, I was there to cheer you on.
You were raised to praise the living Lord to whom you now belong.
If you find someone to share your time and you join your hears as one,
I'll be there to make your verses rhyme from dusk till rising sun.
In the middle ages of your life, not too old, no longer young,
I'll be there to guide you through the night, complete what I've begun.
When the evening gently closes in and you shut your weary eyes,
I'll be there as I have always been with just one more surprise.
I was there to hear your borning cry; I'll be there when you are old.
I rejoiced the day you were baptized to see your life unfold.

SNIFF THE SCENT OF MEMORIES

I was traveling alone on a quick trip that took me through the city in which I grew up. Jacksonville had evolved into a bigger, busier and different suburb from the one I knew eighty years ago. The interstate on which I was traveling did not exist, but when I neared the 8th street exit I had the irresistible urge to turn off and descend into a world gone by. Although change was everywhere, I could sniff the scent of memories all around me.

Passing the complex of new hospitals built on the corner lot where we test flew our model airplanes. Turning left onto the Boulevard, I passed the place where I spent my first eighteen years in a wonderful, two story frame house. In its place was a large, two-story parking garage, whose concrete façade faded into a thousand memories. A block away was the grammar school that began the process of chipping away at my immaturity. It was still in the business of teaching, but sadly the playground that held so many memories of recess and sandlot ball had been transformed into a paved parking lot for school buses. Just past the school was an empty store, destined for destruction. In days past, it was a candy store, operated by a wonderful little lady named Mrs. Gilhouse. While eating forbidden sweets, we would watch the man from Japan do marvelous maneuvers with a yo-yo. . .sometimes two at a time, and try to sell his wares.

At Sixth and Silver Streets there still stands the church in which I was baptized and where I grew up. As the neighborhood changed, the church changed hands and denominations but is still a beautiful building and a place of worship. Across the street from the church is the home of my best friend. In a sea of change, his house still is much the same as it was when we played in his side yard and climbed the tree in front of the house.

Main Street and the area around it are completely changed. Gone is the Capitol Theater, the corner drug store, the sawdust floored grocery and the five and dime store. The one landmark that remained the same was the fire station at 5th and Main. In some areas, where I used to deliver the *Saturday Evening Post* and, later, the *Times Union* morning paper, I felt insecure and took pictures through the car windows. Other areas felt almost like they did when I was riding the streets on my bicycle and playing in the alleys.

Wherever I was, I would see the streets and homes as they were in the 1930s and 40s and was thankful for a wonderful childhood, now living only in dreams of days gone by. I am glad that I was lured from the highway into past times where I could drive familiar streets and sniff the scents of many memories.

TO MY HAM FRIENDS

It was like the old days. The other Saturday I spent part of the morning answering contesters around the world. I am not really into contesting but I do enjoy chasing a little DX, so it was rewarding to find so many bands wide open. In a thirty minute period I made thirty-five contacts on 20, 15 and 10 meters in South America, Europe, Asia and the Arctic. I am sure many of you did much, much more. For me it was fun and it let me know my equipment was still working. CU on the air. . .K4JUG

SPRING IS HERE. . .WELL ALMOST. . .MAYBE

It has been a long winter, not really a hard or bitter winter. Guess it has been rather nice compared to what has been happening up north. There was only one small snow and a few sprinklings of ice. Guess we should not complain. But we are ready for warmer weather. I was away for a few days and when I returned the trees were turning green and the early flowers were out. The Bradford pears form a triumphant arch through which to drive. The intricate design of petals is almost lost in the profusion of white. The sky is turning blue again and rain is a memory. Even the prediction of a cold spell to blow down on us next week can neither dampen the spirit nor is the belief that spring really here. . .well almost. . .maybe.

I STILL LOVE MY MOUSE

I think I have talked about my mouse before and, if so, forgive me. My soft little mouse is my next favorite toy after my red ribbon.

He was one of the first things I remember after moving into my new home many years ago and has been with me everywhere I have gone. I find my mouse hiding under the bed or in the corner of a closet. I bring him out and play with him. He plays whatever game I suggest. He does not try to run away nor does he object or cry when I put my paw on him. When we are together, I feel that everything is going to be all right. Guess we comfort each other. I still love my mouse and I am sure the mouse loves me. LB

RACING IN THE HOUSE

I know that my staff does not understand it, but there are times when I feel that I must race around the house, running around the four rooms at lightning speed, jumping on whatever is in front of me. I cannot really explain it. Maybe it is my distant past coming to the surface. . .a time when I had to run for my life or had to race after something in the jungle for food. There is no schedule for it to begin. Sometimes it is in the morning when I lead my man-staff to the kitchen and to my breakfast. Sometimes it happens in the afternoon after I have had a long nap and need to let off energy.

The other evening it came on me after I sniffed out a cricket that was hiding in the closet and chased him around the room. After that I just felt like I needed to run and jump. I raced around the house, up and across the bed and into the bathroom where my man-staff was taking a bath. He thought I was going to sail right into the water, but I knew what I was doing. I made it onto the counter, back down, under the bed and into the closet.

After making one more frantic run around the house, I felt that surge of energy draining away. It was now time to jump on the bed where my lady-staff was reading, roll over and wait for her to pet me and tell me how beautiful I am.

As I said, I do not know why it happens or when it is coming, but it sure makes me feel good and relaxes me for a good nap or a good night's sleep. Besides, it is fun to see my staff watch me with amazement and wonder what has gotten into me. LB

BENEATH THE SURFACE

GROWING OLD GRACEFULLY. . .NOT ON YOUR LIFE!

As the years slip by and gather speed with each passing day, I thought it might be helpful to explore some thought on "growing old gracefully." I really wasn't very excited about it, as neither growing old nor being gracefully, was ever my thing. So I did what every eighty-plus explorer does. I went to the internet and typed in "How to grow old gracefully." To my delight there seemed to be an unending supply of advice on the subject.

The first listing included; Fighting fatigue. . .something I had been doing since the age of six with little results. Exercise from the neck up was another suggestion. . .something that is difficult to do when you can hardly remember how to spell neck. Another suggested pole walking. . .pole walking? Not when I can hardly keep my balance using two feet planted well apart and my cane stabbing at the ground in a futile effort to help. Then came, "Dance, dance, wherever you may be. . ." I gave up graceful dancing at the age of six when my feet kept tangling up and I took up square dancing.

The next listing suggested that I get serious about mid-life change. . .come on now, that happened almost fifty years ago and I can hardly remember it. It also suggested I do a backpacking hike through the Grand Canyon. I quickly moved on. Another suggestion was that I get spiritual. Come on now; I have been in ministry for sixty-five years and I should know a few things about getting spiritual. Sure, it might help in growing old but then again it helped when

I going through teenage years. Not much new. After looking through three pages of posts, I turned off the internet in disgust.

There is only one alternative to growing old, and I am putting that off as long as possible. But I will definitely declare that I will not grow old gracefully! I may grow old but I will get there kicking and screaming, scratching and fighting and in full denial. There are lots of adventures yet to explore, although perhaps a little less challenging. There are mountains to climb but they may be more like hills. I still climb ladders (when my wife is not looking). I still use the chainsaw when I can sneak out of the house (but I do it very, very carefully and only cut small branches). I still plan for great adventures on the land, on the sea and in the air, but mostly in my dreams.

Am I growing old gracefully? NOT ON YOUR LIFE!

THE TIP OF AN ICEBERG

The comment was made by a college professor who was talking about his students: "Some thirty or more students are in my class for an hour three days a week for a quarter or semester. I interact with them and get to know them. . .some well and others just as faces, voices and names on papers. But for the vast majority, I am seeing only the tip of the iceberg."

That comment got me to thinking about the people I know or think I know. . .the people we speak to each week at church. . .the mail carrier who has served us for years. . . the one we talk to every day at work or at play. We know only what is visible. . .only that which is opened to us during our encounters. How much more is beneath the surface?

As a pastor, I have had the privilege to dive beneath the sometimes cold surface and see how much more is hidden there. Sometimes I found great pain and hidden burdens. Other times I found hidden talents waiting to be developed. Often I discover a wonderful friend who reaches out to me.

My challenge to you is to watch for opportunities to discover the unseen world of those around you. . .not out of curiosity, but out of a real desire to become immersed in the unseen world of others. Do not force yourself in, but when invited, step in, and you will often find deep friendship that will enrich both of your lives and will take you far beyond "the tip of the iceberg."

IN YOUR EASTER BONNET

We may not have 5th Avenue, but we have the Easter Parade and all the fancy bonnets you could imagine. It starts about a week before Easter. A room adjacent to our dining hall is transformed into a high fashion hat. Over the years a variety of hats have been collected and decorated for a special event. The ladies of our home try on different pieces of head gear; then they select the hat they want to wear and mark it as theirs for the big day.

Before the Easter Parade can begin, there is the traditional Easter Egg Hunt. We are never too young or too old to remember and relive the wonder of finding a brightly colored egg. When all the eggs are found and Easter baskets are filled, it is time to come back inside, don the brightly decorated hats and parade through the halls of Clinton Presbyterian Community. It is every bit as exciting and as much a part of the Easter week tradition as the parade in New York.

Once again we are children, sharing the fun of Easter and preparing for the deeper and more important message of Easter morning.

INK AND TEARS

A few weeks ago we attended a memorial service. As I sat in the pew and listened to the music and the words of the pastor, it took me back to services that I had conducted during my fifty years of ministry. As the pastor struggled to keep composure while talking about a dear friend, I remembered the many times that lump would well up in my throat, making words difficult to say clearly. I remembered sitting at my desk, trying to find appropriate words to describe a faithful member of the church and a dear friend. The manuscript was most often blurred with tears as I thought of things I had learned from wise words of advice. . .of laugher that had bonded friendship. . .of disagreement but always respect. . .of visits with families and much, much more.

There were times I struggled to keep composure, not because the chosen words were not comforting, but because they were so personal. A pastor has the privilege of being part of the greatest celebrations and darkest hours of his congregation and the emotion is as real as life itself. Perhaps the tears on the pages of a memorial manuscript represent the privilege and reward of being a pastor. It also stretches the gifts of empathy and compassion.

As I listened, I remembered other times when I sat in the front of the church with members of my family and heard words about a lifetime helpmate. The same familiar scriptures reminded me of past grief and a somber thanksgiving. The hymns brought back the comfort that was showered on me by friends and congregations and reminded me of the blessings that comes from being in a family of faith. These are good memories even though tinged with sadness.

Occasions like this are appropriate, sometimes saddening, but necessary to pay tribute and remember friends that gave meaning to my life. Even as I write, the page is a mix of ink and tears.

ANOTHER NEW RC FLYING FIELD

Last week I had a chance to get back to the mountains of Sautee Nacoochee. The house looked good, just waiting for family and guests to use it. Of course, the moss lawn in front and the challenge hill in back always need a little TLC. One of the main reasons I came this particular weekend was to be part of the workday at the new RC flying field. It is a beautiful place to fly but still needs a lot of work. A large group turned out with shovels and saws and other equipment. Before the day was over, tables were in place, the frame for the canopy was standing. My only disappointment came when I tried to help with the heavy equipment. . .the gang very nicely told me to go sit down, drink my coffee and stay out of the way. It could be a worse life! The runway is in and, except for a few bumps to be smoothed out, it is very flyable.

Thanks to everyone for lots of planning and hard work. I look forward to spending quality flying time at the new field.

A STORY OF WARMTH AND COMPANIONSHIP

Holly is a good friend who lives near Sautee, GA. Rosie is a newly adopted kitten, rapidly becoming a young cat. The following is an excerpt from a letter we received. Those who enjoy the stories of Lady Bean might relate to the story of Rosie and Red.

I figured that they'd meet each other. . .Rosie and Red. After all, it is November. I suspect that their acquaintance will turn out to be just as warm and compatible as mine is with Red, whom I fondly refer to as my best wintertime friend: *Red, my humble, old-fashioned hot water bottle. Last night, half asleep, I noticed that when Rosie settle down on my bed, it was not where I've become accustomed (well, almost) to share space with her, where she snuggles up to the curve of my legs. No, she was by my feet, pillowed on the still warm lump that was Red.*

(Excerpt from Holly's letter. Used with permission)

MY TIME VS THEIR TIME!

I wish we could get our times together. . .I mean the clocks in our heads. They seem to run on completely different schedules. When I want to sleep, they want to play. When I want to play, they are zonked out in the bed. They say that I need a lot more sleep then they do, but I question that. Much of the time when they think I am asleep, I am just napping, waiting for them to finish looking at that silly screen with strange figures running across it. I keep one eye half open most of the time to be sure everything is safe and that I do not miss a meal time. They just think I am asleep.

What really bothers me is the fact that, when it is dark and everything is quiet in the house, they will not play with me. Every cat knows that nighttime is the best time to play, prowl or howl. Sometimes I just get bored stalking around the house and, just for fun, I pounce onto the middle of the bed. Whoever is sleeping there gets "pounced." It is fun to shake up my staff. Then there is a dis-agreement over meal times. They want to eat only three times a day.

Every self-respecting cat knows that we should eat whenever we are hungry. They worry about gaining weight. My friend, Garfield, spoke for us when he said, "Why should I worry about dieting when my wardrobe always fits."

Maybe someday we will work out this matter of time, but I doubt it. Until then, I will just have to put up with their idiosyncrasies. LB

THE NIGHT OF THE CRICKET

A TRIBUTE TO ROBERTA (1910-2015)

A call from her son brought the sad news that Roberta had died at the age of 105. With that news came sadness at her home-going and rejoicing for the richness of her life and faith.

In the fall of 2002, the telephone rang in our North Carolina home. When I answered, a strong but elderly-sounding voice asked, "Is this little Francis?" After admitting that I once might have been called "Little Francis," we established that it was my great aunt Roberta calling. The last time I had seen Roberta was seventy-seven years ago. My family had driven from Jacksonville to Gainesville, FL, when I was about seven years old and had dragged me along. I was pleased that she remembered me after all those years. She was pleased that we were planning to move to Ocala where she had lived for over seventy years.

We moved to Ocala the next year and immediately went to see her. Her home was small but adequate. In back of the house were citrus trees, and beside the house were plants and flowers. In the garage was an old automobile which she never drove, but started regularly to keep it ready. She was in her mid-nineties and still cut her grass with a gasoline push lawnmower. Roberta was a master gardener and her plants reflected her knowledge. Inside her home were books, clippings, pictures and magazines which told of her passionate interest: the Dorsey genealogy.

We visited Roberta regularly. Each time she would tell us more about my family history. One day she showed us a picture taken on the front steps of the house in which I grew up. It included my grandmother, the one Roberta called Aunt Annie. Also there were my parents and aunts and uncles I had heard of but had never seen. She had traced the Dorsey family all the way back to the 1600s. Each visit would bring another story of things that happened to my family before I was born. Once while she was visiting in our home, I videotaped some of her stories of our family history.

We admired Roberta, not only for her longevity, but also for her alertness, her phenomenal memory, and her interest in the world and the people around her. We will miss her and are thankful for the many hours we spent with her. We are so glad she searched for and found "Little Francis" after so many years. May she rest in peace and enjoy reunions with so many of the beings that she had known only on her family tree.

SEVENTY-SIX TROMBONES

The minister was paying tribute to my great aunt Roberta who had died at the age of 105. This lady had been a member of the church for seventy-six years and had been loyal through ups and downs, through thick and thin. Seventy-six years. . .suddenly I felt like I was part of the finale of The Music Man when seventy-six trombones came marching down the street. We were celebrating seventy-six years of loyalty to her Lord and her church. The minister went on to say that Roberta did not always agree with what the church did. She liked some ministers and she felt that some others might well have stayed in seminary. She was outspoken about her feelings, but for all those years she was a loyal member and supporter.

I am afraid that loyalty is a missing virtue in many church members. People disagree with some issue or action in the church or denomination. I remember a church that split over what color to paint the nursery chairs. It is easier to run from issues than to try to change them. I firmly believe that diversity is one of the greatest strengths of the Christian church. Loyalty and commitment is more difficult than flight. Most often, when a congregation leaves the denomination it is because they have been led away by a pastor who is determined to take the congregation to a place of his own choosing. It is true that after a pastor has been in a pulpit for five years, the congregation begins to look like the pastor and is easily influenced. I regret to see the body of Christ fragmented and losing credibility, as the world looks and sees a church that will not allow diversity, that only their way is God's way, and feel they cannot be loyal to their heritage. We may not agree with all that the national or local church does. That is our right. But let us remember that we are the family of Christ, who may disagree, but whose love for Christ and the other brother and sisters will keep us in the family that brought us into being.

I give thanks for Roberta and those like her who remained faithful to their church for seven or seventy-six years. Maybe it was the heavenly trombone band I heard, welcoming Roberta home.

THE NIGHT OF THE CRICKET

The day had been a good one. Together with friends, I had taken *Karisto* out for a day's sail. We had good wind and ventured past the three mile limit to weave around the gambling boats. Even though we were back at the dock by late afternoon, the exercise and heat had taken its toll and I was tired. Bev had stayed home to do some things around the house and after fixing supper, she was also ready for a good night's sleep. We turned in about 10:30, read a few minutes and turned out the light.

The room had hardly faded into darkness when we heard it. It started rather quietly: Carick, carick, chirp, carick. At first we thought the window was open and night sounds were filtering in, but soon reality became apparent and we knew. . .there was a cricket in the bedroom. How one little critter can make so much noise is a mystery to me. Even turning on the light only discouraged him for a little while and he would begin his song again. I looked around in the obvious places for him to hide, but with the strategy of the insect world, he would never chirp when or where I was looking. Soon I gave up and went back to bed. Luckily, I am a sound sleeper and once asleep could sleep through a hurricane if necessary. Not so with Beverly.

She lay awake listening to the rhythmic undulation of the cricket's call. Another cricket from outside the tightly closed window began to answer our friend. There would be minutes of silence when Bev would almost get to sleep and then it would start again, jolting her awake. On and on it went. She began counting cricket calls instead of sheep. She found that the series of chirps in each sequence were usually even in number, ranging from six to twenty in length. A few odd sequences were heard but most of them were even. Periods of silence might last as long as four minutes, not long enough to fall asleep and not short enough to stay fully awake. Finally, out of the sheer exhaustion of counting chirps, she fell asleep. Morning would come too soon and what rest there was would be fitful.

The next morning there was no sign of the chirping creature that had marked the night like the constant sounding of the sea buoy just off shore. A search of the bedroom expanded to the whole house but without success. Perhaps it had found its way out as stealthily as it had gained entrance. Our visit to Wilmington and the doctor's office made us forget the night's events.

On Wednesday, we got to bed a little later. It was our hope and prayer that the night would bring undisturbed rest. As the light in the room blinked out, there was silence. . .no chirp, no karack. Ten minutes went by and then it came again. . .out of the blue. . .out of the night. . .from behind the dresser. . .the unmistakable irritating sound we had learned so well the night before.

It was war! Lights, action, take the offensive. I realized that if I did not find him there would be no sleep for me or Beverly. Armed with a rolled newspaper, a broom, a yardstick and a giant flashlight with which to see him, flush him out, swat him or catch him, I entered the battlefield. After shaking the dresser and poking the dust beneath it with the yard stick, I stepped back and shined the light on the floor. Glory be! There he was, sitting on the rug by the right leg of the dresser, probably stunned by the activity and bewildered by the spotlight that blinded him. Like a large praying mantis, I pounced on the enemy, capturing him in my right hand and holding it tightly closed. Running to the front door, I threw the frightened, noisy pestilence into the bushes where, I am sure, he was as relieved to find himself as we were to see him gone

The rest of the night brought quiet, rest, peace to both of us, but we will long remember the night of the cricket.

A VISIT TO 1776

Recently we climbed aboard our bus and headed for a trip back in history to the time when the colonies were fighting for their independence from England. Our destination was Musgrove Mill State Park, the scene of one of the many battles that took place in South Carolina.

We disembarked and entered the park's visitor's center, where a park ranger welcomed us. He showed us a topographical map of the battle. It was one of the first battles, or skirmishes, in which the colonial militia stopped a larger company of British soldiers. We examined the weapons that each side used as well as the uniforms and clothing that was worn. We learned a great deal about South Carolina's part in our war for independence.

We boarded our bus again and drove to Musgrove Falls, near where the actual fighting took place. We had to hurry to get back for dinner. The trip was one of many enjoyable trips that Clinton Presbyterian Community provides for us.

I WANT TO BE A WATCH CAT!

In the past I have tried out many occupations. I have told you about some of them, like: being a file clerk, being a bed tester, a food-tester, being a lap cat and a model builder. Now I have decided that it would be nice to be a watch cat. From what I have observed, a watch dog just sits around and watches. That seems like a perfect occupation for a cat. When the sun is shining, I could just lie on the front steps or on the deck and watch what is happening around me. I might even get in a few winks. As you know, we cats spend a lot of time sleeping, but we always keep one eye slightly open. Without exerting much effort we always know what is happening around us. That makes us perfect for the job of watching. My staff always comes to let me in if it rains or if anything unusual is about to happen, so I am never in any danger.

Yes, I think being a watch cat seems the perfect occupation for me. I think I will give it a try, at least until it rains or night-time comes. LB

STEERING BY A STAR

BETTER NEVER THAN LATE?

The other Sunday Beverly and I got to church to find that the service had already started. When we opened the door, everyone was standing, singing a hymn. I whispered to Beverly, "They have just started so we are not very late." We slipped into the only empty pew about half way to the front. To our surprise, everyone remained standing when the music stopped; the minister came down and pronounced the benediction. It was then that I realized that sometimes never is better than late.

I almost feel that way about this issue. It was started in May and was postponed, put off and procrastinated until September. It is not exactly current events but Lady Bean told me to send it anyway.

MY EIGHTY-SIXTH BIRTHDAY

I am celebrating my 86th birthday. It is good to be alive and still reasonably active. I am sitting at my cluttered desk with unfinished projects I gaze at the computer, ham radio, video projects around me.

- I think of the newsletters, blogs and books I want to write.
- I think about the carport full of wood still to be cut, shaped and put together.
- I think of all the model airplanes waiting to be built and flown.
- I imagine all the pictures yet to be taken and edited.
- I dream of places I still would like to visit.

Then I figure up the hours, days, months I need to complete all my books, projects, activities and dreams. It is then I realize that it will take me at least ten more years to finish what I have started, without starting anything new. It is such an astounding revelation that I doze off as I think of it. Zzzzzzz. . .*On my 96th birthday I am sitting in my newly-built chair at my new, shiny and clear desk, am looking at my stack of newly written books. I am looking at my finished airplanes hanging from the ceiling. I have finished all my writings on my perfectly working, wireless computer and I am talking to China on my refurbished radio. The pictures in my ever-changing picture frame remind me of my many recent trips. My room is tidy with no clutter lying on my bed.*

A crash from DVDs falling off of my crowded desk jolts me wide awake. It is my 86th birthday and the multitude of things to do is still out in front of me. I realize that I will be at least ninety-six years old before I finish all that I have already started. Better get to work! But first there is time for me to complete my nap.

FROM THE PAST

The other day while reviewing one of our trips on *Karisto*, I came across this theological reflection that I thought might be of interest. It was written while doing an outside passage from North Carolina to Florida.

STEERING BY A STAR

It was a clear night in late January and the sky was alive with stars. The moon had not yet broken the plane of the horizon and the sailing vessel, *Karisto*, was far enough from shore to be well clear of any land lights or light pollution. The wind was blowing about ten knots off of our beam and *Karisto* was fairly dancing along under full sail. It was the kind of night a sailor dreams about, with enough wind but not too much, and enough chop to send spray back along the side but not over the gunnels.

As I took my watch at the wheel the compass showed 265 degrees. Watching the needle of the compass swing with the changing waves, I would make corrections until the needle showed the corrected course. It was much easier to look up and find a star close on the forward horizon to steer by. One need only see that speck of light in the same position to hold course, at least for a short period of time. Lost in the magic of the night and the dance of the ship through the waves, I was startled by the sound of flapping canvas and was aware that the sails no longer held the wind; the vessel was slowing to a crawl. It was then that I realized that the tiny dot of light, the star I had been steering by, was in reality a reflection of my own running light on the forward rail. I could have steered in any direction and would have been following my own light.

It made me stop and think. How often we make that mistake in our lives. We have set the directions of our lives on lofty and accurate goals, and that goal is somewhere far in front, toward which we should move. But we lose sight of it for an instant and when we look back we catch the reflection of where we are and what we are doing. With the light of that false star we can wander in circles until we realize that we have lost sight of our goal, changed our direction, and perhaps even stilled the wind of noble desire.

It is then we need to check our life's compass and our highest goals, reset our direction and find and follow the true light that will truly lead us home. Paul may have said it best when he wrote, *"I set my direction toward the prize of the high calling of God in Christ Jesus."*

TO MY GRANDCHILDREN

Your grandfather died before your father and mother were born. I wish he could have known you and you could have known him. He was a kind and gentle man who was interested in many things. He had wanted to be an architect but never had the opportunity of college. I often think of him and wish I had the chance to show him some of the things that have happened since his death in 1956. I wish you could take your granddad for a ride in your car or van. He was good at mechanical things and often marveled at how the engine in our 1939 Chevy could keep running mile after mile for its fifty-thousand-mile lifetime. He would be awed at the comfort we take for granted. . .the traffic we accept as inevitable, and the gadgets that are part of the modern car. Take him on the Interstates and over some of the maze of bridges and highways that we travel every day. In his day, he would travel on the futuristic highways on the pages of *Popular Mechanics*.

I wish you could show him your computer or tablet. It would seem like a magic miracle at first, but I believe he would accept and immediately start experimenting with the word processor. He probably would have gotten on Facebook and Twitter. He used to write me letters on an old manual typewriter and illustrate them with stick drawings. Dad's work involved cutting and pasting tiny letters and numbers, holding in place with tweezers as he prepared the copy for photographing and printing. He would have found it wonderful to simply delete, change, save and print on the computer. Long evenings of work would be done in minutes. Maybe you could take him to a modern airport where he could see the changes that have taken place in air travel. Still, I think you would rather travel by car and enjoy the scenery. On our summer vacations to the mountains, dad would often comment on the beauty through which we drove and how much space there was in our great country. He had always planned to travel around the United States after retirement, a dream that was unfulfilled. Maybe you could take him to Cape Canaveral Space Center and assure him we really went to the moon. While there we could visit a large cruise ship, which is floating city. Together, you could visit cities and see how tall and majestic the buildings have become. Show him how we call the world from our cell phones. Let him look at the pictures from the Hubble Telescope. Tell him of the expanding universe.

Let me show him my workshop. Saturday afternoons would find dad in his workshop on the second floor of our wooden garage. Dad could do most anything with wood. His father was a builder and the carpenter genes were certainly passed on. His pride and joy was a large carpenter's work table which he found in a yard sale. It had the big, wooden screw vices on the front and end and was solid and heavy. A few homemade power tools had been fashioned to run on a shaft, driven by an old washing machine motor. I would love to take him to the shop that I have now, show him the power tools and equipment that he never could afford in depression days. With all the tools in the shop, I never could make things fit together so neatly nor look as good as he did with a simple saw, chisel, hammer and a hand sander. I am sure he would put on an old carpenter's apron, stick a pencil behind his ear, and pick up a small square and begin to create something for the house or yard. There are many things I would like you to show your grandfather, but most of all I would like him to get to know you, his grandchildren. Introduce him to your mother and father that he never had the privilege of knowing. He would be very proud of them and of you. He would have brushed away a tear of joy as he hugged each of you. He would swell with pride as you told him of your parents' work, your schooling, and your own work. He would have been so interested at the accomplishments and plans of each of you. All this and much, much more, I would like you to show your grandfather. But somehow, someway, I have the feeling (or is it my hope and faith?) that he already knows and is very, very proud.

KEEP THE WINDOWS OPEN

In the mountain church that we attend there is no air-conditioning for the sanctuary and the windows are always open in the warm months. Slowly rotating fans keep the air circulating. Sometimes it is a little warm, but that is offset by the benefits that open windows bring. Bird songs come drifting in. Like soft musical background, we hear muffled voices and the sound of children playing in the park across the street. A muffle-less car or motorcycle sometimes interrupts the dignity of worship. But best of all, we are letting the world into the church.

Maybe that is one of the problems of the church today. We seal ourselves in a cocoon of comfort and like-mindedness. We say we want the world to come and join us but we are too comfortable with our bundle of warm friendship. By and large, we agree with one another and are not challenged by the new and different. In our age of air-conditioned comfort we have closed the windows to the laughter, interruptions and cries of the world around us. This is not bad for a social group, but it is not what the church was intended to be.

Now I know it is impractical to keep all church windows open, but it may give us food for thought as to the purpose and mission of the church. Maybe I have heard a song, or maybe one should be written, that sings:

Open the windows of my heart
And let the world flow in.
Open the windows of my church
And let the outside in.
That through the open windows
Of my heart and of my church
The love of God may flow to all the world.

WEDDINGS AND FUNERALS AND THE LIKE

We attended the wedding of our grandson the other week. It was a great event with all the beauty, pomp and ceremony that accompany such an occasion. Last year I attended the memorial service for a family member. Both events were quite different but they had one thing in common. They brought family members, many of whom had not seen each other for a long time, together. At one event I met cousins that I played with when very young and had not seen since. At the other it was rewarding to see children, grandchildren and cousins enjoying the reunion of family. There may be planned reunions but they are few and far between and often are not given the highest priority. The silver linings at sad events and the extra joy of happy times can be seen in families coming together, renewing kinship bonds and rekindling the love that makes us family.

THE YARD NEXT DOOR

I really like the yard next door. When I take my man-staff for a walk, I like to slip over there. It has real grass while my yard has a lot of clover and clay. There are some beautiful flowers on the edge toward my house and there is a narrow wooden walkway through the flowers, made just for me. The thick hedge along the road keeps those big, noisy trucks away.

I really like the little boy they call Bryson who comes to visit. But he always carries a couple of sticks in his hands and is always poking the ground, so I am not sure what else he might do with those sticks.

Of course, I have to look back and check on my man-staff. He usually stays in our carport or stands by the van so I can keep an eye on him. Sometimes he wants to go in before I do and he calls me. If I am about ready to go in, I humor him and slowly come back. Once in a while, I have to let him know who is boss. I want to stay longer or go farther, so I just ignore him. Then he comes and stands in front of me. I will turn around but stand my ground. When he touches my rump, I really voice my displeasure with a full-blown Siamese growl. Usually, I give in and slowly move toward home, voicing my displeasure with my deep growl. Sometimes, I have to stand up to him and refuse to move. Then he picks me up and holds me tightly. I kind of like that but would not let him know it for the world, so I keep up my Siamese snarls. (I know he is the alpha cat so I dare not protest too much.)

When we get to the front steps he puts me down so I can walk in and not be embarrassed in front of my lady-staff. (We have an understanding.) There are times when I will walk to the back, ask to take him out again, and we start all over. This time in the back yard!

There are times when I like to stay in my own carport or on the seat of the golf cart, but I really like the yard next door. LB

NO LONGER ALONE

It is with a heavy heart that I prepare this issue. For many years Beverly and I have found great pleasure in sending stories of our lives and miscellaneous trivia in this newsletter. Today it is hard to write, and it is with a broken heart that I share this page from my journal.

FROM MY JOURNAL (November 13, 2015)

The beautiful red, yellow and orange leaves of the season have fallen, blown down by the winds of unexpected events. A short time ago they were new and green and full of life and anticipation. Today green leaves and much, much more are only memories. The stark bare skeletal trees of reality stand as sentinels of the past. For me, the sky is grey and weeping and there is a chill in the air.

Beverly died last night at 11:28.

She has moved from one home to another. She has embarked on a new and wonderful adventure, far better than other adventures we have shared together. She will be welcomed by the saints in glory and will be gather in by her waiting family. She is no longer alone.

I had stayed with her most of the day, held her limp hand and prayed that God would release her from her prison with a one-way window. God answered my prayer. Tonight I returned to her room and sat with the empty house in which she lived for eighty-six wonderful, but sometimes painful, years. She was no longer there and I was glad.

A few days ago, I looked up and saw black clouds all around me. Just as I felt engulfed in darkness, the setting sun's brilliant light suddenly burst above black clouds. It came like a glowing crown upon encircling gloom. The sun-light sat upon the clouds, bringing light to all the world below and the darkness could not put it out.

So it is with the new adventure we call death.

The severe stroke that locked Beverly in a cage that allowed her to hear but not to speak or move occurred during church on October 29. Beverly was treated and cared for in Laurens Hospital, Greenville Memorial Hospital and in Hospice of Lauren County. After almost a month of captivity, the Lord released her and took her to a home prepared for her.

A memorial service was held for Beverly in the chapel of the Clinton Presbyterian Home on November 19th. A second memorial service will be held in the Nacoochee Presbyterian Church, where she was a member, on December 6th.

Perhaps in days to come I will feel the urge to continue this newsletter, but for now I can only pay tribute to one who brought joy, companionship and love into my life. Her life was not always easy or free of pain, but it was always vibrant and filled with happiness. The way she reached out to others and brought joy to those around her is attested by the multitude of cards, letters, and calls from friends in many places.

FROM MY JOURNAL (November 29, 2015)

It is Sunday morning, one month after Beverly and I set out to preach at Cane Creek and set in motion the stroke that took Beverly home. For the first time since then, I am getting ready to go to a church to lead worship and preach. It will be the first time in many years that I have gone alone and I am a little frightened. The sermon is ready and I am looking forward to preaching, but I wonder if my emotions are up to the task. The events of the past days have sapped my strength and I am feebler than ever before. The day looks much the same as it did a month ago. The sun is shining and it is warm for late November. The colorful fall foliage is gone and the drabness of early winter matches my feelings. It is something of a new beginning for me but it will be a lonesome ride. Surely, the Lord will be with me and cover my anxiety with the power of preaching. I look forward to going to a new church, to meeting new people and to sharing a message of thanksgiving and hope. But I will miss the one who always sat near the front of the church and cheered and prayed me on.

Later that day, the service went well. Rocky Creek Presbyterian Church is a lovely red brick country church. The congregation was warm and friendly. As I lead the service, I looked down at the second pew to my left where Beverly always sat. It was empty, but I had the feeling that Beverly was there in spirit. The prayer of thanksgiving for the saints who had died had special meaning.

CONFUSED

Something is going on and I do not understand it. My man-staff is here part of the time but my lady-staff is not. I am lonesome for the noise and activity that usually goes on. Oh, I am used to them going off, but they always come back and each of them pets me and tells me how beautiful I am. Now my man-staff is the only one that talks to me. I know that I bonded with him long ago but I also remember that it was the lady that heard my anguished meow from a cage. She reached out and petted me through the wire wall and I purred. When he came back from looking at some useless dogs, she said with authority. We'll take that one! She pointed to me. Recently I have spent more time with her as we took naps or watched TV while my man-staff was outside or on that noisy radio of his.

Today I searched all over the house, even looking under the beds and in the closets. When I took my man-staff to walk, I even look inside the van. My man-staff seems sad too, so I try to curl up as close to him as I can. He reaches out and strokes me and that seems to help him and me. I will continue to miss my lady-staff and hope that someday I will see her come through the door. I bet my man-staff also wishes she would come home. LB

MEMORIAL SERVICES

Many of you have asked me to give more information about the memorial services for Beverly. A good portion of this newsletter is devoted to answering your requests.

On November 19th, exactly one week after Beverly's death, a memorial service was held in the chapel of the Clinton Presbyterian Community. The Rev. Debbie Johnson officiated and Dr. Jeri Perkins and Dr. Tim Womack took part. Charles Coker played the same piano that Beverly had played for a memorial service just a week before her stroke. It was a beautiful and appropriate service, well attended by friends from the home and the community. The service paid tribute to Beverly and attested to her faith and the faith of her family.

Family came from New Jersey, North Carolina and Florida. There was family in every room and young people sleeping on sofas and air mattresses. We had to take care where we stepped. LB and I were relegated to the basement workshop where there was a comfortable sofa-bed. My nieces, Ann and Melinda, were our hostesses on Saturday night in Ann's lovely home in Sky Lake. There was great food but even greater fellowship as cousins, uncles, aunts and friends got reacquainted. It was a silver lining to a sad occasion. Saturday night was a long night for me. Although there were children and grandchildren all over the house, I felt very much alone.

On Sunday, December 6th a memorial service was held in Nacoochee Presbyterian Church where Beverly was a member. The service was a beautiful tribute to Beverly. All participants did their parts well with words of comfort and affection. Grandson Jonathan played part of the prelude. Beverly would have been proud of him. Rev. Bob Prim, our pastor, led the service and delivered an excellent sermon and eulogy. Granddaughter Savannah read scripture from Corinthians 13. Son, Francis M. Womack, III, spoke of Beverly with tenderness, giving thanks for the joy she brought to his father. Granddaughter Lindsay spoke of Beverly with compassion and love, and son Timothy Womack brought tears and laughter as he told of the many adventures Beverly and Francis had enjoyed together, traveling, sailing and being together since we were married at the age of seventy. He read a portion from his father's journal, written on the night Beverly died. The church choir had wanted to come to Clinton to sing for Beverly, plans thwarted by her death. They sang beautifully at the service. The church was filled with members and friends from the community and from the flying and radio clubs. Following the service, members of the church had prepared a reception with many good refreshments. A table displaying the symbols of Beverly's life was in the reception area.

For a service filled with so much emotion, it was a joyful celebration of Beverly's life and a tribute to her faith as she moved into that new adventure called death.

THE MORAVIAN STAR

I am a couple of weeks late but I finally got it up. To be honest I had forgotten all about it until I struggled up the attic ladder and saw the points of the star poking out of a protective trash bag. It was a struggle to get it down the ladder but finally it was down and cleaned up. The same hook that held it last year was in place just inside the carport. It was soon up and as dusk fell it spread light in the community and in my heart. We had used that same star in Sunset Beach, Ocala, Sky Lake and last year in Clinton. It is the symbol of the season that is upon us.

THE CHRISTMAS TREE

I had debated with myself about putting the Christmas tree up this year. But tradition soon won out. I cannot remember a Christmas that was without a decorated tree. I remember how excited I was to go with my father to pick out and purchase the best tree on the lot. It was tall enough to almost reach the ceiling and dad would us a ladder to carefully place each decoration in an exact place. As roles flipped and I became the dad, I remember many trees and many small hands eager to hand up decorations. There was the year we waited too long to get a good tree and settled for a "Charlie Brown" pine tree. In West Virginia we cut our tree and dragged it home through the snow. In Sunset Beach and in Ocala the tree, alive with lights and spinning ornaments, was the highlight of our many Christmas drop-ins.

Even though it brought a tear or two as Lady Bean and I set and lighted the tree, how could I even thing of think of not having a tree? I will get some friends to help me with the decoration and the tree will bring joy and light together with many memories.

A BOX OF DECORATIONS

I brought many boxes of Christmas out of the attic. (I did not know we had saved so much "stuff.") But one box caught my attention. It was carefully protected and marked fragile. When I opened it, decades of Christmas flashed across my mind. A few remained from my childhood. There were little painted ones done by little fingers on an icy day. I held painted sand dollars and little sailboats from friends at the shore. There were remembrances from every place we served and tokens from places we had visited. As I touched them, one by one, it seemed most of my eighty-six years flashed before me. Most of them will go on this year's tree but they will soon be passed on to family or boxed up for the next generation to dispense. This year they will enhance the tree and brighten the Christmas season.

LONELY

It has been rather lonely around here since my lady-staff went away. I know my man-staff wonders why I am under his feet all the time or in the chair right next to him. I used to be rather independent and would sleep on the sofa or in the toy room rather than in the big bedroom. Now I almost beat him to bed and claim my spot right at the bend of his knees. He never says anything about it and sometime reaches down to pet me. I wonder if he knows why I am always underfoot or under knee?

A long time ago, when I was very young, I woke up from a nap and found that my mother had gone away. I looked for her but never saw her again. Later, my sister and I were taken to a place with lots of other cats. After a few days my sister disappeared and I never saw her again. The next day the lady who would become my lady-staff saw me in a cage, petted me and told my man-staff-to-be that they would take me home. That all happened a long time ago and we have been very happy as a family. I have been able to train them well.

Now my lady-staff has gone away and I cannot find her. I am very afraid that my man-staff is going to go away too. If he did, I don't know what I would do. So I watch him very carefully. I stay under his feet and sleep on his bed. When he goes away, I lie on the back of the sofa by the window and watch for him to come back. I take him to walk regularly and do not let him get too far away. I sit with him on the sofa and pretend I like that silly picture box and when he is playing with his radio I sit in the chair next to him.

I try to show him how much I would miss him. I really hope he does not go away like the others. I purr about that every night. LB

THE BEST NEW YEAR POSSIBLE

Lady Bean and I wish for you and yours the best New Year possible.

- May you find joy and happiness.
- May our world find peace and healing.
- May the Lord bless and keep you and those you love, and those who need your love.

BEVERLY'S REVENGE!

Some of the articles in this news letter have been taken from writings in my journal. If they seem somewhat disjointed, it is because I am still a little disjointed by the events of the past year. Christmas and the beginning of 2016 has been different, both joyful and sad. This issue may reflect some of the feelings of the season.

LAST BOX DOWN!

After coming home from a good dinner at the bistro, I decided to get the rest of the Christmas boxes from the attic. Last time I climbed to the attic, I realized I was not in the best shape, so I put my cell phone in my pocket, just in case.

It was harder and harder to make those last three steps from the ladder into the attic. I felt my feet and legs wanting to give way. I took a careful hold onto the timber braces and ventilation pipe and swung myself onto the attic floor. I selected five boxes that I felt I needed, stacked them by the stairwell and reversed the process of climbing the ladder. By the second box, I realized that I was placing myself at risk of falling with unknown results. I thought to myself, this is the last trip from the attic for these boxes as they will not be going back. Inside each box was a world of treasures, of no value except to stimulate memories of Christmases long ago. I thought of the different attics that had held these same boxes and how easy it was to almost run up and down the steps. Now, each step down, balancing a cardboard box, seemed more difficult than the last. In fact, it was foolish to place myself in danger of falling. At eighty-six years of age, either the boxes would never return to the attic or someone else would carry them. It was a sobering thought for one who had thought himself to be invincible.

There were still a few more boxes up there, but they would have to stay, at least for now. As I folded the attic ladder and snapped it into place, I realized that for me, this was the last box down.

CHRISTMAS EVE AND LOOKING BACK

It has been a strange Christmas Eve for me. I was up early this morning to travel in the rain to Greenwood where the hematologist gave me some blood to boast my low hemoglobin. When I returned, the dining hall was almost empty but I was in time to get some barbecue and potato salad.

There is a lot to do but nothing I really want to do, so I worked on my antenna and straightened the radio desk. At 4:00 I went to vespers in the chapel. Only a few of the residents were there, many with family or friends. I had been invited to my neighbor's home for a light supper. After supper and a nice visit, I came home and the house seemed emptier than ever. I put some tinsel on the Christmas tree and thought about Christmas Eves of the past.

I looked at a picture from an old Christmas card showing our family gathered round the tree when I was about fourteen years old. It opened my memory to many wonderful Christmases of my childhood.

My thoughts raced ahead to the first Christmas Eve in the little four-room house at my first church. Jackie and I had been married less than a year and after the service at the church friends came over and shared our first Christmas Eve. The next year, it was all about our Christmas present of a four-month-old baby boy.

I think of many Christmas Eves with children growing up. I remember the privilege of preparing Santa Claus in the wee hours of Christmas morning and the confusion and excitement of leading the children from their bedroom into the wonder land that was Christmas morning.

I think of Christmas Eve in the snows of West Virginia and in the warmer climes of Florida when children were almost grown. There were the many drop-ins in Sunset Beach with Jackie and our friends. I think of the joy of Christmas Eve when children had returned from college. The Christmas Eve after Jackie died was spent with friends on B dock, gathered in the salon of a large sailing vessel where we told tall tales and shared the loneliness we all felt.

I remember the Christmas Eves with Beverly and the four or five drop-ins we held each year for our friends in Florida. I think of preaching on Christmas Eve and walking out of the church with lighted candles singing Silent Night, Holy Night. . .holding hands in the cool December air for the benediction.

Tonight is Christmas Eve and I am alone with my memories. It would be bad if there were no memories for they give me comfort and even joy. I have been blessed with eighty-six years of Christmas memories. I would be lost without them and I give thanks for the gifts of many great Christmas Eves with a great family, great wives and great children and friends.

THE LAST CHRISTMAS ARTICLE

I was proud of myself. Mary Glenn had packed and taken most of the Christmas boxes to the attic. Yesterday I had completed the job with the Moravian Advent Star and an additional box or two. There was nothing around to remind me of 2015 Christmas and I could concentrate on the New Year.

On New Year's Day I was eating breakfast when I heard it. . .the musical strains of "O Holy Night" filling the room with the spirit of Christmas. There it was. . .on the wall in front of me, the last vestige of the season past. . .the Christmas clock that played a different carol each hour. I listened to the chimes and thought about the many times I had instructed my congregations to make Christmas last all year. Should I leave it up or take it down? Take it down, of course. I removed the batteries, packed the clock in a Christmas bag and sat it in the hall, waiting for my next trip to the attic. I wondered if there were other Christmas items lurking in the house.

NEW YEAR'S EVE AND IMAGINATION

It is New Year's Eve and I have been watching football. I have been alone all afternoon. I guess the emptiness of the house and the sound of a New Year's celebration going on in a nearby community has added to my loneliness. But it was while I was fixing supper that my imagination began to work on me. When I sat down to eat, Lady Bean jumped into the chair beside me, where Beverly always sat. She did not curl up and go to sleep but rather sat straight up as if she was joining me for supper. While I washed the dishes and cleaned up, she turned around and watched intently as if to see things were getting clean. When I went to the living room sofa, she did not settle in to sleep but sat beside me and looked toward the TV. Occasionally, she would reach out a paw to touch me.

Now I really do not believe that the spirit world comes back to visit in an animal of their choice, but if I did, I would swear that Beverly had taken over Lady Bean. I remembered last night when I woke up about 2:00 a.m. and found the cat had left her basket and was close beside me, her head resting on my arm. Then, earlier today, when I was struggling to take a few boxes up the steps to the attic, Lady Bean sat right beside the ladder and meowed loudly as if she was pleading with me not to go up the ladder. Beverly would have done these same things.

Now I know this is all a figment of my imagination and Lady Bean is the same spoiled cat she has always been. I know spirits do not return to comfort or chide me in actions of a cat. It is just my loneliness and need for companionship. But Lady Bean has just climbed into the chair next to my computer and is looking at the screen as if she wants to correct my grammar and spelling. . .just like Beverly used to do.

Guess it is time to stop thinking and go to bed. I'll be all right in the morning when it will be a brand new year.

BEVERLY'S REVENGE

She almost got me back! I was going through her multitude of pocket books when I found a strange object. It had its own cloth container so I knew it was special. After examining the tube with a small opening on one end and a spring inside, I determined it to be either a device for giving the cat a pill or a pill splitter for stubborn pills. Naturally, I had to find out how it worked. It had a pill stuck in on end and the spring was already tensioned. I held it out and pulled the latch that acted as a trigger. There was a loud bang, a tiny, burning projectile shot out of the end, making an arc across the room. The room filled with white smoke and my eyes began to water. As I left the room to catch my breath, I realized that the smoke was tear gas and the little "pill crusher" was really a tear gas gun to protect my lady from those who would do her harm.

She almost repaid me for all the times I fussed at her for being a little late or not doing exactly what I thought she should be doing. As I remember the event, I think of it as "Beverly's Revenge."

I GOT A CHRISTMAS PRESENT!

I wasn't at all sure of what was going on. My man-staff moved my sofa from its place in front of the window and that really upset me because I could no longer lay up there and watch the world go by. Then he replaced my sofa with a tree. . .not a regular tree but one with lights and little hanging things that I was not allowed to touch. The room was full of funny looking things, most of them dressed in red. My man-staff would turn on the tree lights and then go sit on the sofa. He acted very sad so I would go over and get close to him on the sofa. He liked me to put my head in his hand and I liked it too.

On Christmas Day he opened his package that was under the tree. I just watched until he came and took me to the tree. There was a little package with my name on it. It smelled good so I tore into the red paper. Inside was a little cloth animal that was filled with catnip. I pawed it, chewed it and rolled over on it. I looked up and purred. My man-staff said it was from Santa Claus but I think it really came from my man-staff. I was happy. I did get a Christmas present! It was a good day. A few days later, they removed the tree and put my sofa back under my window. That was the best Christmas present of all. LB

THE SPECIALIST

Today I went to a doctor who was to track down something that was causing low iron in my profile. She reminded me of a definition of a specialist that most of you may know: *A specialist is one who knows more and more about less and less.* Now I know that we need those who zero in on certain things. I know they are a very important part of the medical profession. But somehow she reminded me of what we have sacrificed as we have made big gains in medicine.

She looked more at her i-pad than she did at me. She asked questions and furiously made notes. She made no hands on examination since her nurse had already entered the data about my weight, temperature, blood pressure, etc. She compared the data from last month with today's data and even showed me the screen with its charts and wavy lines. I could neither read it nor understand it. When she began telling me about all the tests that she wanted me to take and what they would tell, her eyes began to sparkle with excitement.

What disappointed me was that she never really saw me as a whole person. She never asked about how or when my problems began. Although I gave her every chance and clue, she never recognized my depression. My health was all about statistics and nothing about how I was feeling nor why I was really there.

I guess I long for something that has passed. I remember a doctor that at least knew my name without reading a chart and looked at me as a real person and not a bundle of blood vessels and bones covered with flesh to be examined and dissected. Maybe I am expecting too much, longing for something that can never be, amid today's demands and mountains of paper work.

On the way home, I felt worse than I did on the way over. I will go on with the tests, although reluctantly. Guess I still long for a doctor who calls my name while pressing my tongue down with a wooden depressor and tells me to say: AHHHH!

ASHES

A number of you have asked me about the service in NPC and about taking Beverly's ashes to Florida. Here is the story of these two events. I hope to write more upbeat stories in issues to come. Thank you all for your patience, love, interest and friendship.

MEMORIAL SERVICE IN SAUTEE

Our family began gathering in Sky Lake on Friday, Dec. 4th. On Saturday evening we gathered at the home of Ann where she and Melinda provided a lovely dinner for all of us. It was a great time of renewing relationships and preparing for the day ahead.

Nacoochee Presbyterian Church, where Beverly had been a member, was the setting for her second memorial service. The church was very much a part of our lives, having sung in the choir and taken part in many activities. The family gathered in the fellowship room at 10:30. We were ushered into the sanctuary filled with friends and family.

Rev. Bob Prim conducted the service and reminded us of God's love and faithfulness as well as paying tribute to Beverly for her service to the church. I was very proud of my children and grandchildren who took part in the service. They had accepted Beverly as part of our family even as she had accepted them as her own. The choir sang a favorite hymn of hers before the benediction. It was truly a service of worship as well as a memorial service.

I am sure that Beverly was pleased and smiling, with perhaps a small tear for the outpouring of thanksgiving for her life and love.

Go now in peace, never be afraid.
God will go with you each hour of every day.
Go now in faith, steadfast, strong and true,
Know God will guide you in all you do.

THE BURIAL

On Sunday morning, Feb. 4th I preached at the ARP church in Clinton. The car was packed for a trip to Jacksonville, FL, where we would bury Beverly's ashes. The walnut box, with symbols on the sides, was strapped into the passenger seat. It was the last time Beverly would ride with me to church. After church I began the drive south. I stopped at Bluffton, SC, to spend the night with my friends Murray and Ayers. Another close friend, Don, met me there. The next morning we traveled on to Jacksonville.

After supper with friends from Ocala, we returned to our motel. The next morning we drove to Evergreen Cemetery where friends from out of town met us and we continued to Beverly's family plot. Evergreen is an old, beautiful cemetery filled with large oak trees. My family is buried there as well.

A tent and chairs had been set up for us at the gravesite. Some friends and family had already arrived. We placed the box that held the ashes on a table over her grave. Tim had come up from Vero Beach to again officiate in the service. The service was dignified yet informal. Friends were asked to speak if they liked and a number spoke of the times they had known Beverly. It ranged from childhood, through youth groups to adulthood. The service was appropriate but it was not a sad service; rather, a celebration of faith home-going. After a lunch with family, we returned to Bluffton and the next day returned to our homes. It was a time of closure for me and I appreciated all those who came.

GOING BACK TO WORK

On February 21 I am going back to work. . .I will be preaching in Providence ARP church until Easter. I have been doing supply preaching most every Sunday but it will be good to have a series in one church where I can get to know the people and be a pastor as well as a preacher. I look forward to walking through the season of Lent with some very nice people in the Providence church.

RAIN IN THE NIGHT

It rained last night. It was not the steady rain that brought flooding earlier in the year. It was not the gentle rain that brings good sleep. The rain last night came pounding down, rattling the shingles and shaking the blankets on the bed. It came in two waves, as if it could not sustain the rate of falling water. The pounding water stopped almost as quickly as it came. This morning, I look out of my window and the sun is shining as if to apologize for the night's pounding rain.

It has been a strange year for weather. First there was summer in December. February brought predictions of snow and ice which never really happened. All around us there was snow but I-385 seemed to be a wall of protection for our small town. Weather forecasters were scratching their heads and even apologizing.

It rained last night and it will rain again, maybe even snow and freeze, but sunshine and rising temperatures encourage me to scratch up my garden spot and get ready for spring which, I hope, cannot be far away.

REVERSE MINISTRY

When I first finished seminary I was sure I had the answer to almost everything. I felt my calling was to proclaim, teach, speak out and give wise council. After sixty years of ministry, I still believe, with all my heart, I am still called to do this, but my perception of how this is most effectively done has changed radically. I call it "reverse ministry." In other words, I am called to listen as well as to speak. This is hard for most of us. We are more likely to be remembered for our "much speaking" rather than our intensive listening.

Reverse ministry has been brought home to me in the place in which I live. Many, yes most, of the people here spend a great deal of their time living in the past. . .there is so much more past than future. They want someone to listen to their stories, their history, their feelings, their fears and their concerns. Then, maybe, we can slip in a word of encouragement and a prayer of hope. This is what I call reverse ministry. I have said very little and yet I have preached an eloquent sermon.

One of the ladies in CPC prides herself on being able to give a good shoulder massage. She moves around the dining hall after lunch massaging many shoulders. It feels good. It is her gift to each person, perhaps her only gift. The other day, one of the diners squirmed and told her he did not need her help. He may not, but she needed it.

By accepting the small things that others have to say or give, by listening when we would rather be talking and by sharing our selves rather than our words of wisdom we are doing reverse ministry. Try it; you'll like it. . .and so will they!

DIFFERENCES

Things have been different around here lately. It is either raining or it is too cold to go outside. I have tried every door in the house. I have also noticed that my man-staff has been acting strangely. He talks to me a lot more than he ever did. He wants me around him almost all the time. I can hardly get a good nap in the afternoon because he keeps wanting me to get in the chair next to him or sit on the sofa with him while he watches that silly TV. He pets me a lot more than he used to and sometimes even brushes me. I guess he is lonely, too.

I will try to make him feel better by humoring him and staying under his feet, in front of his computer screen or beside him on the sofa. This morning I even sat in the chair next to him at break-fast table.

I dare not let him know, but I kind of like staying close to him, too. LB

Lady Bean has become more and more possessive lately. I always knew she thought she owned the place, but lately she seems to be constantly under foot. She is using her voice a lot more and I feel obliged to answer her. I know she is a little lonely so I let her get on the computer table and in the chair beside me. But when she tries to curl up in my chair, which is made for one person, I feel a little used. I even am awakened at night by a loud purring noise, and have to move over because a cat wants sleep beside me. Maybe I spoil her too much but she is a lot of company.

I dare not tell her, but it makes me feel better to have close company, even if it is only a cat.

KIDNAPPED!

*There's a long, long trail a-winding. . .*that will take us through the adventures of the past few weeks. It all started on Monday, March 7th. I had been packing the car, a little at a time, to keep Lady Bean from knowing she would be traveling to Sky Lake with me. It was wasted effort. When I came back from a meeting and a quick lunch on Monday, she was in her remote hiding place under the bed. An hour of effort brought her out cussing and fuming. The beginning of our trip to the mountains was uneventful until the road disappeared in front of me.

As I came into the town of Pelzer, I felt a little weak and then a curtain came down over my eyes, either from dozing off or passing out. I tried to pull to the side and stop but it was too late. I felt a jolt and the next thing I knew a truck driver was asking if I was alright. The EMS, local police and state troopers soon showed up. I was put in the EMS vehicle and tied up with test instruments. I knew from looking at the front of my van that it was going nowhere on its own. Lady Bean was looking out the window. The siren started and we were off to Greenville Memorial Hospital. (Lady Bean can tell her own story.) Then came six hours in the hall of the emergency room, a private room for the night with heart monitors and a device that gave me a pint of blood. I felt alright, a little shaken, tired and in need of sleep (which I did not get).

Mary Glenn came and collected some of my stuff from the car. There were clothes, radios, computers, a suitcase, etc. that filled the small hospital room, much to the displeasure of the nurses. Tuesday morning, they offered their hospitality for a few more days but I declined, much to their dismay. I checked myself out and neighbors rescued me from the hospital.

Wednesday the car was towed to Clinton where repairs would begin the next day. I was feeling OK. . .a little sore in the chest. . .tired and glad to be alive. The next week was filled with visits to doctors for check up. That will continue for some time as the try to increase my energy level. Maybe I am just getting older and should have less energy.

The van will come home on Monday, March 22 and I will soon try again for a successful trip to Sky Lake.

SPRING IS BEAUTIFUL

Spring is bust'n out all over
all over the meadows and the hills. . .

Some mornings are still cold, reminding us that winter does not want to turn loose, but there are signs of spring everywhere. As if defying the cold mornings, the Bradford pears have put on their springtime white. They are like beacons along the roadways. The tender new green of tiny leaves is bringing a fragile beauty to barren brown branches. Tiny flowers appear almost overnight and may be overlooked trodden under foot if we are not careful. The blossoms of the tulip tree bring a richness to the world while a new carpet of grass has suddenly grown beneath us. Birds are looking for the bird houses we made during the winter. There is the sound of children in the project not far away. I hear the music of the ice cream truck as he is surrounded by devotees of the driver's wares.

I welcome spring and what it brings. But spring brings a tinge of sadness. I wish I could share its beauty and walk hand in hand under the flowering trees. But spring also brings comfort and hope. Spring is beautiful and I will rejoice and be glad.

MONTREAT PAST

Montreat is a conference center of the Presbyterian Church located in a horseshoe valley high in the North Carolina Mountains. It was originally controlled by the Presbyterian Church, US, the Southern Presbyterian Church. Lake Susan, formed by a mountain stream, is in the middle. Ministers, missionaries and church people built modest summer homes and retirement homes. Assembly Inn, Anderson Auditorium, dormitories, lodges, a cafeteria, the Foreign Mission Building and other facilities were built to facilitate the summer conferences and visitors. A two-year college made use of the facilities in the winter.

Many would come to Montreat every year, some staying a week and others staying the whole summer. With activities such as conferences and study groups, the Boys' and Girls' clubs with planned events, it was heaven on earth for those of us who came with our families.

With reunion and changing times, Montreat has changed and although conferences are still held, affordable homes and vacations have become a thing of the past. Montreat is a town for those who can afford mountain homes.

In memory, I go back and relive the wonderful days and inspirational experiences that shaped my life. This story is one of many that I treasure. It is taken from my Easter sermon given at Providence ARP Church.

I had not thought of Miss Lucy in years until, in a worship service at the General Assembly, she was mentioned as an example of faith. Miss Lucy was a fixture in Montreat, as much a part of the setting as Lake Susan or Anderson Auditorium. You could expect to see her anywhere. . .or more accurately, you would expect to see her just where you would not expect to see her. That was what made Miss Lucy so unique.

She was always doing the unexpected, saying the unexpected, wearing the unexpected and turning up in unexpected places. She was different, irrepressible and serendipitous.

I first remember her during those long ago, wonderful summers in Montreat. I was in that "no man's land" age; not old enough to drive yet too old to be tied to apron strings. It was an age for rock-hopping, sandlot ball, belonging to the boys' club and bashfully admiring residents of the girls' club.

We all knew Miss Lucy. We laughed at her with the cruelty of immaturity. We made fun of the prim and proper way she walked. . .the way she stopped to admire a little mountain flower. . .the way she talked to the babbling stream and seemed to be listening for it to answer her. We spoke to her to hear laugh and to hear the unusual things she would say. We made fun of the way she dressed, like a style-less Mary Poppins. She seemed old to us but she must have been in her thirties.

Montreat, and our lives, would have been incomplete without her. One time in particular stands out in my memory. There must have been four or five of us wading, splashing and just enjoying the cool water of a pool held in the rocky hand of a mountain stream. Suddenly, she was there, standing by a Mountain Laurel on the path above us. She was smiling her outrageous smile. We stopped playing and waited, knowing that she had something to say.

"Now wasn't it nice of God to make such a beautiful place for you boys to play? I know you want to thank Him for what he has given you." That was all. With a knowing nod she turned and was gone down the roadside path. We exchanged grins, voiced a few unflattering remarks and returned to our business of play.

Since that time I have heard a thousand sermons, listened to a hundred theologians, read a library of books and have forgotten most of them, but I remember clearly that unexpected witness of Miss Lucy:"Wasn't it nice of God to make a beautiful place for you to play?" She saw what many of us fail to see: That in a world filled with terror and war there was hope; that in a land of pollution and ugliness, God provides havens of exquisite beauty for those who will look for them; that in broken lives and dreams, there is the promise of a better, happier day. She saw that beyond the thunder and judgment, the agony of a cross, the loneliness of death, there was an empty tomb, a resurrection and life eternal.

TRAIN CARS

Today I was stopped by one of those long, slow freight trains. Usually I would have tried to find a way around the train or would have found some diversion on this side of the tracks. But today I was caught in traffic and there was no way out.

As I counted cars, I was struck by their variety. There were box cars, their contents bolted shut; there were tank cars that could have held a variety of liquids. I watched gondola cars filled with grain, feed, wood pellets make their way slowly across the tracks as the line of cars grew longer. There were flat cars with huge pieces of machinery carefully strapped down. The open gondola cars offered a glimpse of their content, just enough to make me curious. There were empty coal cars, returning after delivering their load of energy.

I began to wonder where each car was going. Maybe they will be pulled to a "hump" where they will be sorted and assigned to other trains. Perhaps they are destined for the long ride on this train. I see graffiti painted on the side and I wonder if the well-done flowers and scenes were done by an artist of the company to discourage less attractive art.

The end is in sight. I miss the red caboose that has been replaced by a small electronic robot attached to the knuckle of the last car. These may be more efficient but I miss waving to the conductor who sometime stood on the rear platform and waved to children of all ages.

KIDNAPPED!

You will not believe what happened to me! I was curled up on the back seat of the van, just behind my man-staff. During the last hour I had let my man-staff know that I did not like riding in the van. I had used my best and loudest Siamese voice. Finally I got tired of complaining so I went to the back and pouted and slept.

Doomsday started with a loud crash that knocked me off the seat and into my bowl of water. Then everything went quiet. I jumped up front but my man-staff was asleep and people started looking in the window and talking. I heard man-staff start talking and sitting up and I thought things were going to be all right. Not so. Someone opened the door and helped him out of the car. I heard a couple of loud noises like a high pitched scream that went up and down. I went to the back and hid under a big airplane. There was lot of noise. Soon a big truck with my man-staff inside went screaming away. I knew that they had kidnapped my best friend.

After what seemed like a long time, two men came looking for me. I tried to hide but it was no use. They put me in a box, then in their car and kidnapped me. When we got to where they were to hold me for ransom, they took me inside where I heard other cats and even dogs. I got a shot, I don't know why, and they put me in a larger cage.

After a long, miserable time, two kind men from my home came and started negotiating with my captors. They must have paid a lot of money to buy my freedom. They put me in a small cardboard box and we started up the road. I let them know I did not like the box or the rough road but I soon gave up. I wondered if they had paid the ransom for my man-staff, too.

When we pulled into my carport, they put the box and me inside and let me out. It was good to be home but I could not find my man-staff. Maybe they wanted too much money for him and his friends were trying to raise the money. There was no food or water in my house. The biggest surprise was that my sand box was nowhere to be found. It must still be in the van.

It was a long night. I was hungry and thirsty and had to cross my legs and hope my box would get here soon. The next day, I heard people at the door. I meowed loudly to greet them. It was my man-staff! They had rescued him from the kidnappers! It was great to have him home, but I still had bathroom problems. He must have seen my distress because he soon brought me a band new box with sweet smelling gravel. Oh, what a relief!

I have slept most of the day and also most of this evening. I see my man-staff is getting ready to get in bed so I think I will get up with him to say a purr of thanks that both of us were safely rescued from the wicked kidnappers. LB

WHAT IS THE MATTER WITH US?

Lady Bean, what is the matter with us? I am trying to write something on the computer and am about to fall asleep. You are lying on the foot of the bed, sound asleep. You have been sleeping more than usual and so have I. It seems that ever since Beverly went away, we have both lost the incentive to do much of anything. You take me to walk and I struggle on tired legs to keep up with you. But you do not go far and come back to the house without me having to carry you. Maybe we are both feeling our age and taking the path of least resistance.

Maybe our pasts are much more enjoyable than our futures. Maybe we both need to see the vet or the doctor. Maybe we are just feeling sorry for ourselves.

What is the matter with us, LB? Maybe the house is too empty and, even though we have each other, we are both quite lonely. If you come up with an answer, please purr it to me.

THE CAT AND THE BUTTERFLY

A VISIT TO THE OLYMPICS

Last week we all climbed into the old, blue bus. There were about twenty-four of us including the athletes and cheer leaders and support staff. Some athletes had been practicing for weeks and others thought they were good enough without practice. Participants came from all over South Carolina. . .the only limitation was that you had to be from one of the five Presbyterian Retirement Communities of SC.

Events did not include the high jump, the 100-yard dash, swimming, nor ski events. Rather they were appropriate for those who were limited by age, arthritis and other ailments. They included spelling, Bocce, miniature golf, walking, and Wee bowling. Teams had been selected by each home and except for spelling, included a women's team and a men's team. Athletes and supporters came to the home in Columbia, SC, sporting different colored shirts ordered just for the event. The competition was fierce.

Following competition, lunch was served in the large dining room and the winners were announced. Like any major Olympic event, metals where given: Bronze, Silver, and Gold. While Clinton did not win the trophy this year, we did come home with quite a collection of Bronze and Silver. A good time was had by all and next year we plan to win the trophy.

VISITORS

It was mid-afternoon and I was working away on the computer when the door bell rang. I thought it was my neighbor, Tom, but when I opened the back door no one was there and the bell rang again. I opened the front door and there stood five pixies with a taller, adult-type pixie behind them. One of the young ladies held out a neatly wrapped box and said, "Our troop wanted to bring you a present." I took the box of Girl Scout cookies and asked the troop to come in.

We had a short visit during which I showed them my "toy room" with radios and airplanes. They wanted me to fly them right then but settled for me showing how they could make the controls work.

They moved on to visit other lonely people. They left me feeling better and less lonely than I was before. Thank God for little girls and Girl Scout cookies.

THE TUB

A few months ago when I was considering moving to a smaller apartment, my daughter looked it over and said, "Dad, you will never like it. It does not have a bathtub." Although I had never really thought about it, her wisdom was very true and it took me back across the decades to the home in which I grew up.

My childhood home was two stories with only one bathroom and that was on the second or bedroom floor. We all of course took turns. My turn was between five and six in the evening, just before supper. Maybe it was because I was the dirtiest from playing in the back alley or the next door sand lot. That hour was the most private, the most wonderful hour one could imagine. I was allowed to lock both doors, with the understanding I did not leave the key in the lock so they could be unlocked in case of emergency.

The iron tub perched on four legs that looked to me like a tiger's paw. At the end were the water came in was the commode. In front of the commode was a stool that held my comic books. Behind the stool was a low dresser with no mirror. On the opposite wall was the basin for washing faces and brushing teeth. To the right of the basin was a door to the dressing room and, at right angles, the door to the hall.

The water to the tub was hot and had to be regulated. Maybe I was just small but the tub seemed huge. I kept my array of boats on the shelf just above the tub. Many wonderful dreams and impossible plans were hatched while hiding beneath the warm cover of water. A small wooden sailboat, dented from an unsuccessful attempt to christen it with a vinegar bottle, may well have been the prototype for the future vessels *Bad Girl, Alscat, Anago and Karisto*. Often I would be reminded more than once to "hurry up, it is almost suppertime."

Memories of that iron tub must had lingered with me through the years, for even today I love to soak in a tub's hot, soapy water, and make plans and dream dreams. The house in Clinton has a tub, be it ever so small, but the home in Sky Lake has a tub that rivals my memories of the old iron tub in Jacksonville in the 1930s.

I guess Mary Glenn was right. I would never be fully content without a tub to soak and dream in.

THE BATTLE HAS BEGUN

Yes, the battle has begun. It is not a battle between Democrats and Republicans. It is not a battle among neighbors or communities like our Olympics. Not even a battle between good and evil. It is open war between deer and tomato plants. I started with bad-smelling sprays, but the deer thought it was perfume and nibbled away at tender plants. I tried strands of old electrical wire but they got under, around and even over it. I finally went for big weapons (guns or electric fences are not allowed here).

I purchased metal posts and acquired a roll of six-foot chicken wire. Now my 10by10 tomato garden is completely enclosed. I hope they will not jump into such a small area but if worse comes to worse I have bird netting that will go across the top and cover the garden completely. Of course, all this makes it quite difficult to get inside and tend the plants or even pick tomatoes, provided this all works.

I never thought the relaxing, wonderful time of growing things in God's good earth would turn into a battle that might eventually grow to Armageddon.

THE CAT AND THE BUTTERFLY

Some of you may have seen a page from my first grief journal, written during the months after Jackie's death in 1998, where I described the beautiful Monarch Butterfly that could be seen flitting in our front yard each day. It became something of a symbol for Jackie's life. Whenever Beverly would see a Monarch in our yard, she would smile and say, "There goes Jackie, checking up on us."

Soon after Beverly's death, Lady Bean jumped on my bed and put her head on my arm just like Beverly used to do. The thought of reincarnation into the cat flashed across my mind. Well, this afternoon I was watching Lady Bean enjoy her afternoon outing on this beautiful spring day. She lay down in the grass and rolled half way over and looked up. Suddenly a big, beautiful butterfly flitted down just above her. She did not get up but lifted a front paw as if to wave a greeting. The Monarch circled around a few times and then was gone. I could not help but wonder if Jackie and Beverly, somewhere on heaven's porch, were laughing together and directing a cat and a butterfly to remind me of them and to tease me.

It did not exactly fit my theological understanding of eschatology, but it brought a smile and good memories.

A FUN GAME

He thinks I don't know what's going on. He must thing I am pretty dumb. For the last few days my man-staff has been sneaking around, getting things out of the closet and putting his noisy radio in a box. He's thinking I am asleep just because I am curled up on the bed with my eyes closed. Everyone knows that a cat can see from the bottom of a closed eyelid.

Today I almost told him that I knew he was packing the car. I went outside with him, walked around the car and then went to sleep under the front of the car. Now I must admit I am not sure if he is going to leave me home with the nice ladies from the clinic or if he is going to make me go with him. Either way, he is going to have a hard time finding me when he is ready to go.

It seems to me he would have learned that I always win the first round of "find me if you can" even though eventually he gets down on the flour and pulls me out from under the bed. It is a fun game and I sometimes delay him for an hour or so. It serves him right for making me ride over rough roads with noisy trucks going past. I let him know that I am unhappy with loud and consistent Siamese howls. He definitely knows he is being cussed out.

Finally I see familiar trees arching over the car and smell the good mountain air and I know we are almost to our mountain home. I get excited and jump on the windshield to better watch for Moss Manor.

I wish our houses were closer together so we could just walk to them. LB

ICE CREAM

MEMORIAL DAY 2016

As I left my mountain home, they were putting small American flags beside the entrance. Arriving home, I found many residents excitedly awaiting the bus ride to Furman for the Memorial Day Concert in the outdoor amphitheater. The airways are filled with music befitting the holiday weekend. It is appropriate.

Memorial Day takes me back to the church in which I grew up. It was 1941 and I was twelve years old. Early that year, I remember seeing a large flag being hung on the front wall of the church, just behind the choir loft. On the white background there was one gold star and a growing number of blue stars. I remember my parents telling me the story of that gold star. My first cousin, Harry, just nine years older than me, had joined the Royal Canadian Air Force even before we declared war on Germany. During a flight over England, he crashed and became one of the first casualties of World War II. The blue stars on the flag would represent those in active service.

After the war, that banner, now with other gold stars and filled with blue ones, would be hung again in the front of the church. Every Memorial Day, I see that flag in my memory and give thanks to God for all those who have lived and died serving our country.

THE TREES ARE DOWN

It was a quick trip to my North Georgia home. A friend was using my house so I stayed with my niece while there. It was good to have time to visit with her and she was good enough to feed a hungry, wayfaring stranger. The purpose of my trip was to see that some dead trees were taken down and disposed of properly. The tree company came with four large trucks, a shredder and a Bobcat with tracks and a small crane. The power company had cut a large tree that endangered their lines but let it fall on my property and left it there. Another large tree that was about to fall, was cut and hauled away. The one I hated to see go was the wild cherry in the center of the front yard. We had enjoyed its shade and spring blossoms. It was almost dead and I think it was merciful to take it out of its brittle misery.

The woods near the street look so much better. The front yard looks a little empty and I will have to decide what should take the wild cherry's place. There is still work to be done and I look forward to spending some time in Sky Lake. It is good to have the old trees down and gone.

THE ICE CREAM TRUCK

My home is not too far from a housing development where there are lots of children. Since there are no children in our retirement community, it is good to hear them laughing and playing on these long spring afternoons.

Two or three times a week I hear unique music. . .music that takes me back to the summers of my childhood. It is the sound of the ice cream truck with its unique bell and music that call to the children. *Come and get a cone or small tub of that delicious, cold substance called ice cream.* It makes me want to rush down and elbow my way to the front of the line. Someday I might just drive my golf cart down and pretend I am a child again. After all, I am in my second childhood.

THE IRONING BOARD THAT WON'T GO DOWN

I have a problem with my ironing board. About a year ago, a small angular piece of metal fell from the bottom of the board. We used to pull or push this thing when we wanted to put down or stand the ironing board. I cannot get it to go where it used to be. I cannot get the board to fold flat so it will stand at the end of the closet. Both my neighbor and I have racked our brains. We have used pliers, screwdrivers, hammers and wrenches to no avail. If I cannot get it to fold, I could use it but I have no room to store it. I could get rid of it but what would I use to iron on? (Of course, I haven't ironed anything since 1992.) But then, who knows when I might need the ironing board. If you have a solution to my problem, please advise.

TOO MANY PILLS!

Just before breakfast, I open my pill box and pour them out on a napkin. There are about seventeen of them and I am supposed to take some before breakfast and some after eating. Some I could even take with breakfast as they are supposed to taste like some kind of fruit. Some I handle very carefully as they must be made of 20-carat gold. They come in different shapes and colors, as if my stomach could care. They come in the mail, from the local pharmacy and off the shelf with no RX. My doctor implies that if I stop taking any of them my constitution would rise up and revolt against me. But I am solving the problem. I am changing doctors.

Maybe my new doctor will start all over with pills. If the count gets up to seventeen again there is always another doctor down the road.

TALKING TO THE CAT

More and more I find myself talking to Lady Bean. She is usually close by, sitting on my radio, curled up on the sofa next to me or under foot, daring me to step on her. I need someone to talk to and she seems to enjoy my ramblings. Talking to her keeps me from feeling so lonely. In fact, she sometimes answers me with a meow or a loud purr. What bothers me is that sometimes I think I know what she is saying. Guess I need a visit to my local shrink. But I know he will tell me that I am just getting old and not to worry about it.

"Lady Bean, what do you think I should do?" *Meow, meow, purr, purr.* "Thank you, LB, I guess you are right."

A STRANGE THING HAPPENED

My man-staff and I had a wonderful time in the mountains. I love the long hall where I can run and slide. There are lots of sofas to sleep on and I can even slip into the guest rooms and hide between the pillows. (Don't tell the guests.) The big back deck is a wonderful place to lie and watch the leaves move on the tall trees. Once in a while a deer or two will come down the hill toward the deck. I do not bother them and they do not bother me. My man-staff lets me walk around the house on the outside. I like to go out of one door and make him open another door to let me in.

Getting here and going home is another matter. I do not like to travel so I still play the game of "find-me-if-you-can" just before it is time to leave. He gets really upset. The trip is boring and shaky and the noisy trucks keep waking me up. I complain a lot but sleep most of the way and endure the trip. I still remember the time the car banged into something and I got kidnapped and held for ransom.

On the way home, something happened that was strange. We had gone a long way and I was asleep in the front seat. Suddenly, a little bell seemed to ring in my head. Something was wrong. I was not sure exactly what. I started my loud, Siamese yowl. The van stopped for a light and the bell in my head got louder and I howled louder. We went on a little farther and the bell in my head quieted down. I was about to go to sleep when my man-staff said, "Back there was where we had our accident." That was it! My internal GPS must have gone off to warn me of kidnappers. I sure am glad we made it past that danger.

Guess I should have warned my man-staff but honestly, I did not know exactly what was happening. Next time I will. Soon we made it home and I was glad to get back to my other home in Clinton, SC. LB

299

THE PRIDE OF BEING AN AMERICAN

⌀

REFLECTIONS ON TURNING EIGHTY-SEVEN

I am getting a little panicky. My desk is still piled high with things to do and time is running out. My book is not finished, papers need to be filed, planes are waiting to be flown, sermons are to be written; plus there are demands from the home here in Clinton and LB wants me to finish her 3rd book!

Putting the desk aside, this is a good time to reflect on last year and the years long gone. I have had two great wives, both taken away too soon. I have great children and grandchildren. My childhood was worth reliving, if that was possible. Each of my friends and each of my churches have added something to my life, and perhaps I have left something with them. Certainly there are things that I would have done differently but then, anything different would have changed my life completely, and I would not have wanted that.

Forty-five years with Jackie and watching children grow from babies into adults was something I would not change for the world. Experiences with a growing family, the empty nest and even tragedies bring treasured memories.

A childhood sweetheart rescued me from depression and gave us both sixteen wonderful and exciting years. We sailed the Caribbean and visited places in the world we never dreamed of seeing. Beverly's death this year still hangs heavily on my heart and I am lonely.

Sometimes at night, I find myself with a growing family, watching games, camping in a large tent, canoeing and caving. I dream again of the Presbytery camp where Jackie and I fell in love. In my dreams and memory, I see Beverly at the wheel of *Karisto* while I handle the sails. Sometimes I wake up laughing and sometimes crying. It is good to remember, both in memory and in my dreams.

On my 87th birthday, there is much to remember. Many adventures decorate the walls of memory. I am grateful for my health, such as it is, and look forward to as many new adventures as I can pack into the next few years.

A NEW RAILING

The deck has always been a great place to enjoy the out-of-doors, to eat an early breakfast or evening meal. From it, we have watched the deer come down the bank and eat our flowers and plants. But there has been something missing. There was always a danger of walking off the edge. Now that danger has passed. There is a new railing all around. I was told that if I ever wanted to sell the house, I would have to have the railing put on in order to meet code. If I would have to do it then, why not enjoy it now?

It is up, still waiting to be stained or painted. So come on over and enjoy the new railing.

POWER WASHING AND TRIMMING BUSHES

Whenever I come up to the mountains, I hope to relax and enjoy doing the things I want to do. . .like writing and working in my basement workshop. I have found that this just does not happen. The moss lawn needs to have a weed-whacker haircut, the hedges need to be trimmed, and the dwelling, walks and driveway need to be power washed. A few other little things need to be done, like cleaning out the garage, disposing of junk from the attic and pulling weeds. Keeping a house up and running is a full-time job, and I don't live here full-time.

I guess the reality of maintenance takes precedence over relaxation. Still, it is good to spend time in Sky Lake.

THROWING OUT PICTURES

For at least seventy-five of my eighty-six years I have loved pictures. My father built a darkroom in the house in which I grew up and I learned to take pictures with my box camera, develop the film and print or enlarge the pictures. I took pictures of homes and tried to sell them to earn spending money. In college, I worked as a photographer to help with expenses. By selling pictures to football and basketball players, I made enough money to buy my first car.

I moved from black and white photos through slides and presentations to digital pix and videos. I always enjoyed taking and keeping pictures. Now it is time to reverse the process and it is harder than taking them. I have to throw them out.

Pictures are the milestones of our lives. Through them we walk our journey of history, we see our families grow and multiply. We retake too many of the trips that we have made. As I pour boxes onto the bed to sort them, I am lost in memories, not only of places, but of the people and loved ones that jump out at me. There are pictures of my weddings, pictures of walking hand in hand with those I loved. There are pictures of the homes we lived in and of things we did while there. There are pictures that bring laughter and pictures that feel the moisture of my tears. I love them all but I cannot keep them. They are of an age gone by. . .of people my children do not know. They must go and with them goes a piece of myself. It is hard to throw out pictures but I know that if I do not look at them one last time and bury then with loving care, they will be trashed with no compassion.

It is hard to throw out pictures, but it must be done.

THE FOURTH OF JULY

A few days before July 4th, a nearby church choir came and gave an excellent presentation of appropriate hymns and patriotic music. They reminded us of our heritage of freedom. We all felt both the pride of being an American and our duty to be responsible citizens. *BANG!*

On the night before the fourth there were a few firecrackers going off in adjacent neighborhoods. Lady Bean and I handled that fine and listened to patriotic music until we dozed off. But on the night of the fourth, it was different. We watched the national capital event and then the fireworks. About 11:00 we went to bed; LB in her bed and me in mine. It was a little before midnight I heard an explosion that shook me wide awake. Then I felt thirteen pounds of cat land in the middle of my stomach. Her jump must have started nineteen feet away and scraped the ceiling on her trajectory. She bounced from my bruised anatomy to a place deep under the cover.

I got up, had a glass of milk and a cookie and went back to bed. Lady Bean never budged until late the next morning. And that is the way we celebrated the 4th.

SUNFLOWERS AND TOMATOES

It has been hot in South Carolina! We did not like the heat but the sunflowers did. The hotter it got, the taller they grew. Now you can hardly see the lamp post for the stalks and big leaves. I thought they would never bloom but finally they came through with a burst of yellow. They welcome visitors in the front and guard the pole for my antenna in the back.

Speaking of the back, it is also that time of summer when tomatoes fill the vines. I put a six-foot fence around my small plot to keep the deer away. I could have saved a lot of work since I haven't seen a deer all summer. Come to think of it, the fence may be the reason I haven't seen a deer. I try to give tomatoes away and the neighbors run when they see me coming with the round, red, juicy vegetables. I must say, I have enjoyed tomato and bacon sandwiches almost every evening.

ICE CREAM IN JULY

When the temperature tries to blow through the top of the thermometer and the cool evening breeze has turned into a furnace, it is time to turn up the AC and break out the home-made, hand-churned ice cream. We did that on the fourth of July and it was good. My neighbor prepared the mix and her husband cranked the churn.

Well, a few invited guests could not come, so a friend and I invited the missing to come tonight and have ice cream. The problem is that I have never made ice cream mix before but I had the recipe. I peeled and pureed the peaches, mixed the other ingredients and put them in the container. I poured ice and salt between the drum and the churn, and then plugged in the electric motor that would take the work out of cranking. I prayed for success.

Ten minutes into the process the motor ground to a stop. I shook it. I took the motor off. The motor ran fine. When I put it back on it would stall. Finally, as a last resort, I read the manual. It told me that the dasher was probably frozen at the bottom. I pulled it out, scraped off the partially-frozen cream at the bottom, reinserted it, plugged in the motor and bingo; it worked perfectly.

The ice cream was great. The party was a success and I have enough left for another party. Come on over!

SLEEPING AROUND

I sleep around a lot but I am really a very nice cat. I guess it is just my nature to find many places to sleep. After all, when you sleep up to eighteen hours a day just to live up to the feline tradition, it is natural to find lots of places to spend your time.

In the morning, I get up from wherever I happen to have ended up the night before, and go immediately to my man-staff's bed. I get a running start and jump so that I land as close to his middle as possible. It is fun to hear him let out a surprised grunt and then fuss about being awakened early. I cuddle up to him, purr loudly and he forgives me and strokes me. About an hour later he gets up. I stay in bed until breakfast is ready and then stroll into the kitchen.

When he lets me go outside, I love to sleep under the car, in the car, under the back seat of the golf cart and just about anywhere that is cool. When we come back inside, I usually go to the sofa where I can watch what is happening outside. If the cleaning ladies or the bug sprayer come I go under the bed. I have special hiding place where I go to sleep until all noise and danger is gone. Sometimes my man-staff goes out front. I go with him and pretend to sleep on the porch. I am really watching him to be sure he does not get in trouble. When he is working inside, you will find me asleep on or behind his radio or in front of his computer screen. Later that night, I usually sleep on the bed with my man-staff until he gets too restless and disturbs me. I have other secret sleeping places that I will not disclose for obvious reasons.

And that is how I spend my eighteen hours a day sleeping around. LB

DOLDRUMS ON THE SEA

A VISIT TO SKY LAKE

It is always good to come back to Moss Manor. It was the last real home that Beverly and I shared together. It holds many memories. It started out as a vacation home and ended as a full time dwelling. As I look at the pictures on the walls of the hallway, I see a panoramic view of memories, family, trips, voyages, children, wedding etc. I remember the first night we spent here. There was no furniture and we slept on a double air mattress.

The steep hill outside still fascinates me although I can no longer climb its tiers and plant flowers, pull weeds and enjoy the challenge of the mountain side. The deer still visit and lay waste the few flowers that are left. The turkey gobbler still stops to stretch and pluck a few blueberries. A black bear occasionally checks us out and knocks down the remaining blueberries.

I enjoy the privacy of living almost out of sight of neighbors, yet I have great neighbors to visit and to entertain. On three sides no human being or home is visible. Down the driveway and across the road I can see the homes of dear friends.

Moss Manor, with its moss lawn that always seems to need a haircut, with its large Japanese maple trees, its woods and mountain ferns, holds a special fascination. From our deck, there is no lofty mountain view but there is the magic of being held in the hands of the mountain sides.

Three bedrooms, two baths, a long hall, a sunken living room with a stone fireplace, a dining room, a kitchen with adjacent breakfast nook leave little to be desired. But my favorite is the finished basement where my radios used to be permanent fixtures and where my RC airplanes fly from the ceiling and the walls. In the two rooms are two big sofas and a sofa bed. It is complete with its own bathroom, tub, shower and a small refrigerator.

To top all this, there are friends in the Sky Lake Community and in the neighboring towns. The Nacoochee Presbyterian Church, with its special family of faith, is a wonderful place to worship.

Although Moss Manor is a little over two hours away, Lady Bean and I will be there as often and stay as long as possible.

LIKE IT WAS YESTERDAY

It is trying to rain but not quite making it. There is thunder and sharp lightning. . .the kind that sends the cat scurrying for safety under the bed. A few big drops of rain come down and settle into a staccato symphony on the roof. Another flash of lightning separates me from my sermonizing and sends me back to time long gone.

In memory, I found myself a little boy again, taking an afternoon nap when the storm rolled in. My bed was parallel to the windows on our sleeping porch. My head was tight against the window sill and was looking up at dark clouds and looking down at rain making circles in the bird bath. The wind was shaking the big pecan tree and once in a while would drive drops of rain against my window screen. While I still resented afternoon naps, I felt very secure in my bed and by my window. The wind, the rain, the rolling clouds and thunder was a drama being played out on the stage of my back yard. The participants in that drama would fascinate me until they, like a too-long sermon, lulled me into sleep.

Another bolt of lightning and some pounding rain shakes me out of the past and reminds me that it is good sleeping weather. It is past my bedtime so I will take advantage of the lullaby off rain and turn in. Good night to all.

THE VAN HAS A STROKE

One day it was fine, the next day it was a different story. Overnight my van had a stroke. It started the day before I was to return to Clinton after a great stay in Sky Lake. I started the car and the engine roared to life, but the windshield wipers came on and very little else. The windows would not go up or down. The turn signals did not work, the radio would not play, the air conditioner would blow but it was warm, outside air. Worst of all, the windshield wipers would not slow down or turn off and I could not open the tailgate to pack. Even disconnecting and reconnecting the battery did not correct it.

Finally, after packing things over the back seats, I was ready to go. Early Friday morning, I pulled the cat from under the bed and we started home. Warm air rushed in through the open windows. The windshield wipers sang a squeaky tune as they beat across a dry windshield. There was no display of speed, gas or other instruments on the dashboard. Lady Bean added her dislike to the noise and confusion. After nearly three hours of misery we arrived in Clinton much to our mutual relief. I was thankful for a safe trip. Lady Bean was just thankful to get out of a noisy and hot van. The local Chrysler dealer could not get me in for three weeks.

Over the weekend none of the accessories worked, but I could still drive the van. On Monday I took it to a mechanic in Clinton. About three blocks from his shop, suddenly everything started to work again. (It was like going to the dentist when suddenly your tooth stops hurting.) He checked things with his analyzer and found nothing. He said, "Bring it back when it stops working."

I have driven the van for over a week. I have made two out-of-town trips, and except for a few hick-ups the first day it has worked perfectly. It was like an act of miraculous healing and I rejoice in a cheap fix, but every time I start the car I am fearful that the windshield wiper will signal a recurrence of the stroke.

If it happens again we will do an exorcism and lay hands of healing on the van's stressed-out computer. If that does not work, I will visit the mechanic.

no

MEMORIES

Seventeen years ago, I fulfilled a life-long dream of sailing the Caribbean and visiting the tropical islands. Our thirty-seven-foot vessel made its way from NC to FL, around Key West. . .then up to St. Petersburg. From St. Pete, we began the highpoint of the adventure. We joined sailboats of many sizes and configuration for a race to Cuba, hosted by a yacht club in Havana. On race day we passed under the Sunshine Bridge which was the starting point of the race. . .cut our engines. . .and raised our sails.

The fleet looked like white-winged horses straining beneath white stallions, eager to begin the race to the island of Cuba. But alas, even as the race started, the wind ceased. A puff now and then helped us struggle away from shore and crawl into the Gulf of Mexico. We rested in a flat sea and watched the white, puffy clouds billowed up around us, looking like giant, white hot air balloons being heated and expanded for a trip aloft. The smooth water was broken only by the long swells, born a hundred miles away, traveling like a liquid army marching across the surface of the Gulf. . .with sails hanging limp and useless above us. They looked like so many sheets hung out to dry.

It was then that John Miller, the musician of our crew, broke out his guitar and began to strum and sing a ballad he had written commemorating the occasion. Its chorus went like this;

> *Send wind! We've got doldrums on the sea.*
> *Send wind! Set* Karisto *free.*
> *Send wind 'n we'll get to Habana town;*
> *Send wind, or we'll crank it up 'n put the pedal down.*

We finally motored into Havana and enjoyed a great week in that old and crippled city, learning the culture and visiting with the people. Wonderful memories from days long gone.

I must pay tribute to my partner in *Karisto* and true friend, Rev. Robert Miller. Robert died last spring. He was with us on the Cuba adventure. He will always be in my thoughts as I remember the many sailing adventures we shared.

A TRIP THROUGH HELL

I had heard the word "hell" used in a number of different ways. I knew it was something awful but now I have been through it and I know how bad it really is! The nightmare began when my man-staff stared putting things in bags and then in the car. He tried to do it without me knowing what was going on but cats are not stupid. I thought I would have to ride in the car, complain a little, and then go to sleep.

The next morning, we got up earlier than usual. I decided not to hide, but to enjoy my last hours here on the deck. As soon as it was light, man-staff came, picked me up and put me in the van. . .I thought I knew what was coming. But this time it was different, very different. The things that keep the rain off the front windows were flapping back and forth. The windows were down and it was already hot. When my man-staff finally climbed in he was fussing about things that did not work. We started down the mountain.

It was alright at first, but when the road straightened out, the wind came rushing in and fluffed up my fur. It was noisy and I could not sleep. When I tried to get in his lap, he would push me away and make some noise about having to watch his driving because the lights did not work. Soon, big, loud trucks began to pass just outside my open window. The sun came up and the air coming in was hot. I added my Siamese yowl to the mix and my man-staff added a few words too. It was like that all the way home. . .wipers flapping and squeaking, warm air rushing in, and trucks trying to get in my window.

Finally, I felt some familiar bumps in the road and saw some trees I recognized. We stopped beside my other house and I was allowed out of the van. It had been a trip through hell and I will know exactly what people are talking about when they use that word again. LB

LONELINESS

A TRIP TO ALASKA

In September my daughter, Mary Glenn, and I set out for a cruise to Alaska. From Black Mountain, where she lives, we went to the Asheville airport and onto a Delta shuttle. In less than an hour we were in the sprawling Atlanta airport and from there across our country to Seattle. We traveled by bus to the port and checked onto the Carnival *Legend*.

Our voyage up the Inland Passage allowed us to see the rugged, ice-capped primitive mountains of the Alaska western shore. From our cabin balcony we were fascinated with the panoramic scenery flowing by.

During our stop in Skagway, we took the train, called the White Pass Special, which carried us high into the Alaskan mountains. We moved through scenes of snow-capped mountains, deep ravines, old wooden bridges and narrow tunnels. A new scene greeted us at every turn. On the summit we were greeted with a blue lake of melted snow held in by mountain peaks on every side. Our return trip was just as fascinating, as the scenery seemed to change. Back in the town we walked old streets, visited unique stores and tourist traps. It was good to get back to the ship and have a good meal for dinner.

The next day we visited the glaciers. The ship treaded its way through a narrow channel leading to the Tracy Arm Fjord Glacier. Ice that had broken from the glacier greeted us long before we could see the ice wall itself. Mary Glenn took a smaller boat that would move to the very face of the glacier. There she saw ice falling into the water and had the unusual experience of seeing bubbles coming from the water near the base and then watching a large piece of glacier ice pop up from the sea. It had broken from the glacier below the surface. After many pictures, our ship picked up the wandering passengers and moved to the town of Juneau. There we were bussed to the Mendenhall National Park at the base of the Mendenhall Glacier. There the park service provided excellent facilities for viewing the huge wall of ice that flows slowly and continuously toward the sea. Alaska is a big, beautiful state and we were only touching the fringe of it.

Our next stop took us to a site for whale watching, eating and viewing. After boarding a smaller boat, we set out to see whales. We had already seen a number from our deck on the *Legend*, but this was to be up-close and personal. Before seeing whales, we passed a floating buoy that had become a dry oasis for sea lions. Soon we spotted the tell-tale water spout that signaled a whale would soon appear. We watched anxiously and soon he rolled out of the water and flipped his tail as he disappeared. This was repeated a number of times.

Then our boat took us to the Opca Point Lodge where we disembarked for a lunch of salmon, grilled over an open fire. We explored the island and all too soon it was time to load up and head back to the bus and eventually to the big ship. These adventures were supplemented by activities on board and entertainment in the ship's large theater. The whole Alaskan adventure was a great experience. Perhaps the best part for me was spending a week with my daughter.

SHADES OF THE TITANIC

It was Sunday evening and Mary Glenn and I were seated at the upper level of formal dining. We had ordered our meal and were remembering the events of the past few days. We had come very close to the glacier and had watched huge, iceberg-like chucks of ice float by next to the ship. We reminisced as we neared the end of our adventure. Suddenly we heard a loud crash and felt the ship shutter as if it had crashed sideways into a dock or another ship. The Carnival *Legend* turned hard to the right and began to list to the left. Dishes began sliding from the table, crashing to the floor. The portholes to our left disappeared into the ocean and only sky could be seen to the right.

There was panic as passengers staggered to the one exit on a sloping floor. The wait-staff kept saying, "Don't panic!" But they too were pale with uncertainty. Some reports had us listing thirty degrees to the side. For a long ten minutes panic reigned as the ship slowly stabilized. During the time the ship was leaning far to the left, dishes continued to crash, the water poured out of the pools on the upper decks and people donned life jackets and headed for the lifeboat stations. The captain came on the speakers to assure us that it was a mechanical problem and we were all right, but with his heavy accent few could understand him.

It took at least fifteen minutes for the ship to straighten to the point that the horizon could be seen on both sides. It was a welcome sight. When we finally left the dining room, we saw many passengers wearing life jackets and some standing on deck by the life boats. We later learned that one of the rear steering and driving pedestals had broken loose and had sent us on a dangerous course. Having turned over on top-heavy sailboats in the past, I was very concerned that the decks and steel above us were near the point of no return. Although Carnival minimized the degree of list, I felt we were dangerously close to the point of no return.

Oh well, it gives us something to tell about and to climax a great trip to Alaska.

A TOUCH (BE IT A LIGHT ONE) OF FALL

It has been a hot summer, the hottest on record in our area. The land has dried up from lack of rain. My tomato vines gave me some delicious tomatoes then died an early death. When rain does come, it comes quickly and vigorously. Then it disappears behind burning sun. It has been a good year to stay inside, enjoy the air conditioning and catch up on the many things that have been put off until later. Well, later is almost here. There is a touch of fall hanging over the heat that still hangs on. The mornings and late evening welcome us out of our cool escapes. Fall is just around the corner, but the season is dragging its feet.

To escape the lagging fall and welcome in the color of the coming season, Lady Bean and I returned to the mountains of North Georgia and Sky Lake. As I approached the community of Sautee, I did see a few trees that had turned red, but they were in the minority. Even in the mountains, fall was slow in coming. Yet under the green canopy of foliage the air was cool and it was good to sit on the deck in the evening and anticipate the season that is bound to come. We follow as early falling leaves drop off and fly erratically to the ground. There is a border of gold around the leaves of the Japanese maples. It is good to open a window at night and have to pull up more cover because the temperature is in the sixties.

Regretfully, I will be leaving Moss Manor about the time the leaves really begin to burst forth in color, but I do look forward to the equally wonderful fall season when I return to South Carolina.

WHAT IS LONELINESS?

How do I define it? It is not what many think it to be. It is not the loss of a spouse or child or companion; this I can accept, as death being part of life. . . tragic or timely as it may be. I have my faith and an acceptance of God's providence.

It is not living alone, though that may be lonely at times. It is not even an empty house in which I rattle around. . .for there I can find much to keep me busy. . .words to be put on paper. . .things to be fixed, planted or built. . .treasures to be given or thrown away. I can adapt and handle most of these things.

What then is loneliness? Loneliness is the little things that happen suddenly and burst upon the conscious and unconscious. . .which come without warning. . .that meet me around a corner or curve in the road. Loneliness is a picture from the past, flashing on the screensaver. It is waking at night after a dream filled with memories and reaching for a hand that is not there. It is rounding a curve on a lonely road in the dark and meeting a full moon. It is seeing a shooting star and being transported to a night of sky-watching on board *Karisto*.

Loneliness is seeing happy couples or families eating out while you eat alone. It is writing something and having no one to tell you it is good or where corrections should be made. It is having no one to take care of, or not knowing that someone will take care of you. It is wondering who will call 911 if you desperately need help. Loneliness is watching a piano gather dust, looking at a lifetime of treasures scattered around the house and realizing that most of them go to Good Will. Loneliness is living with surprises. Some are pleasant, some are sad. Loneliness is not made up of calculated thoughts nor measured actions; it is defined by memories that jump out from unexpected places.

What is loneliness? Loneliness is a thousand little things meeting me around each corner. . .unexpected, sometimes far apart. . .yet often enough to fill a remaining lifetime. Loneliness is a burden and a privilege. It is made of laughter and a tear that will not fall. It is a debt and a precious gift. It is a moment and a lifetime. It is a shadow and a reality. Loneliness brings meaning to lifetimes of togetherness.

Loneliness is all this and much, much more.

A SURPRISE HARVEST

Last year I erected a trellis-like structure that covered almost half of the carport side. I planted amaryllis, Florida juniper and other flowering vines. Along with flowers, I planted Kentucky string beans, and the cut-end of a sweet potato. Everything but the flowers grew well. They were somewhat overwhelmed by the beans and potato vine. Although we got a few servings of beans, it was the sweet potato vine that really took over the trellis. It seemed to grow a foot each day and soon a multitude of runners obliterated the view of my neighbor's carport from my kitchen door. I was most pleased by both purple and white flowers.

The other day, I was admiring my potato vine when I saw, staring at me from the vine, a big, long growth that looked a great deal like a cucumber. After consulting with my neighboring farmer, we agreed that it was indeed a cucumber. The mystery of the white and purple flowers became clear. There must have been a few cucumber seeds hiding in the bean seeds.

As of today, we have not dug up the sweet potatoes but we have enjoyed a few good cucumbers. The lush, green foliage of both is beautiful and makes wonderful shade.

I DON'T LIKE RIDING

I have two great homes and I enjoy being in both of them. One is small with soft beds and sofas. It also has a place just outside where my man-staff keeps the car and other junk. I love to chomp on the grass in the yard and sleep on the hard floor or in the back of his golf wagon or even in the car when it is parked and still. Sometimes I take him to walk and when I get tired, I just sit down and he carries me home grumbling all the way. I grumble too because I think he likes me to.

My other home is larger with a long hall and at least four doors. If it is raining I check them all to be sure the sun is not shining on at least one of them. It has a deck with soft cushions in the chairs. They make great sleeping places. Animal friends come by and we look at each other from a distance. My basket is in my man-staff's bedroom with a big, soft blanket just asking me to climb in. Since a big dog comes to visit us, I have asked my staff to serve my dinner near my bed and out of danger. I like it there even if the dog is not visiting us. We get along fine. He sometimes wants to play but all I have to do is "ppssiffff" at him and he gets the message. I sometimes stay and guard the house while my man-staff goes off for a day or so. I really don't mind if he is not gone very long but I am glad when he comes back. I am always afraid my food will give out.

I love both my homes but they must be a long way apart. We have to travel a long time to go between them and it is the "in-between time" that I dislike. I hide just before we have to leave. I know he will eventually find me but I need to make a point. I DO NOT LIKE TO RIDE! It is noisy, boring and the van shakes and tilts and is just not suited for a dignified cat. I let him know my feelings with my best Siamese yowls.

I don't know why he did not get homes next door to each other. We could have walked and done away with the long, miserable ride. After many hours, I either see the tall pine trees and the magnolia tree or I see the green arches and Japanese maples over me. It is so good to get out of that car and see whichever home is there. Best of all, I know that the "in-between time" is over. LB

LADY BEAN TO THE RESCUE

It has been a long time since this newsletter has made to your computer. I guess the most comprehensive reason is that I have just not felt like writing for the past few months. Sure, I have kept busy but I cannot hide behind activity as an excuse. A lot has happened that I will sketch in some of the articles in this issue. To be honest, I have missed both writing and taking pictures and will try to do better in the coming year. Enough excuses. . .let's get started on the December 2016 issue of the newsletter.

MERRY CHRISTMAS TO ALL

Here it is less than two weeks until Christmas! Cold weather finally arrived, the drought has been partially broken and it looks more like Christmas weather. I look out the window and see a light mist falling. It is too warm for snow but too cold to be comfortable outside. Santa arrived in town last Saturday with decorations and lights everywhere. It is truly a wonderful time of year.

I hope that you and yours are enjoying the season and plan for a great Christmas Day, regardless of weather. I will be right here, preaching at Providence ARP Church, but I will be thinking of you and remembering the many good friends and good times in days past.

THE BEST AND WORST CHRISTMAS EVER

Have you ever had a Christmas when you received every gift you wanted and then some? I have! It was Christmas 1935 and I

318

did not realize that there was a great depression. I was six years old and lived in a two-story house with the bedrooms upstairs and the Christmas tree downstairs. Even if I woke up early on Christmas morning, I could not go downstairs until everyone was up and ready. When it was finally time, we all came downstairs. I came three steps at a time and bounded into the living room.

There, under the tree, was everything I had asked for. There were games to play, toys to surprise me, a little toy sewing machine (why I wanted a sewing machine, I will never know, but it was there). When I had torn through the paper on presents, I looked in the corner and there was a shiny new sidewalk bicycle. It was beyond my wildest dreams. I had received everything and more. During the year that followed things changed: my father had to change jobs; my mother began teaching more piano students. But I was sheltered and, for me, little changed.

The next Christmas I was seven and I asked for, and expected, lots of presents just like the year before. When Christmas morning came and I came down expecting everything I asked for, I found only one small present I asked for. The packages I opened were mostly clothes, not toys. To say the least, I was very disappointed and it must have been quite obvious. It was the only Christmas I ever remember seeing my mother cry. My grandmother, Nannie, took me into the back room and sat me down on the cot where she would often read to me about *Tom Sawyer* and *Robinson Crusoe*. I do not remember all she said, but it was something like this:

"Christmas is a lot more than getting the toys you asked for. Your parents work very hard to provide what you need and most of what you want. None of us are getting many gifts this year. There is just not enough money for our house, for food, for clothes and lots of presents. Maybe it is time for you to remember that Christmas is really not about what you get but about what God gave us in the baby Jesus."

A lot of that did not sink in right then but as I grew older I have often thought about that little lesson on Christmas giving and I appreciate it more and more. After eighty years I can still hear the echoes of her words and it is more meaningful to me each year.

Maybe my worst Christmas was actually my best.

A BIT OF HISTORY

The middle of September Lady Bean and I were in Sky Lake for almost two weeks, with a quick trip back to Clinton for Sunday with a return on Monday. Both of us enjoyed the home, the basement toyshop and good memories. Good friends made it a special two weeks.

I hesitatively tell about the following experience as this newsletter is supposed to be more than a personal history, but I guess you need to know. It was a little after noon on Thursday when they rolled me out of the emergency vehicle to rush me to the hospital in Greenwood and into the emergency room. I had spent a good fourth of my life in the halls and rooms of hospitals, visiting and waiting with families but this was the first time I had ever ridden in the back of an ambulance and checked myself into a hospital.

It started a few hours earlier when I felt too weak to stand up. Thinking it was my heart, I called 911 and set the process in motion. The forty-five-minute ride was made brighter by nice attendant who rode in back with me and hooked me up to cups and needles. Turned out it was not my heart, but loss of blood and anemia.

After two days, three doctors, three units of blood and at least two dozen needles in a great hospital, I was ready to go home. They treated me well, but I do not want to do it again. I found myself in a car with my son and his wife who had come down from New Jersey to check on me. We were heading back for Clinton.

Carol spent Sunday cooking and freezing portions of the most delicious Italian food one could ever want. She divided into portions and froze it for future meals. We had a great visit before they headed back to New Jersey. On Wednesday my youngest son flew in from Vero Beach, FL only to find that there was not a rental car at the airport or in the area. I prevailed upon a neighbor to both get and return him to the flight. My second son, John, with his wife Debbie came a week later, checking up on their sick dad and bringing frozen food. My daughter, Mary Glenn, had been standing by to swoop down at any indication that she was needed. (I think there must have been some planning/plotting in the family.)

It is great to have a caring family!

During November, Lady Bean and I spent another great two weeks in Sky Lake. During that time, I was able to finish the booklet in which I put on paper my feelings during and after Beverly's death. Putting things on paper helped me through a difficult year. It is good to have it finished and behind me. Now I am trying to catch up with all the Christmas activities in the home and at the church. For me, it is like the old saying, *"the hurrier I go, the behinder I get."*

A CHRISTMAS TRADITION CONTINUES. . .DROP-INS

I thought that last year would be my last. But when the Christmas season rolled around, it just did not seem right to have Christmas without friends. So. . .this year I have invited those who are able to spend a part of Friday afternoon drinking hot cider, munching on cookies and talking with each another. More than that, on Sunday I have invited the entire congregation of Providence ARP church to come and enjoy a few minutes in the pastor's home. . .another Christmas Drop-in. I guess as long as heath permits and Lady Bean allows it, the tradition will continue.

YESTERDAY

It was Saturday night and I was sitting at the computer putting the finishing touches on my sermon. I felt a paw and an urgent meow beside my chair. Lady Bean was reminding me that it was time to go into the living room and spend some time on the sofa with her. *Mary Poppins* had just started on the TV and almost before I had my shoes off, Lady Bean had settled close beside me and was putting her head in my hand. Like stepping into the sidewalk painting in the magical park, I was suddenly whisked back some sixteen years to our home in Ocala, Florida. I was sitting on the same sofa. The TV was sitting on the same artificial fireplace. The Christmas tree was in the same relative position in the room. It seemed like we had just come back from bringing our new, young cat, named Bean, from the shelter. She had ventured from under the sofa and had finally felt secure enough to curl up next to me and place her head in my hand.

It was a scene that would happen over and over in the years to come. As I snapped back to reality, I found that Bean had become Lady Bean and had put on quite a few pounds. Her vibrating purr now is combined with a snore. The room is smaller as is the Christmas tree. But most of the decorations are the same and each holds a special memory. The kitchen is in a different place and there is no one beside me on the sofa except the cat. It is interesting, no, wonderful, how little things can send me back on a trip down memory lane. It is also surprising to find that although time and space is different, some things never seem to change. Maybe the combination of past and present makes reality.

HOW I SAVED THE DAY

It was not too long ago. My man-staff had opened the front door and asked me to guard the house while he was doing some silly work inside. I was very glad to oblige and promptly lay down on the front steps to fulfill my duty. I was almost asleep. . .we cats never really sleep, we just pretend. . . when I heard it. My nose stood straight up I tested the air for an unusual smell.

Then I saw it.

I had heard about mountain lions but I had never seen one. He was big and fluffy and was jumping and rolling around on the grass. I guess he was sizing up my house and my ability to protect it. He looked right at me, stood up and started wagging his bushy tail. Of course, I arched my back in a defensive move and waited with cat-like patience. The lion barked and kept waging its tail. I knew it was a trick to throw me off guard. He inched closer. We were almost nose to nose. I knew the moment of truth had come. I summoned up my courage and gave the longest "hisssssss" possible. Then I swiped his nose with my clawless paw.

Would you believe that he jumped back, put his tail between his legs and ran to the house next door while yelping like a dog? You know, now that I think about it, he looked like a dog, but I'm certain it was a lion. I sure hope the neighbors have a brave cat to guard them. My man-staff must have heard the noise for he came to the door and petted me. I'm sure I heard him say, "Well done, great guard cat."

We came inside together, but I will long remember the day I saved my house and man-staff from the big, bad mountain lion. LB

THE DAY THE CIRCUS DIED

AN ENSIGN IN THE FAMILY

It was my first trip to Rhode Island. . .a rather crowded one, at that. The plane was small and my seat even smaller. When I arrived, Mack and Carol, father and mother of the ensign to be, met me and we were off to the hotel. Festivities were scheduled for that night in the same hotel, and I enjoyed being with the family and the anticipated event.

Thursday night it snowed and Mack drove me out to see where the millionaires lived. Friday was the big event at the base. We were entertained by the naval band and watched proudly as Francis M. Womack, IV became an ensign in the US Navy.

Saturday morning I enjoyed riding in an official car around North Brunswick. The family had prepared a gathering of friends and classmates on Sunday night, with over seventy-five in attendance. It was a great tribute and send off for Ensign Womack. I enjoyed visiting with the family until Tuesday when I again squeezed into the airline and winged my way home.

A LITTLE BOY AGAIN

Saturday morning it was snowing pretty hard. Mack, who is mayor of North Brunswick, took me down to city hall where we picked up an official car with lights all over it. We drove around town checking the road and stopping for motorists who slid off the road. He let me operate the gadget that turns on the red or blue blinking lights, horn and siren. (It was almost as much fun as the time I rode the Amtrak engine and blew the whistle.)

A STORY OUT OF THE PAST

It had been a busy week in Charlotte, where I was serving a church. Snow had come earlier in the week. Now it was sloppy and messy outside and the weatherman was predicting more cold rain. We had put off going to the grocery story for two reasons: the weather and tomorrow was payday. It was Friday night and after sitting around the fireplace, telling a few stories, we got ready for bed, looking forward to sleeping late on Saturday. We had tucked our four children in bed, the oldest being seven. As I climbed into bed, I could hear rain on the roof and wind in the trees. It was a perfect night for sleeping.

Suddenly, lightning split the air and a roll of thunder shook the house. We heard eight little feet and four paws coming down the hall and felt four children and a dog pile into our bed. Just as we all settled down, the phone rang.

"Hello Francis, this is Frank, do you remember me from Seminary?"

Yes, I remembered him. Frank was a good friend in school. . .a little strange but a good friend. He had left the south to teach Hebrew in a school in Bangor, Maine (you have to be a little strange to leave the south to live in the cold of Bangor, Maine.)

"Francis," he continued, "We are passing through Charlotte with our three children and we cannot find a motel. . .could we come and spend the night with you?" What do I say? "Sure, ole buddy, come on out!" An hour later they find our house and we met his wife and three children for the first time. I asked, "Have you had anything to eat?" I knew it was the wrong thing to say. . .but it was said.

"We haven't eaten since an early breakfast and the kids are starved!"

I looked at Jackie and she stared back. I could feel her saying, under her breath: "I told you we should have gone to the store!" There is nothing in the house to eat. What do we do? I put on my

325

raincoat, slipped into my overshoes and went next door. . .to the house with the doormat that read: ONE OLD GROUCH AND ONE BEAUTIFUL PERSON LIVE HERE

(As I stood in the cold, ringing and knocking, I remembered the scripture, *"trouble me not, the door is now shut. . .my children are with me in bed . . .come back tomorrow."*) I prayed that the beautiful person would answer the door. . .no such luck. The Ole Grouch opened the door and growled, "It is midnight and snowing. . .whatever it is you want, it can wait until morning." He would have closed the door except my foot was in it. After a few exchanges, my neighbor relented: "I'm awake now! Come on in if you must!"

The beautiful person joined him and she helped me fill my basket from her refrigerator and added some fruit and cereal. The night was saved. My friends were fed. But I will never forget the drama of that night. (This has happened before. Jesus told almost the same story in Luke 11: 5-13. It even has a surprise ending. Read it!)

THE CHILD'S CATECHISM

I had slipped into the pulpit early to get my papers straight. Voices from a children's Sunday school class floated up from the front rows of the empty church. I heard the teacher's question and then the unison response:

Q: Who made you?
A: God
Q: What else did God make?
A: God made all things
Q: Why did God make you and all things?
A: For His own glory
And on it went.

I sat down and quietly listened as children learned "A Catechism for Young Children." It took me back eighty-one years when I was being taught the same answers. They were simple and easy to remember, not draped in the confusing tapestry of advanced theology, and they formed the framework of my theology and ministry. I could quietly answer many of the questions with the children.

I wonder how many churches of today, still teach this version of the Westminster Catechism. I hope there are simpler, more understandable versions of the many creeds and statements of faith that are the basis of Presbyterian theology. Maybe in a world of confusion, it is time to strip away long and complex verbiage and go back to a version of "A Catechism for Young Children," since we are all children of God.

THE DAY THE CIRCUS DIED

Tonight the local TV news was advertizing the last performance of the Ringling Bros. Circus in our area. Soon the Greatest Show on Earth would hang up its high-wires, say goodbye to the clowns and close its doors forever. Soon that great circus would be a thing of the past. People were lamenting and paying tribute to entertainment that had been around some 150 years. I, too, was saddened to hear it, but for me, the circus was already dead.

It died when the huge canvas tents came down for the last time. It died when the circus moved inside or into concrete stadiums. It died when majestic elephants could not be used to pull the ropes that unfolded the tent and lifted it skyward. It died when I could no longer walk through the circle of side-shows nor jump as the caged lion roared at passersby.

For me, it died when I could no longer watch the circus train unload, nor savor the mixed smells coming from animals and the circus mess wagon. For me it died when I could no longer climb the shaky bleachers and sit on boards smoothed by a thousand posteriors. It died when I could no longer feel the tent shake as the human cannonball hit the net. The tent, the wires, the nets, the three rings with something different going in each of them; the transient nature of it all, the little car that held so many clowns. . .it all changed for me when the big top came down.

I guess it was inevitable; nothing on this earth lives forever, not even elephants and circuses. But I am glad for the memories that linger as long as I do. I will pull out the old movie of the circus and the circus train and live in memory what will soon fade into the past. I pay tribute to Ringling Bros. Barnum and Bailey Circus, the Greatest Show on Earth, as it dies again, but will live forever in a million memories.

CHECKING UP ON AN OLD MAN

Many of you have asked, "How are you getting along?" The other day a young person asked, "How does it feel to be old?" The truth is, I really do not know, because I have never having been this old before. I am not sure how to define "old."

I tell them, "I'm doing fine for an old man, better than many." The truth is I am exploring a new world. . .one that is different from anything I have ever known. The fact is I refuse to grow old gracefully. My doctors tell me I am OK but they reserve the right to poke around and try to find all kinds of ailments. My schedule is determined by doctor visits.

I still like to explore new interests, but it is harder to get started than it used to be. So many things are contradictory. I live among people, have good friends and enjoy fellowship, but I feel very much alone. I still have my many "toys". . .my computers, my radios, my cameras and my airplanes, but I find myself losing interest in the things that used to give me so much pleasure. I seem to have exchanged anticipation for past memories, and the dark shadow of loneliness is always hanging around. However, I find great pleasure in the church I am now serving and give thanks that I am still able to be a pastor. It is a model of a small church worshipping, living and serving as a family of faith.

You asked how I was doing. . . this tells you far more than you want to know. I am well, doing fine in a new and lonely adventure called aging.

A WEATHER CAT?

I have been many things in my lifetime and have used most of my seven lives wisely. I have protected the house, I have been the

328

author of at least two books and I have been a traveling companion and caretaker. I have even served as a warming-pad in cold weather.

I like to get an early start and usually get him up before he is ready. I lead him to the kitchen, get a quick bite of food, go to the door and stand and look at him. He gets the message and I go out. Now I do not mind these things, but I really think that my man-staff is going too far when he wants me to be his weather cat. He tells me that he can tell how cold it is by the length of time I stay outside. He measures it in something called degrees. He also says that if I come in wet, he knows it is raining and if my fur is fluffed up, it is windy.

I want to do my part as a family member, but don't you think it may be going too far to treat an almost-perfect and dignified cat like a weather station? I think I will go on strike for a raise or at least more treats. LB

ADDING LIFE TO YOUR YEARS

SNOW IN CLINTON!

As I look from my carport through the frame trellis that will soon be filled with vines, green leaves and yellow jasmine, I see a snow coming down in mid March. Snow began falling while I was still getting my early hours of sleep. The grass, bushes and trees soon wore a crown of white that glistened as sunshine fought through light, grey clouds. It is always amazing how the world around us can silently change.

The ground was too warm to make the roads dangerous, so at the appropriate time I was off to church. The hardy souls and faithful worshippers were welcomed by a carpet of new fallen snow. By the end of the service the ground, grass and tree limbs had reappeared in their natural color. We were glad to see the blanket of white seep slowly into our thirsty landscape. We hoped and prayed that this late freeze had not killed all the early flowers and destroyed the tiny peaches just forming in their flowers. It was good to have the snow come and it was good to see it go with sunshine taking its place.

TAX TIME

Papers and forms, O My!
Receipts and figures, O My!
W-2s and 1040 s, O My!

Well, I have put it off as long as I could. I must pull out the 2016 tax folder and dedicate the dining room table to papers and clip and the calculator. I used to put things off until March 14, and later to April 14. Then I would meet all my friends between 10 p.m. and midnight in a long line at the Post Office, trying to get that timestamp on my tax envelope. Things have changed in the latter years, as I now send them to a tax company, get them back to sign and return. It is a little easier, but still brings the stress of being honest yet getting the most out of my deductions.

Tonight, I brought them up to Moss Manor where there is no one to disturb me or hear me vent my frustration. The papers are out on the table. My trusty calculator is handy; I have sharpened the pencil and am ready to look up my financial record on the computer. It is time to start.

But wait! I still have to meet the radio net. . .there is something I want to see on TV. . .I need to get my airplanes charged up for tomorrow. . .I can always do taxes tomorrow; after all, it is not really due until April 18[th.]

One of my cardinal doctrines is procrastination.

THEY GOT IT WRONG!

Did you see the blazing front cover of last month's AARP Bulletin?

They must have missed the boat when Ponce de Leon was looking for the fountain of youth, or maybe they are trying to rediscover it. Whatever they were trying to say, I think they got the "cart before the horse" or the "years before the life." Sure, we want to live as long as it is appropriate. For some it may be a long, long, and sometimes miserable life. New medicines, foods, and lifestyles are making that possible. So what is wrong with the cover? I would move two words around to make the cover read:

LIVE
LONGER!
50 PROVEN WAYS TO
ADD **LIFE** TO YOUR **YEARS**

Written this way, I would read the article with interest and anticipation. I look forward to a few more years ahead of me, but only if there is some quality of life in those years. I have watched too many people exist without living. Except for Methuselah, I do not remember anyone who became famous because of the number of years they spent on this earth.

Some of the doctors I see are intent on giving me longevity but at the cost of the quality of life. When I tell them that I do not want to live beyond the point when life has no meaning for me and others, they look at me as if I am from another planet. The doctor's work is to prolong life, and that is good. My work has been to bring a new quality to life and to prepare people for the inevitability of death which is not all bad.

Stephen Vincent Benet wrote, "Life is not lost by dying; life is lost minute by minute, day by dragging day, in all the thousand small uncaring ways." There are a number of books out there that give us guidance on how to improve the quality of the years we have left. The Bible is one of them and I recommend it highly.

Maybe next month they will catch their mistake and write an article about fifty proven ways to add life to your years, but I really do not expect it. After all, maybe that is our job. If so, we had better get to work.

VALENTINE'S DAY

I came to church and made a note on the bulletin to wish ever one a Happy Valentine's Day but little did I expect the surprise that came to me. As was my custom, I had come into the sanctuary before church to greet and welcome those who were a little early.

I looked up from greeting folks and there were two lovely little ladies from the Sunday school carrying a strange looking twig tree with strange leaves. They came to me with smiles and handed the tree to me. "It is the valentine from our class to you." On the tree were paper hearts and notes with valentine greetings written by young fingers. I was both surprised and honored. Never before had I received such a creative valentine from such lovely children.

Immediately I placed it on the piano in the front of the church. Maybe Valentine's Day is not a church holiday, nor is the tree even appropriate for a solemn worship service, but I am sure that the Lord was just as pleased with this expression of love as I was. I took it home where it enriched my living room and my spirits.

Thanks to those who care.

TRIMMING THE GRAPE VINES

I had grown up in the city. I grew up thinking milk originated with the milkman and his horse-drawn wagon. Even in my third pastorate I could not tell the difference between an emerging stalk of corn and Johnson grass. So it was a new experience when I was asked to help trim the long row of grapevines. With clippers in hand, I started out.

"Cut each new growth just past the second sign of potential growth," I was told. I started clipping in earnest, being carful not to step on the fire ant mound that surrounded each support. For about an hour we pulled and clipped. We created enough reeds to make a Christmas wreath for each door in the community. I was glad when the foreman, Tom, said, "that's enough work for the day, let's go home."

The next day I gathered up some of the cut branches, took them home and began another grapevine wreath. Guess it is just my 1930 upbringing. . .waste nothing, save everything. . .that nudged me to keep them. Guess that is why my house is overflowing with "stuff."

THE BANNISTER

In the home in which I grew up, there was a long staircase leading to the second floor. From the top, there were three short steps to a landing where the stairs made a right angle to the first floor. To the right was a wall. To the left was a polished railing about three feet high that ended in a square newel post on which sat a beautiful old vase. For a youngster, about four feet high, the long banister was the perfect place on which to sit side-saddle and slide, almost to the post, and then dismount with a jump to the floor. It was my preferred mode of travel.

One day, I failed to dismount in time and crashed into the post. The beautiful old vase came crashing, too. I gathered the many broken pieces and tried to glue and tape them back together. When my mother appeared, the scene dissolved into tears, anger, understanding, forgiveness and restraint.

If only I could ride the banister again. If only broken things like bones, hard feelings, hearts and dreams were as easy to repair or replace as that vase at the bottom of the stairs.

WALKING STIFF

The other day I noticed Lady Bean coming back from her walk around the house. I was following right behind her. She was walking like her legs were stiff and every once in a while she would look back at me and give a complaining meow. I thought to myself, "My, don't we make a fine pair? She's showing signs of arthritis and old age and here I am, shuffling along, trying to keep up and keep my balance." Lady Bean finally sat down in the grass and just looked at me. She was too proud to ask but I knew what she wanted. I reached down and scooped her up in my arms. Of course, she complained and growled softly as if protesting but snuggled closer to me at the same time.

We staggered to the front of the house together. She demanded that I put her down so that she could proudly enter her home victoriously. I followed more slowly, thinking: "What a grand pair we were, growing older and more decrepit all the time and both of us too proud to admit it." Our motto is the same: **Never Grow Old Gracefully**!

MY OWN VALENTINE CARD

I got a valentine. . .just for me. . .addressed for me. . .with a beautiful picture of a red heart on the cover. I have seen them before; I have knocked them off of the dresser, but I have never had one of my very own. The only problem is that I do not know who "my special valentine" is. He or she did not sign it. Guess I will just have to pretend it is from each of you. I will keep my valentine next to my basket. I hope the valentine cards you got meant as much to you as mine did to me.

HOMESICK!

My man-staff and I made a trip to Sky Lake. I like to come to my other home, up here in the mountains. I remember lots of happy times. . .times when I could explore the mountain with my man-staff. I still like my basket here. It just fits me and is high enough so I can see around the whole room. It seems that I remember someone being here with me most of the time, taking naps or working in the kitchen, but now I am alone most of the time.

My man-staff feeds me and then goes off carrying his big toys. It is very quiet here. Even when my man-staff lets me go outside, it is either wet or cold. I do like to sit in the living room with him and watch the fireplace. It is like a television for me. But once in a while it pops or makes a loud crackling noise that frightens me, so I come back to my basket.

It is nice to be here but I miss my other home, the sounds that come from big trucks outside or wood being sawed next to my house. I really miss the bunch of green grass that I like to munch on. I hate to admit it, but I will be glad when my man-staff puts me in the van and takes me back to my other home. I don't think I will even hide under the bed when he begins to pack. LB

RIVERS OF MEMORY

ON TURNING 159

Today I turned 159. To celebrate the occasion I received two new shoes as my old ones had worn rather thin. The doctor operating on me did a good job. He checked my temperature, my insides and poked me in the strangest places. He even suctioned out a few things from me. He said he thought it was cat hair. When he was finished, he said, "For your age, you are looking mighty good." That made me feel really proud. Wonder what I will feel like when I turn 160?

No, there is no mistake. I really am that old! Oh, you thought this was Lady Bean or her man-staff talking. . .sorry about that! I did not mean to deceive you, but I am their trusted friend, their blue van talking. . .you know, the one with all those wires sticking out of the top. I have just turned over 159,000 miles.

We've been through a lot together. It was hot when we lived in Florida and I used to get sand in my shoes from beach sand. When they took me to the mountains, my front shoes wore down on the sides because of the many sharp curves and turns I had to make.

Since I came to South Carolina I am a little bored because I sit in the carport most of the time while he uses a golf cart. One time there was more excitement than I wanted. It was when I banged into a truck and they had to do plastic surgery on my front end. But now I am all spruced up and ready to go. I even took a practice run to Wilmington the other day. I suspect we will be taking a long trip, soon. I hope so. Maybe when I get back I will have turned 160,000 miles

ANTICIPATION

Looking forward to an event can be as exciting as the event itself. Do you remember in days of old, how much wonder and excitement there was in those long days before your birthday or Christmas? You could imagine that you were getting almost anything. Since most of us have grown into the age of reality, the edge sometimes seems to have rubbed off of things to come. The new and different almost seems routine. But think again.

Whether it is a trip to a foreign country or an event when family gathers, anticipation can be as much fun as reality. There is not a mishap or a faulty plan. Everything is just as we want it to be. While the world may not be perfect, the event we look forward to can come close. In our plans, in our dreams, in our anticipation, everything will be perfect.

Beyond that, anticipation can last a long, long time. The reunion, the wedding, the trip may last but a few days but our plans, our dreams, our anticipation can last for months before it actually happens. Looking forward, the actual event and remembering can be rolled into one in our memory and may last a lifetime.

There will be adventures to come, be they small or large, be they of our choosing or a surprise. Look forward to what might come your way. Enjoy it when it comes. Treasure the many memories until they slowly fade into oblivion, and then begin again.

Anticipation is a wonderful part of the adventure of life.

THE FLORIDA ADVENTURE

In June of this year, I had the privilege of attending the wedding of my granddaughter, Ashley. It was a wonderful event as Ashley Womack became Mrs. Britt Phillips, making a couple that seem meant for each other. But the story I tell is about much, much more. It is about little things that took me out of today and whirled me back in time. This is a story that mixes reality and memory, present and future all rolled in one.

My journey to Florida was both sad and wonderful. It was the first time I had made the trip since Beverly's final journey. I would look over and almost expect to see her beside me and have her hold my cup of coffee. But it was a joyous trip too, because I had the opportunity to share the joy of a wedding, to see old friends, visit churches I had served, be with family and make new friends. Every trip can be an adventure if you let it. This adventure took me first to Ocala, then to St. Augustine and all the festivities of the wedding. Then I would return to Ocala, visit two former churches, retrace my steps through my home town of Jacksonville, and then drive back to Savannah for a night with family and return to my Clinton home.

RIVERS OF MEMORY

The trip from South Carolina to Ocala, Florida, took me over many creeks and rivers. Most of them reminded me of times we anchored in them just before they flowed into the Atlantic. Each creek or anchorage had a story. But three rivers brought special memories.

As the speeding stream of cars and truck race down I-95, I watched carefully for the St. Mary's River that marks the Georgia/ Florida state line. As a small boy, returning from Montreat, when we crossed the bridge I would celebrate and say, "The skies of home look more beautiful that any others." (Home always has the best of everything.) On the narrow, two lane highway, we would soon pass Dinsmore Dairy and I would remark, "That's where our milk comes from." It was the river that sang out, "We are almost home."

Years later, I remember the excitement of a young family crossing the same bridge as we moved our home, complete with four children, the dog and cat and kitchen sink, from West Virginia to Florida. In Jacksonville I took a detour to cross the St. John's River. That river held so many memories. I remembered my first sailboat, the *Bad Girl*, and sailing with my best friend, Ed, and with a young Beverly, the many hours spent on that river with fishing rod or tiller in my hand. I remembered making bridges open for our sixteen-foot sailboat with the tall mast while traffic waited and fumed. The St. Johns was a place of happiness and heartbreak. But that is another, much longer story.

Later in the week, I would cross the St. Johns upstream at Palatka. There I would have time to stop, look and remember. The first real sailing adventure was a wonderful two week voyage with my friend Ed from Jacksonville to Welaka. In memory, I could see the small dock, close to the bridge, where we tied up for the night. As the sun pulled over the horizon, we found ourselves surrounded by a sea of water hyacinths, some tall enough to look down into our open sailboat. The morning was spent with one of us on the bow pushing the heavy, green and purple floating enemies to the side while the other worked the small outboard back and forth. Some adventures never leave you.

The Mug Race was another wonderful memory. As I crossed the bridge, I could almost see sailboats of all descriptions, large and small, sailing or drifting under me. Here was the beginning of fun races for all classes of sail, hoping to make Jacksonville by afternoon. Canoes with sails to ocean-going ships were all part of it. My mug sits proudly before all other mugs in the kitchen cabinet. It is strange and wonderful how a bridge and a river can bring back so many great memories.

In Jacksonville I took a detour to cross the St. John's River. That river held so many memories. I remembered making the bridge open for *Karisto* while traffic waited and fumed. I remembered starting on the first real sailing adventure. Ed and I spent two wonderful weeks chasing adventure as we traveled from Jacksonville to Welaka on our sailboat. The world was ours and we were off to new adventure and the beginning of many sea adventures to come. The St. Johns was a place of happiness, of dreams, and of adventure. But this is another, much longer story.

THURSDAY NIGHT IN OCALA

After four hundred miles of driving, it was good to spend the night with good friends with whom we had traveled and shared a common interest in photography. It is good to talk of old times. How often we dwell upon a past that can never be again and lose the wonder of a new experience and adventure. We drove through the rapidly expanding community that had been our home. Driving by the house in which we lived and shared many good times, I saw it as block and mortar. It left me with a cold feeling. It was just a house among many, no longer ours. It existed in a different world and memories were not there but in my heart and memory. Yes, you can go home again but it is no longer home except in memory.

Thursday night was a time to catch up on family, church, health, friends and activities. A good night's sleep, a good breakfast, and I was off to St. Augustine.

THE OLD CITY

Most of the wedding party had already arrived and were at the beach putting the final touches on their tans. I was pleasantly surprised at my motel, which faced the river and was only a few blocks from the old fort. After settling in, I went to the upstairs porch and looked out over the river with the old fort to the left and the bridge of Lions further down to the right. I sat and dreamed of times past. I could almost see *Karisto*, the sailing vessel on which we traveled every year. We would usually anchor just off the old fort, see the lights and hear the sounds of the city. I am sure the children visiting the fort would pretend the cannons were aimed at us and pretend to fire. The tour boats would pass between *Karisto* and the fort. Cameras would capture the fort, then take pictures of us eating supper in the cockpit and enjoying it all. Other sailboats were anchored there now and I am sure they were enjoying the same excitement that we felt.

Looking south to the ancient Bridge of Lions, I remember circling in the water while waiting impatiently for the timed opening of the drawbridge that allowed us through and on down the intra-coastal waterway. I spent some time looking at the sailboats anchored along the edges of the channel and wishing I was able to relive the days long gone. Later, Mary Glenn and I walked down to Castillo de San Marcos, the oldest Masonry fort in the US. As we walked around the fort, I was a child again; exploring the towers, the store rooms and cannon. I could almost hear my mother telling me to get down to where it was safe.

St. Augustine is far different from the town I knew in the thirties, but it is just as fascinating. We returned to the sea wall, watching the early sunlight dance between the anchored sailboats.

THE REHEARSAL PARTY

Weddings are always wonderful, exciting and much too busy. It is a time to visit with family, yet there is never enough time. There is so much one would like to say and share, yet things are rushed, separated, and often confused. Still there is a brief time for reunion, memories and nostalgia.

The rehearsal dinner was held at the marina beside the Bridge of Lions. It was casual but everything was beautiful. There was a full moon that reflected off the water and brought new dreams and thankful hearts to all. The bride was as beautiful as the groom was handsome. The meal was great. It was a great evening. For me there was a special nostalgia as Beverly and I had docked at the marina and eaten at the same restaurant a number of times as we traveled south on *Karisto*.

THE DAY OF THE WEDDING

The day of the wedding is a busy one for the bride and bridesmaids who are getting their hair done. The groomsmen are straightening their wedding garb and the minister is either going over his notes or going fishing. The parents of the bride and groom are attending to last minute details. For family and friends it is a morning of leisure. A visit to the old lighthouse is in order, and with various means of transportation most arrived for a climb to the top. There is sightseeing and lunch together. The old city of St. Augustine has many things of interest to see and visit. The older of us looked frantically for the Fountain of Youth; yet even those finding it experienced few results.

THE WEDDING

Although no pictures were to be taken by guests, those attending will long remember the simple and deeply meaningful service. The bride and groom pledged themselves to one another and family and friends pledged their support in the years to come. Dr. G. Timothy Womack pronounced Ashley and Brett husband and wife and introduced them as Mr. and Mrs. Britt Phillips. The guests burst into applause.

THE RECEPTION

The reception that followed was filled with music, dancing and fun. Waiters and waitresses were continually bringing finger foods and other goodies. Drinks flowed freely from an open bar. Tables were designated and I soon found the family table. Good-time confusion reigned. Some friends from long ago required a memory search to find where they fit into my life. Sometimes I searched in vain. Maybe it would have been easier if they (and I) looked as we did sixty-five years ago. The dance area was a small rectangular area near the center of the room. It was packed and if I had been willing to enter the packed space, I could not have fallen, even if I tried. I wished Beverly was here as she always carried cotton for our ears to dampen the booming, almost deafening sounds of rhythms like "YMCA" and other action songs of a generation beyond mine. There was action everywhere but there was loneliness as well. It was a great occasion and I was glad to be part of it. I slept well that night.

VISITING CHURCHES

The bothersome alarm clock rang me out of bed early Sunday morning. I was driving back to Ocala to visit the churches where Beverly and I had been a part. The Reddick Presbyterian Church was a small church I had served alternately for almost five years. They knew I was coming so at 9:30 a.m. the congregation came early to prepare and serve a nice breakfast in my honor. It was a joy to see friends with whom we had grown close in friendship and ministry. We shared our stories of joy and sadness.

Ten o'clock and time for service came too soon, and the breakfast broke up in favor of worship. It was a good visit. It was the first time I had been to Reddick since Beverly had been on the piano bench. Both I and the people at Reddick felt a little emptiness. Soon I was on the way to my next church stop.

A VISIT TO COUNTRYSIDE

The minister was well into his sermon when I arrived. Immediately I noticed a different environment. The church doors were locked during service. Perhaps it was for safety, but it gave me a bad feeling of being locked out of a place of faith. I was let in by a watchful usher. I sat with friends and looked around at the place when I had on occasion filled the pulpit. I saw faces, old and new, and empty places where a friend used to sit. I listened to the sermon and truly worshiped but it was a different place than the one I knew where Beverly served as an Elder. Maybe it was I who had changed. Maybe it was the same or better and I did not recognize it. I enjoyed renewing old friendships but for me it was a lonely place of memories.

After the service I visited with old friends and hurried off to eat dinner with a small group of them. That afternoon we drove through the community I knew for seven years and yet I did not know at all. The winds of time blow continually, dimming memories, bringing in new homes and new people. In the whirlwind, in the dust and debris of change, my memory mixes with the dust of passing time. Good times and tragedy mingled. On Top of the World in Ocala is only a fading memory. It is just a place in which we lived.

Sunday night Brad, Mary Lou and I spent the evening talking about family, looking at videos and sharing experiences. It was good to be with friends but I was glad to leave a community I really did not recognize. Change is both the wrecking ball and the building blocks, but only change is permanent.

343

JACKSONVILLE

I left the St. Johns River to my right and turned north on I-95, a highway that I helped to build as a summer job in 1948. I drove through the neighborhood in which I grew up and passed the parking garage that covered the space where my boyhood home once stood. I passed my high school and the drive-in "Pig Stand" where Beverly and I would share a single limeade with two straws. Rain was coming down in buckets. A few blocks away across the railroad track was Evergreen Cemetery. I turned in, confident I could find Beverly's marker. I looked and looked but finally gave up and returned to the office to get a map. I was not far off. There were the stones for Beverly's family and her new stone. I placed a rose on each of the family markers and two roses on Beverly's stone, one for her and one for Jackie, my first wife. I was sure they were together, looking down and laughing at my crude gesture of appreciation. I was glad the rain was falling to hide my tears.

TO SAVANNAH AND HOME

It was good to visit Judy and Frank in their lovely home near Savannah, GA. Judy had been part of the family since I first met her at the tender age of seven. She had been with us in St. Augustine for the wedding. We talked about old times when I was married to Jackie, her sister. We planned for a time in August to gather in Sky Lake. They were gracious hosts and I needed to unwind after six days of travel and celebration. After breakfast on Tuesday, Judy led me to I-95 and I was once again off to the races on the highway.

WHY DID HE LEAVE ME?

My man-staff was so slow in doing the newsletter that I wrote two articles and urged him to hurry up with his.

Why did he leave me? Everything was getting along just fine. The weather was getting warm and I was getting to go outside more often. I often slept in the car, when it was not running, of course. I had even been a good cat when I rode in the car. Everything was just fine.

Then I noticed he had the big red box out. That always means trouble. He thought I did not see him but he put a lot of big boxes in the car and even hung his coat on the side. (I kept careful track of everything in the car while he thought I was just sleeping in the sunshine.) I thought he was going to take me to my other house. Although I was under the bed, I was ready to go when he pulled me out. But this time he just looked under the bed and said goodbye. Then he was gone. The next day I watched for him to come back. I knew I was in trouble when nurses started coming every afternoon to check my food.

Why did he leave me? I really was ready to go. He was gone so long I began to worry. Finally, after what seemed to be a couple of months, I heard the van rattle into the carport. The door opened and there he was. I asked him, in no uncertain terms, "Why did you leave me?" He never answered but he petted me and let me outside so I stopped fussing. I really was glad to see him and even slept with him all night long.

Next time I see the red box come out, I am going to hide in the car. Then maybe he will take me with him. LB

SURPRISES!

Sometimes my man-staff surprises me. You see, I am a very gentle cat. I am careful where I walk. I usually walk under him or just in front. I am helping him get where he is going, but he is always telling me to move or get out of the way. I ignore him. When I jump into an open drawer or up on a dresser, I am always careful where I put my feet, but if something is in my way it has to go. Sometimes it makes a crashing sound and he comes running. It is not my fault. It should not have been in the way.

The thing that puzzles me the most is this. I get up earlier than he does, and I go into his room to see if he is awake. If he is not, I very gently jump on to his bed. Usually I land, very gently, in the middle of his stomach. He makes a loud noise and pushes me across him. As I said, I am a gentle cat. I am trim for my age. I only weigh twelve pounds.

I jump carefully. I just do not understand why he shouts out and sometimes gasps for breath. . .he is a strange man-staff. But I have

gotten used to his behavior and it no longer bothers me, because I am a gentle, careful and even thoughtful cat. LB

NOTE

A few days after I returned, we received the news that my grandson, Ensign Francis M. Womack, IV, was on board the Destroyer *Fitzgerald* when it was rammed by a cargo ship in the Sea of Japan. He was not hurt but was in a position on the bridge to see the collision and witness devastation and death. The ship and most of its crew are back in their base in Japan, but for the young men who saw the accident there will be emotional scars. We hold Ensign Womack, his shipmates and families of those who died in our thoughts and prayers.

THE VALUE OF TRADITION

ON TURNING EIGHTY-EIGHT

How does it feel to be eighty-eight? Before I start complaining, I will say that at eighty-eight I feel very fortunate to have the strength and opportunities to do the things I do. I appreciate the many cards. God has been good to me. In this newsletter there are a number of articles that might reflect how I feel.

I am feeling a little sore from pulling a few weeds from the garden. I find myself depending more and more on my cane to keep my balance. The option of using the "electric chair with wheels," the one Beverly left for me, looks better and better.

How does it feel to be eighty-eight? It feels like time is running faster and faster. It feels like it is always time for a nap. I almost panic when I think of all the things I want to do before something happens that will restrict me. Still, it feels good to be able to walk without help, drive without problems, eat what I want, and live in my own house without assistance.

How does it feel to be eighty-eight? It feels like I should go to bed earlier and sleep later. The older I get the more I dream. Let me tell you about a dream I had the other night. I was back in Jacksonville, FL where I grew up. I was planning to throw a party and invite "that ole gang of mine," the group I hung out with, that put up with my foolishness and still liked me. I sent out the invitations, and on the appointed day and time I waited for the gang to gather. I waited all evening and nobody came. Then I got a phone call from California, from a member of our gang, who reminded me that he and I were the only ones still living and it was too far for him to come. I was glad when Lady Bean woke me by jumping on the bed and telling me it was time for breakfast.

What does it feel like to be eighty-eight and still counting? It feels good to be alive. It feels good to have the friends I have. But still, it is lonely near the top when none of the ole gang are left to come to the party. Sometimes it feels like I am living in the past. I can remember things that happened then, far better than what is happening now. Guess I had better stop as I cannot remember what else I was going to say, except: It is good to be here and be able to write.

LIVING IN TWO WORLDS

Last week, I felt like the world and my routine was closing in on me. I felt I just had to get away for a day or so. I drove up to my other home in Sky Lake. Sometimes I feel that I am living in a box. I have great friends here in Clinton. The home provides for me. I have security. But at times, I feel the walls of aging are surrounding me. I watch the process of aging all around me. I feel the door to a new adventure is closing. There is past and present but very little future.

When I go to my home in the mountains, I feel I have gained control of my life again. There I might, possibly, find a new adventure. Now I know that I have just turned eighty-eight, and there are limitations. There are disadvantages to being free, and I know that I will to glad to return to the security of "the box" and visit with my friends. I also see the church that I am privileged to serve as a way of tying my worlds together, of giving both adventure and purpose to an aging pastor.

Maybe I am living in three worlds and I need them all. At least, that is my perspective from my vantage point of eighty-eight.

THE VALUE OF TRADITION

Bonclarken is the ARP assembly grounds in Flat Rock, NC. There you will find a cluster of homes, a small hotel, a lake for canoeing and fishing, a gathering spot for youth and a large gym, an assembly building and a worship center. It is an important place in the denomination, much like Montreat used to be before it became a town.

But more than being a place, Bonclarken is a tradition. Year after year people return to attend conferences and camps. They play and worship and learn. They make new friends and enrich old bonds. They learn the meaning of what the larger family of faith should be.

For the past week, young people and adults from all over the assembly had been attending the annual music camp. They had been part of an environment that is a church conference. They have looked forward to the week for a long time. The climax of the music conference is a closing in which choirs for preschool to adults take part. There are at least five choirs who have practiced all week and are ready to sing. There is a brass ensemble. Good church music fills the auditorium for almost two hours. It was a great and inspiring time of music and worship. . .no sermon. . .only music.

But it was not the music, nor the beautiful setting that impressed me most. Rather it was the emotional words of a young man who had traveled a long way from where he was working to be there for the service. He leaned over to me and said, "I have been part of this music week since I was five years old. I have sung in every age choir and have been part of the closing service. When I get married and have children, they **will** attend this conference every year."

That is Tradition! That is what it means to be a community of faith.

ANOTHER RAINY MORNING AT MOSS MANOR

I woke up this morning to the sound of rain hitting the roof and rushing through the gutter down spout. I knew it was coming for I had watched the large mass of green and yellow crawl across the screen of my tablet. I can remember the days when we would be surprised by wind or rain. It was rather nice not to have the weather laid out before for the week to come. We don't have as many surprises as we used too.

At the breakfast table, I look out at a wet world. There is not just the sound or the look of a wet driveway. I also see the leaves of the Japanese maple trees dancing and bouncing as a drop hits them and they dip to rid themselves of the water. The tiny violets are looking up as if to say thank you while the taller snap dragons are bending down in humble praise.

A rainy day is good. It keeps me from feeling guilty when there is yard work to do and I am inside. A rainy day gives me the opportunity to catch up on a thousand things inside that I have put off doing because sunshine and dry weather have tempted me outside. A rainy day forces me to pick up things I have left strewn around the house. It sends me to the basement workshop where things need straightening, sorting and throwing away. In a sense, it captures me and makes me do what I have put off doing. A rainy day makes it great for sleeping and, all too soon, after getting a few things done, I will join the cat who thinks it is a great day to stay in bed. Rain sings a lullaby for napping.

Although there are things I would like to be doing outside, I am glad it is a rainy day in Georgia, and I am going to enjoy it.

THE DOCTOR IS OUT

The doctor is out. . .The system is in. . .and the system is broken! I guess it was inevitable as we become more efficient and less humane. The doctor seems to be hidden inside a tablet that holds all my data and dictates my prescriptions. I guess it is necessary because the window of time the doctor has to spend with each patient is set by the system. Every once in a while, the doctor escapes the computer and emerges as a person that knows and cares about me as person, but soon must return to the tools of the system.

Now I do not blame the doctor. He is caught up and fixed by the system as much as the patient. Behind the iron mask of the system, there is, more often than not, a person who really cares and would like to fulfill the Hippocratic Oath.

The system is broken! The doctor is out! In our town and in other places I have known, the system is growing and the doctor is simply being absorbed. Across the street from each other there is a small hospital and a doctor's complex. Each belongs to a different system or corporation and neither will recognize the other, nor allow access for treatment. While each fight for power and profit, both patients and doctors lose.

Who is to blame? The government and the insurance companies with their mound of paper work and regulations? The corporate office that provides better technology but is more concerned with the bottom line than with healing? The doctor who must sell his or her soul in order to survive? Or the patient who is caught in the middle and must pay for the broken system?

I do not know the answer. I cannot blame the doctor. I believe most doctors really care about their patients but are shackled by the system. I appreciate the equipment and technology that the system can provide and individual doctors cannot afford. I hurt for the patient who cannot afford the system and cannot find the doctor because "the Doctor is out." I pray for a time when the corporate war will cease and the doctor can climb out of captivity. I hope and long for the time when I can really feel that "the doctor is in" and "the system has been fixed."

I KNOW HOW TO GET HIS ATTENTION!

My man-staff is much bigger than I am, physically, so I have to use my brains, and whatever else I might have, to get what I want. There are a number of ways to do this:

- *If he is not paying me enough attention, I jump up on the desk where he is busily typing and look at the same thing he is looking at so intently. Now, I cannot make out anything on the screen, and I doubt if he can, but he either has to pet me and talk to me or pick up my thirteen pounds and move me. Either way, I have gotten his attention.*
- *If it is time for him to go with me to the sofa and let me curl up next to him, I get beside his chair and talk to him in Siamese language. After a while he gets tired of hearing me, so he closes his machine and goes to the living room to watch TV. I curl up next to him, put my head in his hand and begin to purr.*

- *If he sleeps later than my breakfast time, I carefully and gently jump on his bed. I land as close to his middle as I can. That usually does the trick. He gets up and eventually gets my breakfast.*

Whatever the problem, I have a solution, and I always win. LB

PEANUTS

SEPTEMBER'S SONG

> "Oh, it's a long, long while from May to December
> But the days grow short when you reach September
> When the autumn weather turns the leaves to flame
>   One hasn't got time for the waiting game."

I love the time of year when the long, hot summer gives way to the cooler nights of fall. Leaves are not yet dressed in their October splendor, but there is a tinge of orange and yellow if you look closely. A few brave leaves turn loose and flutter like drifting butterflies to the ground below. The scuppernongs are beginning to take on a golden hue and sunflowers bend low with the weight of next year's seed. Open windows signal the approach of nights without the noise of the air conditioners. They let in the harmony of nature's symphony of nature's many instruments.

I like to open my mind to the wonder of this season of the year. . .the preview of wonders yet to come. . .the crescendo of the passing year. But like the song reminds us, they come with fall memories of days gone by. . .of Septembers of the past, now only memories. . .of times to be relived in dreams but never again to be experienced in the Technicolor of life.

From my vantage point of age, the words of the song take on new meaning: "The days dwindle down to a precious few. . ." I feel an urgency to draw every bit of energy from each day. There is so much left unfinished, so much to be put down on paper, so many places yet to visit and so many new friends yet to meet. The rush of time drives me to my desk and to my map and to tables filled with new faces. With the prospect of cooler days and darkening colors, I feel the frustration of slowing down, of people I knew so well and yet cannot recall their names; of too many senior moments. In the morning I write down what I hope to accomplish. When night comes, most of them are still on the paper. . .undone.

September is an exciting time of year; a prelude to birthdays, to Thanksgiving and Christmas and then, perhaps to a new year, full of opportunities. . . .or. . .maybe. . .a time of running out of gas and just relaxing. . .leaving things undone in the hands of a new generation of writers and dreamers and doers.

Yet, having said all that, I love this time of year and I look forward to the months ahead, to new friends and new adventures and even to Septembers yet to come. So bring on your color. Turn on the cold of winter. Bring on the flowers of spring. Hopefully, prayerfully, when next summer ushers in September, it will usher in a new and wonderful September song of memories and adventures.

GRAPEVINES

In our complex there are two long rows of grape vines. They were planted years ago by one of our residents and have expanded and thickened each year under the care of a number of our residents. Today the vines are loaded with concords and scuppernongs. Residents have been picking the most obvious and easy to reach grapes. I have been climbing carefully under the wires which hold the vines and finding there the light brown ripened grapes. I am sure I have eaten more than my share and still have a few in the icebox and in the freezer for future consumption.

PEANUTS

As October rolls around it is time for peanuts. Now, all year long I have been eating salted and unsalted roasted peanuts, but in my opinion, the best of all are good, well-salted, boiled peanuts. This time of year we find raw or green peanuts in the stores. For the last few days the house has been filled with the fragrance of peanuts simmering away in my crock pot. It takes about fourteen to sixteen hours to get them to the point where they are firm yet still somewhat soft and pliable. It is like fishing to dip into the pot of dark, brown brine and bring out the succulent, perfectly-boiled peanuts.

When I take them to the dinner table, they become a test for those who have been converted to southern living and those have just come south for the climate. For those who enjoy them, boiled peanuts are the oyster of the vine and will be eaten with gusto and pleasure. My neighbor tells me that the chewed and rejected hulls make excellent mulch, so nothing about the peanut is wasted.

CHURCH IN THE HILLS

On Sunday we closed the ARP church building in Clinton for one Sunday. It was the first time the church had been completely empty on Sunday morning since I had been worshiping with them. I understand a visitor came to worship in Clinton and was surprised that the doors were locked and the building deserted. Where was everyone?

For that one Sunday, the church had moved. Since the building is not the church, the people who worshiped in that building, who are the church, had relocated for one Sunday to Bonclarken. Located in Flat Rock, NC, Bonclarken is the assembly ground for the ARP denomination. It is a place that every ARP must visit on their journey toward heaven. It is almost a heavenly location held in the hand of the mountains and brims with homes, church conferences and summer camp experiences. It is a place of learning and tradition. It is glue that seems to hold the denomination together as a people of God. On that particular Sunday, most of the members and friends of Providence ARP church made the hour and a half journey to gather in a pavilion on the edge of the lake. They came ready for worship and prepared for a picnic that would follow. It was a good service, a wonderful fellowship and a time we will all remember.

The following Sunday we were back in Clinton, worshiping in the building called Providence ARP church. We will be in Clinton each Sunday until maybe next year, when we will again, for one Sunday, take the church to Bonclarken to worship and eat together.

ANOTHER STORY FROM MY DISTANT PAST

Long ago, I was a teenager, like some of you. Nothing had gone right that day. My parents were out of town and Nannie, my grandmother, was at home with me. I had just been cut from the football team; my teacher told me I was failing algebra; my best girl friend had moved to another city, and my Sunday school teacher had called to tell my parents that I had misbehaved. To say the least, I felt mighty low.

Nannie sat me down beside her on the couch and told me the Bible story about Joseph. She ended by giving me a hug and saying, "God's a-workin' in you." It didn't help much then, but I have never forgotten what she said. . .and I have found it true. Things happened to prove her point because every one of the disappointments I told my Grandmother made a big difference in my life.

Because I was cut from football I joined the swim team and helped win a state championship. Because I failed algebra, I was advised to take creative writing and more English, both of which were necessary in my future. Because my first girlfriend moved away, I had at least seven more girlfriends before I met the one that I am sure the Lord sent to me, and I married her. Because I misbehaved in Sunday school, the teacher took a special interest in me. We became good friends and she encouraged me to become a minister.

God was working in ways that I did not recognize. And "God's a-workin" in your life, every day, whether you recognize it or not.

WHY CAN'T HE BE SATISFIED?

My man-staff is very unstable, by that I mean he is constantly moving from one place to the other. Worse yet, he insists on taking me with him. I do not mind being in either of our two homes. They each have their advantages and disadvantages. One sometimes has a dog that is noisy and bothersome. The other sometimes has a black cat who always wants to come inside. I could enjoy living in either home, but my man-staff wants to live in both and it is a long, bumpy, noisy ride in between. I wish he would make up his mind and let me sleep in peace.

I guess he is just unstable and can't be in one place very long. LB

HOLY WATER

HALLOWEEN DROP-INS

Drop-ins have been part of my life for sixty-three years and I am not going to let it stop now! Usually they were held in December with all the Christmas decorations up, but last year there was a scheduling problem. This year I decided to use Halloween for the occasion. I climbed into the attic. (You will hear about that later in this newsletter.) I found a garbage bag with a witch's head sticking out. After getting it down and sorting out the good from the bad, I decorated the living room. There were witches and pumpkins, spider webs and straw people. There was even a live spider that had taken residence in the artificial web. . .he must have lived on last year's candy.

Invitations were sent out to the whole church for Sunday. Another invitation went to the independent dwellers here at the home for Monday. What worried me was, "What shall I do for refreshments?" All I could cook was breakfast, popcorn and boiled peanuts, and I did not feel any of them were appropriate. Neighbors and church members came to the rescue.

When Sunday and Monday arrived, along with friends from the neighborhood and the church everything was ready. There was hot cider, coffee and a punch bowl full of ice cream floats. Sandwiches, cookies, nuts, apples and dips poured in. All I had to furnish were the cups and plates. I did make a few biscotti, just to save face.

Both afternoons the house was filled with laughter and good friends. From my point of view it was a great success. Lady Bean even allowed children and adults to pet her. My thanks to all who helped, brought goodies and washed cups. Thanks to all who came and made this Halloween special for me.

As I write this article on the day after, the house is quiet and seems empty. I am a little lonely as LB is sleeping off the excitement in the other room. Guess I will just file these memories with other good ones and wait for the next gathering to scare away the ghost and goblins of loneliness.

REMEMBERING ON ALL SAINTS DAY

It is Wednesday, November 1st and it is All Saints Day on the church calendar. It is a time to remember and to celebrate those who have preceded us in death and are now with other saints in glory.

Today I remember how I have been blessed. Both Jackie and Beverly were all that I could have asked for. They both died during this season of the year.

It was twenty years ago and we had just finished an Interim Pastorate in Morehead City when Jackie, my first wife and mother of our children, died suddenly. During the service on the next All Saints Day, the young people carried banners they had made celebrating the life of those who had died during the year. I still have Jackie's banner with the symbols of her life on it. It is one of my treasures.

Two years ago today, Beverly, a childhood sweetheart and second wife, was in the hospital following a stroke that left her trapped in a body that would not work. Though immobile, she was aware of what was happening. I was glad she was not sentenced to live for long in that prison. Within a month, she would join Jackie.

Today I remember and pay tribute to both of them. Both meant the world to me and I am a better person because of them. I thank God for choosing them for me. Today I visit days past and wipe away a tear. I sometimes fight depression. But I will not live in the past nor let memories dictate my future. My life may be marked by loneliness but there is the newness of each morning. There are new friends, new opportunities to be of service and new adventures to fulfill my life.

All Saints Day is good, but I am glad it comes only once a year.

NEVER AGAIN

They warned me not to go there but I wanted to start decorating. I carefully put my cell phone in my pocket, pulled down the attic stairs and started up. Going up was not too bad. I moved around the boxes of stuff, around things I had forgotten were there and finally found the old, black garbage bag I had come for. I put the bag right on the edges so I could reach up for it. Then I started to go back down. Oh, there is the rub! It was easy enough to get up but it took me twenty minutes of trial and error to position myself to descend. I lay flat. I kneeled. I rolled around. I searched for hand holds. It seemed impossible to get in a position to safely find the first step and put weight on it. I even thought of calling maintenance to come help me, but that would be too embarrassing. Finally, I edged one foot on the second step, found a hand-hold in the floor and prayerfully, carefully moved down the ladder, hoping my foot would not slip or the handrail give way. The floor never felt so good. That was my final trip to the attic! Until. . .

NUTS!

My next door neighbor called me. "You want to go pick up the pecans the wind has blown down." He must have known I was about out of nuts for my biscotti.

The tree was on the edge of the property. Nuts were all over the ground. It was just a matter of bending over and picking them up. There is the rub! Bending and coming up, over and over again. One time is bad enough but over and over? I even thought of sitting down but just maybe I couldn't get up from the slippery grass.

After what seemed an eternity of bending over and straightening up, we had our two baskets filled. The nuts were of the smaller variety and were very good, but shelling would have been a real task. Luckily, my neighbor knew someone with a shelling machine. I'm not sure what it will cost to get them cracked shelled and cleaned, but I know it will be well worth it.

THE COFFEE CLUB

There are many different coffee clubs. Some meet at the fast food restaurants, some use the lobby of their apartment building, some even rotate from home to home. But regardless of where they meet, they have one thing in common. They drink coffee, or something, and they talk. Their topics of conversations are wide-ranging.

I believe I am part of the perfect coffee club. Early each morning, about the time the sun is shaking off the dew, I stagger out of bed, get a cup of coffee from the kitchen and sit down in front of my ham radio equipment. There, out of the speaker and through the mike, I visit with a number of my friends from different places. This kind of club has many advantages:

- I can still be in my pajamas.
- I only travel from one room to another.
- There is never an argument about where we will meet.
- If there is a hearing problem, I just turn up the volume.
- Politics and religion are forbidden subjects.
- I do not have to remember names, just call signs (required by the FCC).
- When I leave the table, I am magically in my own home.
- I learn something new, important or not, fact or trivia, every day.
- If I do not show up, I am missed but not chastised.
- If get tired of the conversation, there is always the "off" button.

I enjoy my coffee club. It breaks the loneliness of an empty house. It reunites me with friends in different places. So here's to our coffee club! May it long continue! Get yourself a ham radio license and join us.

BLESSING OF THE ANIMALS

I had never been to one before, but when the new Episcopal pastor announced that there was going to be a "Blessing of the Animals" in the yard on the side of the church, I was interested. The only problem I encountered was that Lady Bean refused to go and be blessed. I am not sure whether she thought a blessing by a priest might change the way she behaved or that it might make her clean up her language. At any rate, she did not want to go.

I had promised one of my Episcopalian friends that I would show up with an animal to be blessed and could not go back on my promise. I got the cat carrier from the attic, took a large facial picture of the cat off the wall and remembered a box that held my grandmother's mink stole. The picture fit perfectly on the carrier door, a pillow made the mink stole look bigger inside the carrier. The final touch was to take a piece of the mink that had broken off and tape it to the back of the cage to simulate a tail.

Sunday afternoon I was off with my pseudo-cat to receive a blessing and a little holy water. There were a good number of dogs, some big ones, there. There were two cats that were up for adoption or giving away. The Reverend was decked out in his formal white robe with stole attached. All the dogs received a blessing and no one was bitten. At last it was my turn to take the substitute Lady Bean-in-the-box to be blessed. The Father looked a little aghast but took it in stride. He looked through the small side holes of the carrier and exclaimed, "You really do have a creature in there!" I said nothing so he bowed down and shook a little holy water on the picture and on the mink inside. Snacks for animals and owners were provided by the church.

The whole service was a rather inspiring event. I am sure it meant much more to the owners than to the dogs and cats. I am sure that as long as our animals make us happy, the Lord will continue to give His blessing to creatures of the land, birds in the air and fish that swim in the sea. I took a few drops of holy water home to Lady Bean just to be sure that if this kind of service was necessary to get her into "cat heaven," I did not want her left out.

She was not the least impressed with our effort on her behalf.

THE ICE MEN

The other day I was corrected when I asked someone to get something out of the ice box. "It is called a refrigerator," I was told. Hanging on the carport wall is set of "ice tongs." Few people recognize them or know how they were used. But I remember and they take me back to the mid 1930s.

In our kitchen was a real icebox. It looked similar to the refrigerators we use today except, instead of having a freezer on top, it had a place for a block of real ice. Each day, a mule drawn wagon, covered with loose canvas, would make its way through the alley in back of our house. I remember the singing call from the driver: "Ice man! Anyone need ice? Ice man!" That was the cry that brought me and my friends running to the alley. When the iceman would pick up a block of ice with tongs, like the ones on my carport, and carry it to someone's kitchen, we would all reach into the back of the wagon, looking for broken slivers of ice. They were every bit as good as an ice cream cone and they were free.

When the driver returned and clucked for the mule to go, we would hang on the back of the wagon, getting a free ride to the next stop, where we would be run off by a good-natured driver.

It was an almost forgotten event from childhood. A tiny segment of an age gone by. A pleasant memory from the distant past.

THE CARE CAT

There was a time when I didn't worry about my man-staff. He had someone to take care of him. But for the last few years it has been just him and me. Oh, we got along fine. We would take long walks in our neighbors' yards. Sometimes I would get too far in front of him and he would have to run to chase me. Now, we still go outside but neither of us does any running. He tells me we both have something called "arthur-right-us," whatever that means.

Being a smart and sensitive cat, I began to see that he was moving more slowly and was sometimes unsteady when he walked. I had to move my tail whenever he walked by. I had to move out of the chair quickly when he wanted to sit down. I realized that I needed to take better care of him.

When he stares at that silly screen too long, I remind him by jumping up and sitting in front of him so he cannot see the screen. Of course he has to pet me and talk to me and I like that. When I know he really needs to take a break, I stand by his chair, meow and paw him. He gets up and we go into the front room and he watches TV while I sleep beside him with my head in his hand.

That is good for both him and me. LB

MY CHAIR!

I wish my man-staff would learn that this is MY chair. Just because my chair sits in front of his desk, that does not make it his. It has my smell, my hair and usually my body in it. It is MY chair!

Sometimes I let him use it for a while. He likes to play with his toys that are on the desk. I even let him sit on the very front edge while I sleep on the rest of it. When he gets up, I reclaim all my territory. Then he will roll me out of the way and bring another chair for himself.

It is strange how long it takes him to learn what is mine. We go through the same thing with the bed. I will stake out my claim on the most comfortable place, usually on the pillow. When he comes to bed, I get pushed over or shoved down near the foot. It is humiliating to be treated that way on my own bed and in my own house.

I guess I just have to be patient with him. Maybe someday he will learn . . .but I am not sure about that. . .he is a slow learner. LB, **owner of everything**

MOVE OVER

WHAT IS IT ALL ABOUT?

I was getting a book from our library when a new resident of the Presbyterian home picked up the copy of Moss/Magnolia Manor News that I leave in the library. "Who writes this and what is it all about?" she asked. I tried to explain and maybe she was satisfied, but it made me stop and think. What is MMN all about and what am I trying to say?

Moss Manor News derived its name from our mossy lawn in Sky Lake. It began as a way to keep my family and friends informed about what Beverly and I were doing in our new home in the North Georgia Mountains. I told of our adventures in the gated community of Sky Lake. It listed friends who came to visit. But it morphed into something different as you have seen. Yes, it still told of things we did and adventures we experienced, but it also started to include things from the past, treasured memories, a little theology, a column by a cat named "Lady Bean" and anything else that comes to mind. Someone suggested that it was a slice of life, seen from the age of eighty-eight and counting. I believe Moss Manor News is a way of sharing myself with family, with friends and with whoever wants to read it. In sharing these ramblings with you, I feel I am talking to friends from past and present days. Writing fills a void of loneliness and hopefully brings some meaning, a little knowledge and perhaps a laugh or two.

I am not sure this answers the question that she asked, but it might help.

A VISIT TO THE PAST

The other Sunday I visited a Sunday Service in a church I had served in the 60s. But before I tell that story, let me back up a little and tell a story that kept circling in my thoughts as I drove toward the church.

We moved the day after Christmas. The house in which we'd lived the past three years was empty. The van was crammed full. Of course there were four children, ages one to six; there was the family dog, two tanks of tropical fish and the lady who had helped us clean up and who we were to take home. A Christmas tree that the children would not leave behind was tied on top. At the last minute we caught Tom Terrific, the cat. We closed the doors and started the engine. That was the signal for Tom Terrific to realize what was about to happen. He let out a howl and did three horizontal cycloramic circles around the car, leaving claw marks everywhere. In a gesture of self-survival, I rolled down a window. Tom Terrific sailed out and disappeared into the woods behind the house, never to be seen again.

At a motel that night there was a notice, no pets, which we pretended we did not see. During the evening, a baby bottle broke against the aquarium and in the noise and confusion, the motel owner appeared. He was kind enough to pretend he did not see the pets and finally order was restored and we got a minimum of sleep. The next morning we arrived at the church and manse that was to be our home for the next ten years.

Now back to my story of visiting the church that I served fifty-plus years ago. My daughter, who had been four when we came to serve the church, arrived about 10:30. We walked through the cemetery in back of the church where my wife was buried and where my name was also on the stone. The markers of many past friends greeted us as we walked.

Upon entering the church we were surprised at the changes. The pulpit area had been enlarged and some front pews removed. A piano was now in the pulpit area and a set of drums stood to the side. A set of bells were set up to the right. It was the same building but looked so different. There were about four old-timers who knew who we were and welcomed us. Others were most cordial. The minister welcomed us. The service began with music from bells and choir. I was impressed at the quality of the music and with the number of local mission activities in which they were involved. I thought there were more people in the bells and choir than in the congregation. Hymnbooks were supplemented by a large video screen that gave words of hymns as well as other parts of worship. As the anthem was sung, the faces in the choir seem to change to those that I remember long ago. The sermon was a solid message from scripture. When I sneaked a look around at the empty pews, I could not help but remember days when the church was full and chairs were set up in the isle. It was good to worship and to remember, but there was sadness, too. Everything was so different from what I remembered.

This became the church that held such wonderful memories. It was the place my babies became young men and a woman. This was the church that wept with me in tragedy and joy; that listened to faltering sermons and pronounced them good. This was the church I always felt was my home church. There were so many good memories poring through my thoughts. In its cemetery I will, one day, rest beside my wife and mother of our children.

I was glad we came, glad to remember and to meet new people. I am also thankful that I can hold the congregation in my memory as it was the day I left for another work. I pray for the church, that once again its pews will be filled and that its hand will continue to reach to the community.

It was a sad but good visit to a church I served many years ago.

A NARROW ESCAPE

My recent visit to a former church brought back many memories. As we walked through the cemetery behind the church, stopping at the headstones of many friends, I spied a large, flat marker that brought to mind an event which brought a smile to my lips.

Just below the cemetery, back of the manse, once stood a rough, slab stable in which Sham, my daughter's horse, took residency. Sham had once lived in a riding stable and knew how to open most any gate. He was a good old horse with a mind of his own.

On a Sunday afternoon long ago there had been a funeral for one of the dear saints of the church. After the funeral and the graveside service, the family left while flowers from the church were being placed on the gravesite. I stepped next door to the manse to await their return. As I watched for them, I happened to look back at the gravesite. There, to my horror, I spied Sham eating at the arrangements of flowers on the grave. Out the back door I raced. I stood on the grave marker beside the munching horse, held on to his mane and jumped onto his bare back. Leaning forward, I grabbed Sham's ears, kicked his surprised sides and steered him to the barn, hanging on for dear life.

I was walking back from the barn, catching my breath, when the family car drove up to admire the slightly munched-on and rearranged flowers. They did not notice any rearrangement. I said a silent prayer of grateful thanks.

Years later, as we walked through the cemetery, I remembered the episode and almost laughed, but at the time it was a serious matter. It was a very narrow escape!

I JUST COULD NOT QUIT!

Last year, I stuffed the tree in its battered box and carefully packed ornaments in boxes. Then, when I saw how much space the boxes took up, I vowed that next year would be different. I would celebrate the Christmas Season with a single Moravian star. Christmas drop-ins were to be things of the past. But as October rolled around I forgot all about my promises and even decorated and had a Halloween drop-in.

Now it is almost Christmas and old habits die hard. I realized I had invited all of the independent residents who lived in the houses back of the main building, but a lot of people who could make it up my three front steps had been left out. Residents who needed walkers or were bound to electric chairs had also been left out.

With a lot of help from a friend, we built a temporary ramp which allowed people to be pushed or powered inside. I decided to ask small groups that usually ate at the same table to come over for a Christmas visit and some refreshments. It has worked well and I have enjoyed visiting with different groups.

This year is probably the last for drop-in, but who knows; old habits and traditions die hard.

THROWING AWAY SLIDES

I am running out of space. The shelves in my closets are full of boxes full of trivia that I just will not throw away. Maybe my reluctance to discard comes from my childhood during the depression of the early 30s when string and bent nails were saved and socks were darned.

In the corner of the closet I found a carousel projector and a stack of boxes containing slides. You may remember slides; they filled in the photographic gap between black and white film and the digital age. The projector would not carousel as it should and the bulb soon blew out. I was left with the task of looking through the slide against a light bulb. Most of the slides that I really wanted had been scanned into the computer. Still, there were hundreds more that I knew I would never view again. As I sorted through the boxes, I made a pile to give to the children, a few special ones to keep and a larger pile to throw away. It was like putting a piece of my life in the trash. As I looked and remembered, I threw them in a pile on the floor. There were the scenes from mountains, flowers and seascapes that had faded over the years. There were trips that we had taken and groups of people I could not place. I knew I would never look at them again, but still it was like throwing away pieces of my personal history. I was tempted to gather them up and put them back in a box on the closet shelf. I bravely withstood the temptation and with relief, tinged with sadness, I threw them in the big, circular file to be carried away.

I guess, like discarding paper pictures, it is a necessary rite of passage in the aging process.

CHRISTMAS MEMORIES

Memories are the best thing anyone can have when they are alone at Christmas. There are so many of them. They are almost better than the crowded, busy reality of the present. Because there are so many memories, I can pick and choose, linger where I want and skip over those that give me pain.

I live again my childhood days when we were all required to wait upstairs until Dad gave the signal to descend into the magic of the tree and Santa's gifts. I can be a child again and visit friends, mostly gone now, to see their gifts and share their excitement. I can be in our first manse with a rickety Christmas tree and feel the mystery and excitement of little children, too young to understand, yet filled with wonder of the season. I can enjoy being in the snow with a family rapidly growing up but never too old for Christmas. I can remember the empty nest, and the Christmas when all but one, who was in service overseas, made it home for Christmas.

I remember fun and teasing and love rekindled at reunions. I remember the time when my wife and I celebrated Christmas together because our children needed to be with their families and start their own traditions. And I could visit sad Christmases when I felt alone although I was sometimes with my children. There is so much more that rushes back at Christmas time. It is good to be alone and have time to remember, to revisit, to shed a tear and even break out in laugher.

God is good and has given me a multitude of Christmas memories. I relive thoughts of churches and Christmas Eve services, of friends and family gathering. And more than that; I am still making memories of Christmas adventures, like Christmas drop-ins, serving a church and of course, being with many, many friends.

I wish everyone a Merry Christmas and a Happy New Year.

WHAT DO YOU MEAN, MOVE OVER?

It happens again and again. I settle down for the night while my man-staff plays with some of his silly toys. When he finally gets tired, he comes in and says, "Move over!" What does he mean move over?

I was here first and I have warmed up my spot and I am not moving. Sometimes he accepts my ultimatum, but there are times when he has forgotten how to share and I am spilled onto the floor. Even then, I will not be defeated so I wait for a strange noise from his nose and I jump back and reclaim my spot.

That is not all. He is very bad at sharing what he has to eat. I will sit very nicely beside his chair at supper and politely ask for some of his food. I really do not want to eat the tasteless stuff he eats but it is the principle of the thing. He needs to share what he has. Sometimes he sits on my sofa and brings a plate of food with him. All I want to do is to smell and have a small taste of his food, but he will not share. All I get are the crumbs that fall from my man-staff's table. He just does not know how to share. I would gladly share my dry food with him, as long as there is plenty more for me. After all, I let him live in my house and we should share and share alike. LB

ECHOES OF THE HEART

As the song says, "It a long, long time from Christmas to Valentines," or did I get the time-frame wrong? This issue of MMN has been a long time in coming. So. . .get ready for a ride back in time and wonder with me: "Where did January and half of February go?"

THE DAY AFTER CHRISTMAS

Christmas has come and gone. Christmas Day began early with a threat of rain but nothing materialized. After a quick cup of coffee and a brief chat with my friends by means of ham radio, Lady Bean and I made it into the living room where our presents were still hiding under the tree. We had both either sniffed or felt the packages but, by tradition, had waited until Christmas morning to open them. The church had been good to us and we found many good things to eat. Lady Bean had more fun with the empty boxes and scattered papers than with her toy or treats.

Soon the neatly arranged room was a scene of chaotic tissue papers and empty boxes. Only the tree remained in regal splendor. By 10:30 I was in the car and on the way to have Christmas dinner with my daughter and her family in Black Mountain, NC. By 12:30, we were enjoying Christmas together. It was good to be with family and to enjoy a good Christmas dinner. By 4:30 I was on the way home. Lady Bean was glad to see me, particularly because she wanted her supper. The entire facility was quiet as most of the residents were already in their rooms. It was good to be home but it seemed lonelier than ever.

It is the now the day after Christmas but Christmas seems a decade away. The cat slept late today, leaving me alone to clean up yesterday's confusion. There was really very little to do and the living room was soon ready for company that seldom comes. My mind wandered back to childhood days when there was so much to do, toys to play with and friends to visit. It was a time when Christmas day stretched out for a week.

My reverie moved on to the days after Christmas spent playing with children and repairing broken Christmas toys and to days of the empty nest, when grown children were busy creating their own Christmas traditions. I moved from living in the past to my computer keyboard where I am putting in print the feelings of the day after Christmas. It is lonely in the house but I am glad to have friends and neighbors who are perhaps also lonely with their dreams and memories. I think of the two great ladies that enhanced the wonder of the season.

I am thankful and proud of our children and their children. I have been so blessed. Still I reserve the right to be lonely and nostalgic on this cold winter day after Christmas.

ECHOES OF THE HEART

I had put it off as long as I could but it was time for the Christmas tree to come down. Even Lady Bean wanted her sofa back under the front window. All decorations, except those already boxed and ready for the attic, had to come down. I began de-decorating the tree.

I lifted the stuffed angel from the top. She had been given to us many years ago for a donation to a Christmas charity. As the decorations came off, one by one, I tried to remember when each was first hung on the tree and what it meant. It was a kind of game to make the task go more rapidly.

There were the old faded ones that should be thrown away but that hung on the tree as long as I could remember. As they came down, I could hear the echoes of childhood and the laughter of friends long gone. There was the little red convertible we bought when we could not afford a second car. There were special ones that reminded me of special times and special places. The painted cutouts of wood reminded me of the Christmas after an accident when the children stayed inside and painted them.

The nativity scene came last. The figures of Mary, Joseph, shepherds and animals and kings and the baby Jesus were carefully wrapped and packed. I smiled as I wrapped the donkey, the one with a broken ear, done in by a child that wanted to help. I carefully wrapped the ones that had been given by friends from many places. I wrapped them carefully with warm memories. The lights came down, string by string and I thought of the many Christmases these lights had warmed our hearts and brightened our homes.

The job was almost done; only the manger scene beneath the tree remained. Sad, I thought, to have to box up the manger figures and have only the memories. But these memories are important; they never really fade away unless we let them.

HAND WRITING ON THE WALL

I have received a letter in the mail from the past. . .or so it seems. I eagerly tore open the envelope to see who could be rewarding me with a letter. I nearly dropped the pages in surprise. . .the three pages were written in a foreign language, or so it seemed. The letter was hand-written, each letter artfully connected, separated only by a period and a space. I searched my memory for the proper code to decipher the letter. Finally it came to me. The letter was written by hand in the ancient language of cursive writing.

In this age of texting, messaging, computer writing and printing, many who graduate with honors do not know how to write by hand in cursive form. Even the font that tries to imitate cursive falls woefully short, each letter being boringly the same as when used last. Now I must admit that I am empathetic with those who type pages. With my unsteady hand, no one could read what I intended to be cursive or hand-written printing. But then that is the penalty or privilege of aging. Even when I try to communicate by messaging, I find my fingers are too fat or stiff to hit the small letter on the phone.

Still, I feel sadness as I see the rapid demise of handwritten letters. The handwritten letters I receive seemed to have the personality of the writer. To use the language of theology, I feel the "by-with-and-under" presence of the writer. There seems to be warmth in my hands that hold the letter. It is personal. It conveys the warmth of friendship. It is almost like conversation.

My suggestion to each of you is: Sit down, take pen and paper and write by hand, (in cursive mode, if possible) to someone you care about. Both you and the one receiving the letter will feel the warmth of your handwritten letter. Then, if you must, you can go back to the modern world of texting, typing and printing.

WHERE ARE MY KEYS?

I can answer that question. . .they are where I last put them! A great deal of my time is spent looking for things that I have misplaced. A lot of my time is spent looking for something that I have put up or filed correctly but I have forgotten where that right place is. Sometimes I spend time looking for something that is right in front of me, hiding from me in such an obvious place that it has become invisible. The other Sunday morning I almost panicked. It was time to leave for church and I couldn't find my keys. Was I going to have to borrow my neighbor's truck like I did a few Sundays ago? Luckily I found them in the nick of time. They were in the pocket of the last pants I had worn while driving.

I find a great deal of time is spent trying to remember why I really came into a room in the first place. I try to be efficient by never going from one room to the other without carrying something. When I get there, I find myself asking, "Why am I carrying this object and where shall I put it?" I have spent much time looking for things that have been place in a safe spot where I could always find them. If I had all that time back, I would have finished my book, stayed ahead with my sermons, written all that the cat wants me to write, and have time left over.

Fortunately, I have never lost my car keys and had them to show up in my refrigerator. When that happens, they say I will be ready for another section in our retirement community. By the way, where are my keys?

THE FILING CABINET

Tom and I were down at the back lot. . .the place where all the junk is taken. I am not sure if we were taking something to deposit in the large dumpster or to look for a piece of wood that was needed for a project. While looking around the junk yard, I noticed a beautiful lamp just inside the half-opened door of the container. Of course we had to rescue that from destruction, as if we did not already have enough junk of our own.

As we were about to leave, we saw a four-drawer filing cabinet in very good condition lying behind the dumpster. The next day we were back, trying to make the filing cabinet fit on the back of the golf cart. Luckily, a worker who was much stronger and younger than either of us came to our rescue, so we brought another treasure home.

We were able to unload and stand it up between my band saw and my workbench. For the next two days, I struggled to get the drawers back in place. They had come out so easily. Now they simply would not go back to their rightful place in the open cabinet. Tom came over to help but even with his ingenuity, the drawers simply would not fit and roll in and out as they were designed to do. Frustration was an under-descriptive word!

A few days later, Tom's son, an engineer, came to our rescue. He picked up a drawer. He surveyed the file cabinet. Then he stood back and said in a matter-of fact-manner, "I see what is wrong. You stood the cabinet upside down." We managed to turn it over and, magically, the drawers slid perfectly into place. It was one of those embarrassing moments when all our years of learning and experience failed us. Aging ain't all it's cracked up to be!

A VALENTINE MEMORY

Wednesday, February 14 is a unique day. This year, Ash Wednesday and Valentine's Day fall together in the calendar. But then, come to think of it, both are about love in different ways. One looks forward to the great love God showed for us, the other looks around and back. Both require the giving and sharing of love, one with the smudge of ash, the other with candy and flowers.

We look around us, perhaps exchange a Valentine card. We are grateful for those we care for and who care for us. We are also thankful for memories of past Valentines.

The other day, as I was flipping through the pages of some books I was giving to the Home's library, a card and some old clippings fluttered to the floor. The card was one I had given my wife on our first Valentine day together. A flood of memories came rushing back, and with them came tears I could not hold back. I thought I was over that stage of grief but sometimes it just sneaks up, like an unexpected valentine from long ago.

My thoughts flashed back to the time I was in the sixth grade and just learning that girls might be persons of great interest. We had been given homework to get or make simple valentines to give each person in the class. I remember making a special one for a girl who sat across from me and often smiled in my direction. I remember passing out the simple paper card and saving the special one, for a special person, until last. I was afraid she would laugh at the valentine I had created especially for her. I screwed up my courage and dropped it on her desk without looking at her. I slipped into my desk. The teacher went on with our lesson. Finally, I dared to turn my head and look toward her desk. She looked back at me and gave me yet another big smile. Funny, the little things we remember: A girl in pigtails who smiled back; smiles that turn into lasting friendships; friendships that are marked by cards and gifts; relationships that might turn into hugs and kisses, rings and things.

But isn't that what Valentine's Day is all about? Love, and being willing to say, "I like you, be my valentine." Love. . .and being part of community that cares. . .love. . .and precious memories.

Lady Bean and I wish all of you much love and precious memories

I ALMOST WON

It had been a good two weeks in my place in the mountains. Of course, there were those three days when a couple of staff-like people came and brought two big dogs. I knew one of the dogs and we got along, but the other was a young one and had not learned

how to behave. I stayed in my bedroom with the door closed while they were here.

When they all left, I cautiously explored the house to be sure they were gone. The next ten days I was free to race up and down the long hall. . .to sleep or nap in any of the three bedrooms. . .to go down to the basement, because all the rooms were mine again. I could even go outside but I would not stay long because it was either cold or wet.

There came a time when I saw man-staff putting clothes in the car and packing boxes. I knew I needed to watch carefully. One morning he closed his briefcase and carried my dinner tray to the car. I knew it was time, so I disappeared. I found a cardboard box that was almost empty. I jumped in and luckily the top folded back in place. I heard man-staff calling, Kitty, Kitty, Kitty *or* Lady Bean *where are you. I heard him looking under the beds upstairs. He came downstairs, moved the sofa pillows around and looked under and behind everything. He went back upstairs, fussing and fuming and looking everywhere.*

About an hour later he came back downstairs. He had looked everywhere except in my box. I was so pleased that I had finally won the game that I started to purr. That was my undoing. He heard my purr and opened my box.

The next thing I knew I was in the van heading down the mountain. I guess it was good that I was finally found. But I was very pleased that I almost won! I would have won if I had not been so pleased with myself that I purred. And I am not through yet. Keep reading.

CHIRP! CHIRP!

Let me tell you about what happened to me when we got back to my other home. It was awful! I had just made that long trip from my mountain home to my flatland home. It had not been too bad. In fact I gloated most of the way about the two hours it took my man-staff to find me. Well, we rolled into my driveway and I jumped out as soon as the car door was opened. I went right to the door and my man-staff let me in. Then it happened! I had just walked in the bed room when there was this awful, high pitched chirp. It only lasted a second but it hurt my ears terribly. That awful chirp came again about every two minutes and it hurt worse each time. I thought it was a big insect or something so I got low to the floor and slunk under the bed. But the chirp sound followed.

Finally my man-staff pulled me out and held me tightly. Now as you know, I am not a lap cat but I snuggled tightly to him and tried to hide my ears under his arms. It must have hurt his ears too because he put me in the car where I could faintly hear the chirp. Then he went to get help.

After a long time, a man came with a ladder and went inside. When he came out the awful chirp stopped. He must have killed whatever was making the noise. My man-staff came and took me inside. He said something about a fire alarm battery. That seemed a strange name for an insect, but I did not care as long as that awful chirping stopped. I have not heard that insect since and I hope it never gets back into my house. LB

FORWARDING TREASURES

ON GOING HOME

Thomas Wolf used the descriptive title *You Can't Go Home Again* for one of his books. In it he illustrated the changing nature of our past. May I go a little farther and say emphatically, "I don't want to go home again." Here is why.

The place in which I spent the first eighteen-plus years of my life was on a suburban street in Jacksonville, Florida. I often go there in my dreams or in my memory. I lived in a wonderful two-story home filled with love and adventure. Nearby was a park with a small creek. There were trees to climb and friends with whom to play. On a recent trip I drove through the neighborhood. In the place where my home once stood I saw a large, impersonal, two-story concrete parking garage. Gone were the trees, the homes and the friends of my memories. I quickly drove away because I had not come home. Let me remember the way it was; the life-cradle that shaped me; the neighborhood that still exists in my memory.

No, I do not want to go home again.

Recently I visited a church and community where I had served and in which our children grew from babies into teens. The home in which we spent those wonderful years was still there but it was no longer ours. All around I saw change. New homes and streets were everywhere. The field behind our home had turned from a pasture to a housing development. The church that was keystone of the community was still there, but struggling to survive. No, I will live with great memories but I do not want to go home again.

A few years ago, we visited the small town in West Virginia where my work had taken me. The house in which we lived was there but had been redone and was hardly recognizable. The flavor of a small town had changed into a town of trendy shops, now enticing tourists to come and buy. The military academy and the finishing school for mountain girls were gone and in their place stood bed and breakfast facilities. Our visit brought back many pleasant memories but no, I do not want to go home again.

A few weeks ago I visited a coastal North Carolina city where my home had been, where the children were born and where I worked some sixty years ago. The suburban church I served was on the outer ring of the city. We enjoyed our life and our work in that historic city. At that time it was dependant on the Coastline Railroad as its major industry. There was little traffic and it was an easy ride to the beach. Today, I could hardly recognize where we had lived. Traffic made it look like Charlotte or Atlanta. The city had engulfed the places I knew as almost rural. Apartment buildings were everywhere and were still being built in rapid succession. Malls had sprung up like mushrooms. The small city that I knew had become a rapidly growing metropolis. No! I do not want to go home again.

As I look back, I realize that time changes everything. I know that the steady march of time. . .the tides of change. . .have no empathy for places we thought were carved in stone. Change may be the wrecking ball of progress. So let me remember things the way they used to be. Do not confuse my dreams with reality.

I do not want to go home again.

ON FARMING AT EIGHTY-EIGHT

The other day I tried to get my garden spot ready for spring. A solid cover of green weeds and grass had, over the winter; replaced any signs of a well kept garden. I was feeling fairly good so I pulled out the shovel and began to prepare the soil for things to come. I pushed the shovel through lush green covering until it stopped in solid South Carolina clay. I put one foot on the shovel and stepped up with the other foot so my weight would encourage the shovel to dig deeply. The next thing I knew I was on the ground and the shovel had not moved. My neighbor helped me up and said, "You are too old to be digging in the garden."

I may be old. I may be losing my balance. The shovel and hoe might be laughing at me, but I will not go quietly into the night of aging! I may have trouble standing on a shovel but I will still work my garden. I will find another way.

On my next trip to town I found what I wanted. When I brought my new electric tiller home, I proudly showed it to my shovel and hoe, then plugged it in and proceeded to get my garden ready for spring. Who says I am too old to farm?

I HAVE THE WEIRDEST DREAMS

Last night, somewhere between 3 and 5 a.m., I dreamed a dream. Let me tell you about it.

The dream began with my family living in a big, two-story house somewhere in southeast South Carolina. We had lived there for the last seven years. Now, we were in the midst of moving to somewhere in South Alabama. The movers were on their way with a big van. Most everything was packed up. I looked up at the pull-down ladder leading to the attic and thought, "I have not been up there since we bought the house and I had better check it out."

In my dream, I searched in the attic and found, hidden behind a lot of junk, an old band saw that I thought would fit nicely in my new garage in Alabama. I pulled it to the edge of the attic for the mover to get. Downstairs, the mover from Alabama had just arrived. He was a big Alabama "good 'ol boy" who had made a fortune with his shrimping fleet and just drove a moving van for fun. About that same time the former owner of my house, whom I had never met, arrived. He was a husky fellow who had made a fortune in kick-boxing. He demanded the band saw from the attic. The mover and the former owner got into a big fight. It was so bad that when the kick-boxer climbed into the attic, the mover locked him in, nailed the trapdoor shut and continued to pack my stuff.

Well, the guy in the attic must have called his cousin, the sheriff, because it wasn't long before we heard the siren and the sheriff and his deputies showed up. He rescued the former owner from the attic and demanded that the mover stop packing and go home. There ensued a heated exchange and neither would budge an inch. It seems that my millionaire mover knew the governor of SC, and after receiving my mover's call the governor sent the sheriff packing. Then things really got bad. The sheriff had a cousin named Trump who had something to do with the federal government, so he sent the FBI and some army guys to force the mover to leave. My mover had some good connections too, and had the Supreme Court take the case.

It was a big fuss over the almost worthless band saw in my attic and it was getting worse all the time. I decided to let the millionaire mover and the equally rich former tenant, along with the sheriff and deputies, the governor's representatives, a delegation from Washington and a Supreme Court Justice, still in his black robe, fight over the band saw while I went to lunch.

When I came back, everyone was gone. There was a huge boom truck with its arm extended over my open roof and the old band saw was dangling, precariously, on a cable over the house. The house, the moving van, the boom truck and a couple of army vehicles were plastered with notices saying that nothing could be moved or touched until the Supreme Court made its decision, which could take up to two years.

My sleep became fitful, as in my dreams I wondered how I could live in South Alabama without furniture or the old band saw. Suddenly, my sleep was interrupted by the band saw falling from the cable and landing on my stomach. I sat straight up in bed. The "band saw" had turned into a cat, which quickly jumped from her perch on top of me to the floor. I could not get back to sleep so I got up and began putting it down on paper.

I told you I had weird dreams and this is just an example. I wonder what I will dream tonight.

A BUNDLE OF OLD CARDS

Today, while cleaning out a dresser drawer, I picked up a bundle of cards and notes. They were neatly tied up with a ribbon. Before I threw them in the trash can, I pulled off the ribbon. I found cards that

I had given my wife for birthdays, Valentine's Day, anniversaries and other special occasions. I sat down and read each one. They were just notes, some funny, some sentimental, but with each card came a memory and new tears fell on the notes.

It was a wonderful surprise to find something that was precious to someone precious to you. It was a moment that seemed to bring a new radiance to the room. For me, it was almost a holy moment when for a time heaven and earth seemed to touch. Of course I tied the ribbon back around them and placed them carefully back in the drawer. Maybe I will run across them again when I need some cheering up. It had been a difficult yet wonderful time.

THE DUMP

I have always loved the dump. Maybe I would have made a good model for recycling before recycling became popular and necessary. Maybe it was because I grew up in the thirties when recycling and saving were necessary practices. Whatever the reason, I still like to visit the large dumpster, almost hidden in the woods, where I find what were once my neighbors' treasures. I see the pieces of lamps and desks, of pitchers and pictures; pieces of things that made life comfortable. I rummage through parts of a broken wheelchair that once brought comfort and mobility to a broken and aging resident.

In that dump I see the reflection of my father straightening bent nails with which to make a desk or bookcase for the family. In the dump I find things that are still usable. I pull from a destiny of destruction an old but still usable filing cabinet that will hold my tools and papers. I dust off an attractive lamp that needs a new shade but whose bulb still burns. I take it home and pass it on to someone who can use it.

But most of all, I see in the dump the future home of my comfortable stuffed chairs, my bed, my prized possessions and my treasures. Maybe someone like me will one day, in the not too distant future, visit the dump and recycle the worn-out furniture of my life. Maybe someone else will make use of the things that made me comfortable.

I hope so.

WHAT LONESOME IS

My man-staff sometimes complains about being lonely.

He thinks he is lonesome. . .let me tell you what lonesome is. The other day I saw him put some clothes in his brief case. He slipped around and got out some clothes from the closet. He had not bothered any of my things, so I knew I would not be going anywhere. I thought he would be gone for the afternoon and would be back that night. Well, nighttime came and everything was quiet. My special food saucer was empty so I patiently waited for him to return. I waited all night. The house had an eerie silence and I kept hearing sounds; strange sounds like creaking and moaning. A brave cat like me is never frightened but it was good get under the covers of my big bed. I even missed the funny noise that man-staff makes when he is asleep. It was a long night and I was a lonesome cat. Soon I fell asleep. I am very good at sleeping.

When morning came my man-staff was still gone. I began to worry about him and about the special food he always fixed for me. The day dragged on and on. It was a quiet and lonely place. To let him know how lonely I was I left my "calling card" by the door that leads to my box. You talk about lonely; I was it!

You can imagine how happy I was when I finally heard the door open and his voice call my name. But a cat has to control her emotions, so I hid my happiness by fussing at him for leaving me. For the next few days I stayed under his feet and close to him. It was good to have my man-staff back home. LB

A LESSON ON SLEEPING

The other night my man-staff tossed and turned so badly that I felt I was in danger of being kicked out of my own bed. (You know, I am good enough to let him use my bed.) I heard him stumbling around in the dark and complaining loudly that he could not sleep. Well, I thought, I can help him. I can give him some good advice on sleeping. I sleep almost eighteen hours a day so I am a subject matter expert.

- *First he needs to go to the kitchen and mix up some food from a small can, put it in a blender, and add hot water. He needs to warm it up and put it in a saucer. It would taste best if he lapped it up from the dish. Then he could get in my big bed and go right to sleep.*
- *He needs to find a soft spot in my bed, circle around in it a few times and then curl up and be still.*
- *If there is any light in the room, I would advise him to put his front paw, I mean arm, over his eyes. If he is very comfortable he might purr softly.*
- *He should also take more naps during the day and find different places to take them.*

Well, I hope he takes my advice and man-staff is able to sleep as well as I do. It would certainly be good if he would stay on his own side of the bed. It is about time for me to take my 7th nap of the day so I will stop here. LB

VOICES

THE HILL

Lady Bean and I recently spent two weeks at Moss Manor. It was good to be in the North Georgia Mountains. For the first time, memories did not come rushing out to knock me down with the nostalgia and loneliness. There were memories but they were good and had mellowed with passing time.

Behind the house, just past the deck, the hill that I've mentioned so many times was still there. We had taken the hill from the clutches of the mountain and tried our best to tame it. But since I was there only a fraction of the time, the mountain was again claiming its lost territory. Yes, there were traces of the annuals we had planted and gladiola still formed a border but snake grass had taken over much of the terrace. In fact the terrace itself could stand a little tender care. The steep steps made of railroad crossties were deteriorating and had become the home of large lizards. However, I was determined to give it a try.

My daughter, Mary Glenn, had brought about thirty-six clumps of Pennsylvania sedge grass which I planted on the lower left side if the hill. A number of yellow-orange small zinnias added some color to the hill (they are suppose to be deer resistant. . .we will see). I tried to pull out the matted snake grass on the other side but made little progress. A few perennials were trying to survive but were having a hard time. With my shaky legs and nothing to steady me I was afraid to climb the weed-covered terraces. I remembered and wished for the days I could repel down the bank and have both hands free to work. I did get a few native ferns and a few zinnias in place.

The hill has been a challenge from the very beginning. The more I try to tame, it the more it fights back. I know who will win in the end but I will keep pulling weeds, chopping brambles, planting flowers as long as I can stay vertical.

THE BEAR THAT WAS NOT THERE

It was the summer of 1948 and I had just finished high school. The world was still new and full of adventures. My best friend, Ed, and I set out in my 1929 Model A Ford on a journey that would take us to Montreat, NC, where we would work as waiters in Bridges Lodge for two weeks, then we moved on to Tennessee where we would spend a week with a cousin, fishing and camping on the lakes. From there it was to Front Royal, Va. to stay with Ed's brother. Enroute home we would spend a week camping on the Skyland Drive and Parkway. There are many stories to tell about that trip but this one in particular hangs in my memory.

We packed up the car, with things we had collected tied to the running boards. We got a late start and night caught us near the top of the Appellation Mountains. There we spotted a small, wayside picnic area. A wonderful place to stop, pitch our pup-tent and spend the night. After a supper of hotdogs and cold baked beans, we explored the area. As darkness closed in on us we spotted a sign that read, "Do not feed the bears." A little nervousness set in. We devised a plan to keep us safe. I detached the bulb type air-horn from the Model A. As we crawled into our sleeping bags, we carefully placed the horn between us. In case of a bear, surely a squeeze of the bulb on the horn would cause a blast that would frighten it away.

We finally went to sleep. About 3 a.m. one of us rolled over on the horn. The horn's loud sound startled us out of our sleep, thinking that one of us had seen a bear and was blasting the horn at him. Both of us stood straight up, bringing the canvas tent down and wrapping it around us. In the ensuing struggle to free ourselves from the tent, we were sure that a bear had his arms around us. When we emerged from the chaos we were alone; no bear anywhere to be seen. But there was no more sleep that night. We packed up our gear, got in the Model A, and continued our journey down the mountain and into Tennessee.

I can laugh about it now, but that night, alone on the mountain top, it was a frightening experience with the bear that was not there.

A SECRET

I've got a secret. . .a secret way to sneak out of the house without my man-staff knowing I am gone. Now I am an indoor cat that also likes to go outside. Sometimes man-staff lets me go for a walk when he is with me but he doesn't want me out by myself. But a little freedom is good for any cat and I am no exception. I have learned that the kitchen door takes a long time to close. When he goes out or comes in I stay out of sight until he has disappeared. Then I make my move and sneak through quickly before it closes. Man-staff looks for all over the house. When I am ready, I come to the door and ask to get in. It makes me feel good to put one over on him.

Please do not tell man-staff or he will fix the door. LB

LIVING WITH A TIME BOMB

A few years ago my Doctor discovered something in my blood. It was the type of cancer that could come to life at any time but most likely it will remain dormant for five to fifteen years. She ran me through all kinds of tests. She had ever bone in my body X-rayed, looking for any signs of activity. Nothing was found.

I do not worry about this tiny culprit. I have the feeling that something else will cause my demise before it makes up its mind to become active. But now and again I think about the fact that I am a living time bomb that could go off at any moment. But then, isn't that the same fact I have always lived with? Isn't that something that each of us faces? We all live a minute, an hour, a day at a time.

My father died as he was getting ready to go to work. My uncles died of heart attacks. The mother of my children died while having a routine check up at the doctor's office. My second wife was listening to a sermon in church when the stroke hit her. Why should I feel that

I am any different? Every car I pass on the road brings me within fifteen feet of a devastating head-on collision. So you see, living with a time bomb is not so bad and I pay it no attention.

What does bother me is that there is so much left undone. There is so much more to write, so many things I want to see and hear. There are so many sermons yet to preach. I have so many friends I want to touch again. I am a little concerned about the way I shuffle and lose my balance. I've done most of the things I wanted to do and am still enjoying a reasonably active life. So why should I worry about a little time bomb that probably will not go off in my lifetime and beyond that I don't care if it does.

THE ART OF TOTTERING

Tottering is described as "walking unsteadily or shakily" and "lacking security or stability; threatening to collapse; precarious." I couldn't have described my activity more perfectly. Tottering is what I do whenever I move, so let me expand on it a little.

I like to think of tottering as an art form. It has taken me well over eighty years to perfect the art.

It is also a form of dance that has taken a long time to develop. During my first sixty-five years the dance of tottering was rough and imperfect. I can remember when my steps were sure and my running was almost perfect. Tottering was not in my repertoire. I did not totter even when square dancing. Then, the dance of tottering was not an option. Now, after years of waiting and practicing, I have perfected the art and dance. Now I am dependent on a cane for reference and for a partner. Whenever I lean over to pick up something that slipped from my hand, I totter around the floor looking for other things that need to be retrieved. When I totter in a straight line, I find that forward momentum, as in riding a bicycle, keeps me vertical. When I try to stand still, tottering becomes something of a rumba as I move forward and back, shaking my body as I fight for balance. When evening falls and the lights go out, I totter even more.

Conquering the challenge of tottering has taken much patience and must be practiced to many different rhythms. Now that I am able to master the art and perform the dance of tottering, I take great pride in the fact that I am, for the most part, still standing. I recommend tottering to all of you, particularly after the age of eighty-five. Try it. You'll like it. In fact, there is very little alternative.

THE SHOPPING TRIP

You may remember the article I wrote a few issues ago about never buying my own clothes. Well, the time had come when I needed a few threads, so I went on a buying spree. It was a new experience for me. The first store I visited was Belks. I remember being taken to Belks as a boy and being fascinated with the little car that moved around the ceiling carrying money to the office and bringing back a receipt. I visited the men's department, looked at casual pants and sport shirt. You guessed it. Sticker shock! I knew prices had gone up but I did not expect to pay a week's pay check for a pair of pants and a cotton shirt. Besides, there was no one to ask if they had anything less expensive.

The next stop was one of those big box stores that sell everything from peanuts to wedding apparel. The prices were better but it took me forever to find something that might fit. It seems that as I have aged, my waist has gotten larger and my legs have gotten shorter. After wasting an hour trying to find measurements that might fit, I purchased a T-shirt and a pair of everyday pants. The girl at check-out assured me I could return them if they did not fit. The shirt fit before washing and the pants are going right back to the place I bought them.

After that harrowing experience, I think I will take a few old clothes to be let out and taken up and send a few more to the cleaners for a one time clean and press. Maybe I am living in the past but it is a lot cheaper than buying new clothes.

VOICES IN THE NIGHT

It was early spring. Warm weather was well on its way. I had gone to bed a little before midnight and was trying to drop off to sleep when I heard voices coming from somewhere outside. I sat up to listen. They were muffled and I could not understand words but a group of people were definitely talking. I strained to understand them but I could not make out a single word. Suddenly, the air conditioner under my window stopped and I realized I had mistaken the irregular throbbing of the air conditioner motor for voices. Very sheepishly, I turned over and went to sleep.

It is easy to imagine voices when what we are really hearing is something very different. If I had not realized my mistake before going outside to join the party, I am sure the men in the white coats would be looking for me.

ANOTHER CAT

As I told you in the past, I am a pretty good guard cat. I am always vigilant. But something happened last night that is hard to explain. My man-staff had gone to the car to play with his radio. Naturally I wanted to see that he was safe, so I scratched at the front door until he saw me and let me get in the car with him. (I like the car when it is not moving.)

I must admit that my man-staff is a little strange sometimes. That is why I like to be with him and watch out for him. He sits at his desk and hears voices. He talks to people who are not there. Tonight he was doing it in the car. Voices were coming from somewhere and he was talking into a small cup on a curled string. He's a little strange but he is good to me and I watch out for him.

While he talked, I looked out of the open window of the car. In fact, I stood on the edge of the window. When I looked a little to my right and ahead, I saw a small circle fastened on to the car and in that circle was the head and face of another cat. That cat looked just like me. It acted like me. When I showed my teeth, he showed his teeth. When my fur fluffed up, his did too. I must have frightened him because when I jumped back on the seat, he disappeared. I remember seeing that cat before. When I jumped on the bedroom dresser, she was looking at me from that big window above the dresser. When I jumped down, she disappeared. Once she appeared above the small sink in the bathroom but when I got down and looked back she was gone. My man-staff finished talking and we both got out of the car. I went slowly and carefully into the carport. I was sure the other cat was hiding in front of the car. My fur was up. I was slinking close to the floor. Man-staff wanted me to go inside but I needed to find the cat that looked like me and keeps disappearing. Finally, man-staff picked me up. I hissed and growled but he is bigger than me and he did not sense the danger we might be in. I reluctantly was carried inside. I will keep looking. I will run her off. There is only room in this house for one cat, and that is me. LB

THEY TRIED TO SKIN ME ALIVE!

I knew I was in trouble but I did not realize how much. I was well into my late morning nap when man-staff picked me up and carried me outside and toward the van. My gentle protest turned into a yowl when he dumped me unceremoniously onto the front seat. I had just come back from a long trip and did not want to go again. I had hardly completed ten good yowls when the van stopped. I smelled animals. My man-staff went in for a long time, but he came back and took me inside. I knew immediately where I was. The front room was filled with dogs. There was one tiny kitten who slept through it all. There was a big, brown, wooly dog that tried to make friends with me and another big black dog that wanted to eat me. There was a little wimpy dog that didn't care what was happening. A lady in a blue jacket led us back into a small room. She weighed me and told man-staff to wait there with me.

I had just about settled down when a man in a white coat came in, put me on a table and started poking and prodding all over me. It was inappropriate to say the least. He talked to man-staff, then picked me up and took me into another room. There, would you believe, he started to skin me alive! I must have made such a fuss that he stopped after just skinning a little of my side. He poked and scraped where he just skinned, then returned me to the room where man-staff was waiting. A few more pokes and punches and he told us to go home. Boy, was I glad and thankful for getting away with most of my skin intact.

But I am humiliated. A large piece of my beautiful fur is gone and my bare skin itches. Man-staff says it all happened because of a soft lump under my skin. I wish he had left it there. I just hope

my beautiful fur grows back in a hurry. Until then I will hide under the bed. LB

THERE IS GOLD IN MY HILL

I have written about "the hill" many times before and I may visit it again in the future. From the day we moved into Moss Manor I struggled to carve terraced flower garden from the mountainside behind e our deck. Time and time again I prepared the rocky soil, planted, weeded, and planted again. Each time Mother Nature tries just as hard to reclaim the mountain. Now I am a few years older, and at Moss Manor less often, and see the mountain rapidly gaining on me. But I still try. I rake off last year's leaves, plant a few new plants, pull a few weeds at a time. But I know now that I will not win this battle.

As I look back, I realize "the hill" is not about carving a garden out of a mountain side. It has nothing to do with how many weeds I pull or if the deer eat my flowers. The hill is about having a challenge, about trying and failing and trying again. It has something to do with my goals, my work ethic, my attitude about life in general and maybe a little about my theology. It does not matter if my dream of a terraced garden ever becomes reality. I have already won because I tried and enjoyed trying.

You, too, have a "hill" in your life. It may be far different from mine. But it will be something you struggle to overcome. You may gain a little and lose at little, but you keep on trying. Struggling with your "hill" is what makes it all worthwhile. When you look back at your "hill," may the effort you made to conquer it be as rewarding to you as my hill has been to me. There's gold in them thar hills!

Robert Browning summed it up when he wrote:

"Ah, but a man's reach should exceed his grasp, or what's a heaven for. . ."

TRIBUTES

There once was a young, theological tadpole, just out of school and serving his first church. The first call on his new telephone was from a member of the Presbytery asking him to help with the Junior Highs at camp. They directed him to contact a Director of Christian Education in a neighboring church. Upon arrival, he was asked sit down and wait. The DCE came in, mistook him for a paper supply salesman, and started giving him orders. After getting the identity straight, he was asked to assist her with recreation during a two weeks Junior High camp in the mountains of Brevard, North Carolina.

They were exciting weeks in many ways. At the end of the camp, she asked him to follow her car down the mountain since it was almost dusk. Halfway down the winding road, they stopped at a roadside park with a bubbling spring-fed fountain. In the magic moonlight of that spot they exchanged their first of many kisses. After their wedding the next year, their honeymoon was spent tent camping on the Skyland Drive and Parkway. Together they served over eight pastorates plus four interims and were blessed with four children. She filled each home with care and love.

The story is told that one night when the minister returned about 8:30 in the evening from visiting the hospitals, he found a wife and four little children lined up inside the back door. She said, "Children, I want to introduce you to your father." From that time on, he was home a little more often.

After forty-five years of building a home and working together and retiring, there came illness and Jackie was called home. She left him alone with a lifetime of memories.

During the year that followed, the minister, adrift at sea himself, tried to solve his loneness by taking a year-long voyage on his sailing vessel. With friends he traveled down the eastern seaboard, around Key West to Cuba and back into the Bahamas. It was during that voyage that the lonely old man became reacquainted with a childhood sweetheart who was lonely too. It was the beginning of a new and wonderful adventure. . .a fairy tale come true. Their wedding invitation read:

"Once upon a time there lived a boy and girl in a city near the sea. They went to the same church and sang in the same choir. They attended the same schools and enjoyed many of the same activities. As high school faded into to college, they began to enjoy each other's company and began to date and fell in love in the magic and exuberance of youth. They would walk hand in hand through the gardens and by the waterways and dream dreams together. But the fickle hand of fate and the providence of God moved them to different cities. Each fell in love with another and each married, made a happy home and raised a family. Those years gathered many happy memories for each of them.

As the years passed, the ones they married were taken away to a home prepared in heaven and they were left alone and lonely. Fifty years after the boy and girl were first together, by the Grace of God, their paths crossed again. They again enjoyed each other's company and again walked, hand in hand, through the gardens and by the waterways. Again they fell in love and dreamed dreams together."

Their marriage brought sixteen wonderful years of traveling in their own sailing vessel and on vessels with wings that carried them to many countries and places. They lived on the coast of North Carolina, then moving to Florida's sunshine. They then moved to their dream home in the mountains of North Georgia and from there to the comfort and care of a retirement community in South Carolina. After two good years in that home, sadness came again. You may remember from an earlier issue of Moss Manor News:

"The sky is grey and weeping and there is a chill in the air.
Beverly died last night. . ."

It was lonely for the one left alone, but he felt blessed and grateful for the two great ladies who had graced his life. He now looks back and lives again in memory those sixty-five great years of living with two wonderful wives.

LADY BEAN'S WILL

THE HORSEBACK WEDDING

Some years ago couple came to my office asking if I would officiate at their wedding. After they promised to participate in premarital counseling, I agreed to do the wedding. Just before they left, the lady turned to me and said, "Oh, almost forgot to tell you, we own a riding stable and we would like to have the wedding done on horseback."

So it was that on the appointed day I arrived at their farm. The wedding was to take place in a large barn where they did training and showed horses. At the far end there were bleacher-like stands for wedding guests. I was given a horse that was used for trail riding. She was gentle enough and we got along quite well.

Wedding guests, many dressed in riding outfits and western hats, arrived and filled the stands. As one who would preside, my horse and I were the first to come into the barn, making our way down the side, coming front and center and facing the empty barn with the guests behind us. The best man and groom came in first, riding beautiful show horses. They turned to watch as bride's maids rode their horses down the aisle and took their places in front. My horse stood quietly as this took place. The bride rode in on a beautiful white horse, her train covering the horse's rump. They took their places before me, horses almost nose to nose. The bride and groom had to reach from horse to horse to hold hands. Behind me I could hear the twitter of guests commenting on the occasion.

The wedding was almost traditional. There was the prologue, prayers, the exchanging of vows, the giving of rings and the pronouncement of marriage. All had gone well but things changed when I introduced them as husband and wife and said, "You may now exchange the first kiss of your marriage." At the moment they leaned over to kiss, the stands broke into applause and cheers. My trail horse, spooked by the noise, reared up and bolted between the bride and groom on their surprised horses. My book went flying. My robe trailed behind me like Superman's cape and I hung on for dear life. I finally was able to rein in the horse as he reached the back door. Someone from the stable led us back around the side to the front where I closed the ceremony with the benediction. I was glad to dismount and feel solid ground under my feet.

It was a day I would never forget. I doubt if my horse would ever forget it either.

A DECISION

A while back I received an e-mail from Beverly's first cousin who is about my age. It took me back to the many times we had visited her and enjoyed every minute spent together.

She is a delightful person, a free spirit, who puts a lot into life and received even more from it. We were always amazed at the things she was doing and the places she was visiting. She would visit her children, who lived across the country. We might receive a note saying that she had just returned from watching the animals from a balloon in Africa. She had a passion for the Shakespeare Theater and spent much time working with them. Her life has been full.

The e-mail set me back at first. Her doctor recently told her that she had advanced cancer and she must begin strong Chemotherapy immediately. In her characteristic, independent way, she said, in effect, "I have lived a full life and enjoyed most of it. I am ready for a new adventure and will not be taken down by treatments that will only prolong my life a few years and make them miserable. I have chosen to go to Hospice." She asked for my support in her decision.

Not long after her decision, she, her children and friends came together to share with her a celebration of her life. Perhaps it was something like Tom Sawyer watching his own funeral from the balcony of the church.

I gave her my support. It was her decision. She was not afraid of her new adventure and her faith was strong. Reflecting on her choice, I think it is a good one. I know her cousin, Beverly, will be waiting for her. If I am faced with a similar situation, I hope I have the courage to make the right decision. It might be the one that she has taken.

May God be with her in these days and in her eternal adventure.

LADY BEAN THEOLOGY

I am really a religious cat.

I am not sure what that really means but my man-staff keeps talking and writing about it so I guess it is important. From what I hear, it means something about how we live and what we expect to happen tomorrow. As you know, I have nine lives and probably have used at least eight of them already. But I do not worry much about what will happen in the future. What I worry about is sleeping at least eighteen hours a day, having fresh water in my bowl having regular meals and treats on schedule. Man-staff leaves his special book open on the bed and I look at it but do not make much sense of the scratching on its pages. He keeps telling me that I am a good cat and that's good enough for me.

I remember that my lady-staff disappeared and did not come back. I miss her and I hope she is all right wherever she has gone. Maybe someday I will disappear too. Maybe I will see her then. I hope so. But for now, religion is a mystery to me and I don't worry much about it. I am not sure my man-staff knows everything about it either. If he did he would not have to read and study so much in that book of his. Maybe cats have staff to take care of the things they do not understand.

Yes, I consider myself to be a very religions cat, but I will think about things like that tomorrow. For now it is time to take a nap and let my man-staff read his book.

LADY BEAN'S WILL

I know that I am an old cat. . .not as old as I hope to be, but old enough to know that I have used up almost eight of my nine lives. My sagging back and stiff joints remind me of my age. The other day my man-staff was fuming about having to update his will. It made me think that maybe I should have a will, so here it is:

If I should ever roll over and not get up, here is what I want done.

- *I don't care how you dispose of my carcass, just get it over with.*
- *I leave whatever leftover food I have to that old cat that keeps hanging around outside.*
- *I bequest my cat carrier, my collar and leash to any who will use them. (They are almost new, as I never allowed them to be used.)*
- *I want my man-staff to keep my feeding tower and water bowl. (I know that because of the way that I have treated and trained him, he will have another cat. I also realize that no other cat will ever quite come up to my standards).*
- *I also leave man-staff my house, my bed, and my chair.*
- *I give him permission to use my name in Moss Manor News or other publications. (Mine is by far the most popular column in his writing.)*
- *Because man-staff faithfully typed what I dictated, I give him the royalties that will come from the sale of my books.*

I really do not plan to die but I cannot let my man-staff have something I do not have. That is why I have written this will and testament. Lady Bean (signature witnessed and notarized)

THE MISTY FLATS OF TOMORROW

The writer of the book of Joel had it right when he said, *Young men shall see visions and old men shall dream dreams.*

There was a time when I was young; when I saw mostly visions and everything real was yet to come. When the future stretched out like a never-ending road; when time was measured in unending years ahead and when every adventure was out there. . .hidden in the misty flats of tomorrow.

Now from the vantage point of eighty-nine years and counting, I see the other part of Joel's prophecy: *Old men shall dream dreams.* That time is here and I am old. Visions of what might be have morphed into what has been. I look back and dream dreams of times long past. I remember riding on highways of water and regretting the liquid paths not taken. I remember adventures that seem alive but are yet trapped in my memory bank of time

So it is with most of us who make it to this time of life. Now we can select what to remember and what to forget. We can choose memories and play them one by one, and experience our favorites over and over again. We can in our minds make certain corrections that we wish we had made long ago.

The time when old men shall dream dreams is a wonderful time of life. It is a time when I give thanks for the memories and for those who have lived them with me. It is a time when danger is past, when storms can be washed away, and when dreams can become as real as we want them to be. It is a time when, in memory, I can be as young and agile as I once was.

Yes, it is a wonderful time of life. It is a time when "old men dream dreams" and the past lives in precious memory.

CPSIA information can be obtained
at www.ICGtesting.com
Printed in the USA
FSHW010820081218
54286FS

9 781545 650394